T0185541

Beginning SAP Fiori

Bince Mathew

Apress®

Beginning SAP Fiori

Bince Mathew
Bangalore, Karnataka, India

ISBN-13 (pbk): 978-1-4842-1336-0   ISBN-13 (electronic): 978-1-4842-1335-3
DOI 10.1007/978-1-4842-1335-3

Library of Congress Control Number: 2015958352

Managing Director: Welmoed Spahr
Acquisitions Editor: Celestin Suresh John
Developmental Editor: Matthew Moodie
Technical Reviewer: Rajanidhi Rajasekaran
Editorial Board: Steve Anglin, Mark Beckner, Ewan Buckingham, Gary Cornell, Louise Corrigan, James DeWolf, Jonathan Gennick, Robert Hutchinson, Celestin Suresh John, Michelle Lowman, James Markham, Susan McDermott, Matthew Moodie, Jeffrey Pepper, Douglas Pundick, Ben Renow-Clarke, Gwenan Spearing, Matt Wade, Steve Weiss
Coordinating Editor: Rita Fernando
Copy Editor: Tiffany Taylor
Compositor: SPi Global
Indexer: SPi Global

Distributed to the book trade worldwide by Springer Science+Business Media New York, 233 Spring Street, 6th Floor, New York, NY 10013. Phone 1-800-SPRINGER, fax (201) 348-4505, e-mail orders-ny@springer-sbm.com, or visit www.springeronline.com. Apress Media, LLC is a California LLC and the sole member (owner) is Springer Science + Business Media Finance Inc (SSBM Finance Inc). SSBM Finance Inc is a Delaware corporation.

For information on translations, please e-mail rights@apress.com or visit www.apress.com.

Apress and friends of ED books may be purchased in bulk for academic, corporate, or promotional use. eBook versions and licenses are also available for most titles. For more information, reference our Special Bulk Sales–eBook Licensing web page at www.apress.com/bulk-sales.

Any source code or other supplementary materials referenced by the author in this text is available to readers at www.apress.com. For detailed information about how to locate your book's source code, go to www.apress.com/source-code/.

Printed on acid-free paper

Dedicated to My Parents and My Brother

Contents at a Glance

Contents

About the Author

Bince Mathew is a SAP Mobility Technology Consultant who has more than 7 years of expertise in developing Mobile applications and executing various projects in SAP Mobility. He is an expert in SAP Fiori, SMP, SYCLO, AFARIA and native Android application developments. Bince was given the Best Speaker award for SAP Fiori in SAP Inside track 2014 held by SAP. He blogs about various articles on topics related to SAP Mobility in SAP Developer Network site (SDN) and other developer communities. He is also an expert in the field of Internet of Things and connected devices.

About the Technical Reviewer

Rajanidhi Rajasekaran has 15 years of Techno Functional experience in SAP including 8 years of experience in CRM and 2 years of experience in SAP FIORI. Have worked more than 10 projects of End to End implementation and support in ECC and CRM. Have worked in 4 SAP FIORI projects including developing custom app and also enhancing standard apps. Have worked on SAP 4.6B, 4.6 C, 4.7, ECC 5.0, ECC 6.0, ISU CCS version of SAP R/3 and CRM 5.0, CRM 6.0 (CRM 2007), CRM 7.0 (EHP 1 & EHP 2) version of SAP CRM, Gateway 2.0 SP08, SAP_UI SP09, SAPUI5 1.22.4, SAP WEBIDE, Hana Cloud Platform.

Acknowledgments

This book would not have been possible without the support of the following people.

Friends and Family

My Parents - Without them I would not be in this position to write about this book, it's because of them I am what I am today.

Bivin Mathew (My Brother) - Who always motivated me to find time for writing the book. He kept asking me every week about how far have I completed with my book and that kept me on track.

Arun Kumar (My college friend) - He invested his time for giving me his suggestions on improving the contents of the book.

Sreehari V Pillai - He is an expert in SAP HANA and Ui5. He had helped me with the HANA Topics and gave me some suggestions regarding the custom applications chapter for Fiori. He has also helped me with the custom control development for the fiori application mentioned in this book.

Final Thanks

Celestin Suresh John - Senior Manager Editor of Apress who gave me the opportunity to write this book.

Rita Fernando - Coordinating Editor of Apress, she helped with preparing a complete schedule on the timeframe to complete each chapter and helped me with all the technical hiccups I faced during the chapter preparations.

Matt Moodie - Developmental Editor of Apress, Matt basically pointed out my mistakes with drafting a proper chapter, He helped me to effectively represent my ideas in a formatted and professional way. His comments basically made me understand how to write a chapter with clarrity.

Rajanidhi Rajasekaran - Our Technical reviewer for this book, Rajnidhi pointed out the missing parts and mistakes in the book. He also suggested me with the additional topics that I should cover in the book.

Introduction

When SAP initially launched its ERP software, the GUI for SAP was a very powerfull piece of software at that time. But in this day and age of powerful smartphones, tablets and ultabooks, the old desktop based SAP GUI is getting outdated. In addition to that, the user experience on the old GUI was not able to stand against the fleet of HTML5 based powerfull and more appealing modern UI which is being adopted by many other software products. SAP's solution to their ageing GUI is know as SAP Fiori. It was one of the first initiative by SAP to achieve their new goal of "One UX for all SAP Products". Fiori is based on a framework known as UI5 which is built on top of HTML5. Fiori is also compatable with any device with any screen size.

Today almost every software and websites has a mobile compatible version. 4 or 5 years ago this wasn't the case. Now whenever we hear about an interesting website or a product, we autmotically checks for its mobile app in the app store. The reason for this shift is because, today our smartphones are much more powerfull and even comparable to a 3 or 4 year old PC. Which enables us to browse websites, play graphic intensive games, edit word or PowerPoint presentations on the go and we even consume a huge amount of multimedia content using our phone rather than a pc these days. We need everything on the go and in the palm of our hand. We are using mobile devices on a regular basis, it has become a part of our life. You will hardly find a person who doesn't have a mobile device in this day and age. Nowadays if your software product don't have a mobile version, then you are missing out a huge part of your business in the mobile space.

When SAP came up with the new UX strategy to cater to all platforms and devices, they not only made it compatable with all devices, they also made the UI less complicated. This was very crucial because accessing a particular application with too much data or too many options in one single screen might not be an issue in a desktop or in a tablet to a certain extend, but it's definitely an issue in a much smaller smartphone screen. So they made the new UX simpler and more appealing to the users.

SAP Fiori started with 25 applications which was based on frequently used transactions and processes in SAP. Today Fiori has more than 500 apps and its still growing. And with the release of S/4 HANA, SAP is moving closer to their goal of replacing the old GUI with a new UX standard set by Fiori for all its products. Fiori is being widely accepted by SAP users everywhere around the globe.

Like every niche technology, the developers will need some time to understand the Fiori architecture so that they can utilize Fiori to its full potential. This book will help you to get a more insight to the Fiori architecture, develop custom applications, extend standard Fiori Applications and customize fiori applications. The book takes you on a tour on everything related to SAP Fiori, it also helps you understand to build Fiori applications for Internet of Things, develop native applications using cordova and developing OData services using SAP Netweaver Gateway. The book is divided into 9 chapters, I have tried my best to keep these chapters simple and yet detailed enough for you to understand.

CHAPTER 1

Introduction to SAP Fiori

SAP Fiori is a new offering from SAP, based on the HTML5 framework. A great deal of help regarding Fiori is available on the Internet, but the information is scattered across many web sites and sources. Users who are new to SAP Fiori may find it difficult to get an overall idea of what Fiori is. This book provides an overview and gives you the knowledge you need to configure, implement, and extend Fiori applications.

This chapter covers the history of SAP Fiori and examines SAP's roadmap to a unified user experience (UX) for all of its products.

Why Fiori?

In the past, SAP customers complained about the old-fashioned look and feel of the standard screen and the fact that SAP can only be accessed via its desktop GUI for most transactions. SAP listened to this feedback from all over the world and launched a set of applications, based on the HTML5 framework, that includes the most widely and frequently used SAP transactions: purchase order approval, sales order creation, information lookup, self-service tasks, and so on. These HTML5 applications are easy to access seamlessly across desktops, tablets, and smartphones (see Figure 1-1). This collections of apps is named Fiori.

Figure 1-1. The Fiori user experience as seen on all types of devices

© Bince Mathew 2015
B. Mathew, *Beginning SAP Fiori*, DOI 10.1007/978-1-4842-1335-3_1

The term *Fiori* is an Italian word that means "flowers." SAP wanted a beautiful UI for its current GUI, and it also wanted to create a simple, elegant user experience. Initially, SAP charged a license fee per Fiori user. After receiving complaints from customers about paying for an additional license on top of their existing ERP license, and from service companies who found it difficult to convince customers to pay the additional cost, SAP announced at the February 2014 SAPPHIRE event that Fiori would be free for any customer with an SAP license. This decision resulted in a higher adoption rate for Fiori and increased market demand for Fiori-based custom UI5 applications.

One drawback of current SAP transactions is that some transactions are complex, and the same transactions are used to perform multiple tasks. As a result, transactions may have many fields and configurations and become difficult to use. For example, suppose a sales and distribution (SD) consultant accesses transaction VA01 to perform SD-related tasks (see Figure 1-2). The transaction works fine if the user is familiar with the complex steps and fields required to complete the task. But a sales representative whose priority is making sales rather than spending time creating a sales order in the complex GUI, this transaction may be difficult, and many of the fields and options may seem confusing and irrelevant.

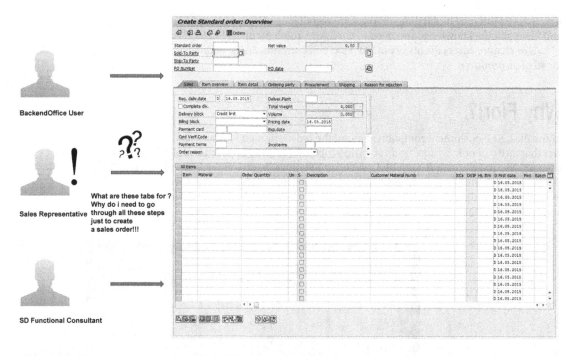

Figure 1-2. *An example scenario with the VA01 Create Sales Order transaction*

To avoid such cases, SAP simplified its complex UIs and split them into multiple simple UIs whose elements make sense to the user. For example, when a sales representative uses the Fiori Sales Order application shown in Figure 1-3, all the elements are useful. The sales rep can create sales orders without using the SAP GUI—the rep can even create a sales order on the go, from a mobile phone.

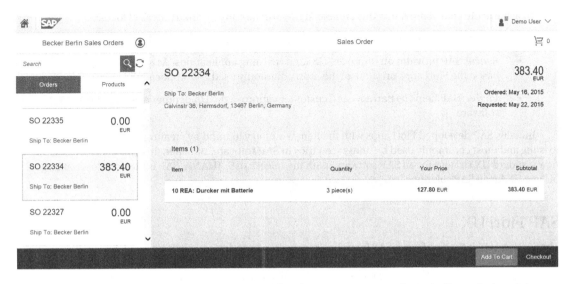

Figure 1-3. *The Fiori Sales Order application simplifies the VA01 transaction by including only the minimum required fields to complete the task*

In addition, to perform simple operations, SAP users sometimes have to execute multiple transactions. SAP split these complex transactions into smaller apps, simplifying them and making them specific to the roles of particular users. At the same time, SAP merged repetitive transactions. Using this approach, SAP created role-based applications: the first wave of Fiori applications (known as Fiori Wave 1 apps) consisted of a set of 25 applications targeted at users such as managers, employees, sales representatives, and purchasing agents.

Introduction to the SAP UX Strategy and the SAP Fiori UX

The new UX for SAP simplifies the old GUI and makes it compatible with any device of any screen size that supports HTML5, including mobile devices. This change was a big step for SAP—it adopted an entirely new technology and strategy for its UI.

SAP UX Strategy

Enterprise resource planning (ERP) software was developed to provide increased functionality. Although ERP solutions have powerful features, end users sometimes find the UI complex and even intimidating. Most of the time, users don't use ERP software based on its features and its ability to handle complicated tasks; they give priority to UI ease of use and the ability to complete their required tasks with the least amount of effort.

For example, consider Facebook. A user may find it easy to use the Facebook web site when they have access to a desktop or laptop. But when the user is on the move, accessing the same fully featured web site via a mobile device can be complex and frustrating. Using the Facebook mobile app gives the user a simpler UI and easier layout to update their status, check notifications, see what their friends are up to, and so on. The most powerful and sophisticated UI is not always the best answer for providing users with a good UX. For this reason, SAP put its users first and developed an intuitive, consistent, simple UX. It saves users time and increases their productivity. The UX provides benefits like these:

- Fewer user errors
- Decreased user training costs
- Higher satisfaction rates

3

To achieve the goal of providing this enhanced UX, SAP has three primary areas of focus:

- *New*: It's all about providing consumer-grade user experiences for new applications.

- *Renew*: SAP provides an improved UX for its existing applications. As a start, SAP based the Fiori apps on some of the most commonly used SAP applications.

- *Enable*: SAP helps its partners and customers improve the UX of other existing SAP software.

Initially, SAP developed Fiori apps with the Renew strategy in mind by creating a new UX for the existing and most commonly used business scenarios in SAP software. But later, this approach evolved into a new standard UX strategy for all SAP software. With the release of S/4HANA, SAP is moving closer to its goal of "one UX for all SAP solutions."

SAP Fiori UX

The SAP Fiori UX is the new face of SAP for its business users across devices, platforms, and deployment options. It provides optimal usability and simple business interactions and ease of use. Fiori is not just a new UI or a new theme on top of existing SAP transactions; it's a new concept of providing user-centric applications.

A traditional SAP transaction generally has numerous screens, fields, and tabs that encompass multiple features and types of functionality and can serve multiple users. These transactions end up with many fields, navigations, and features that don't apply to all users—rather, each part, tab, or area of the transaction is targeted at a different type of user (see Figure 1-4).

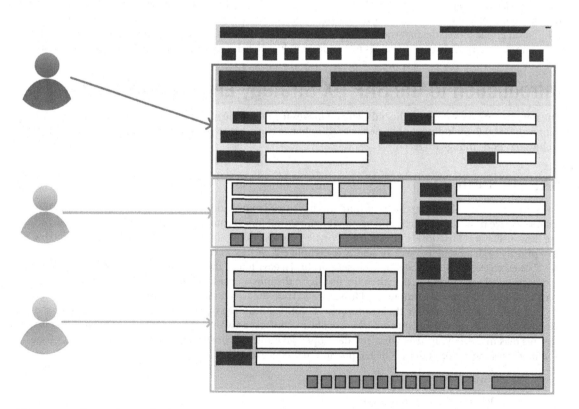

Figure 1-4. A sample standard SAP transaction

With SAP Fiori, apps are developed from a user's perspective: the apps are user-centric. These apps are simple, relevant to a particular user role, and designed to carry out specific tasks and activities. Basically, Fiori apps break the big, standard SAP transactions into multiple small, easy-to-use apps that make more sense to individual users (see Figure 1-5).

Figure 1-5. *Standard transaction converted into smaller, simple, role-based, user-centric Fiori apps*

In addition to having apps for specific tasks, with Fiori, the user has access to a fleet of apps based on the roles that particular user handles. For example, suppose a user is handling multiple roles in an organization: the user is an employee but also approves finance-related activities as a manager. As a manager, the user needs access to certain approval-related apps; and as an employee, the user needs to request leave, update timesheets, submit claims for travel expenses, and so on. Fiori gives the end user a single point of entry to access all apps relevant to their roles: the Fiori launchpad (Chapter 2 goes into more depth about it). When users log in to the Fiori launchpad, they see all the apps that have been authorized for them, based on their roles (see Figure 1-6).

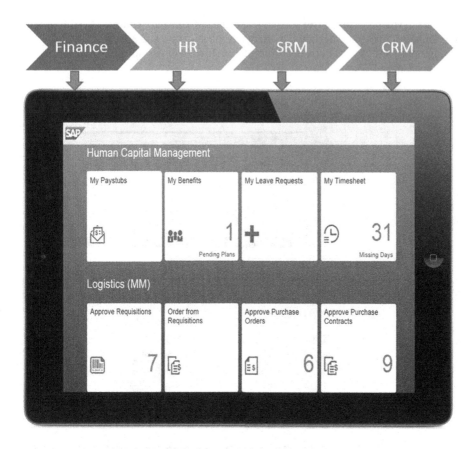

Figure 1-6. *Sample Fiori launchpad running on a tablet*

Apps in the Fiori launchpad are displayed as tiles, as shown in Figure 1-7. Each tile is like a shortcut icon on your desktop that opens an app when you click it.

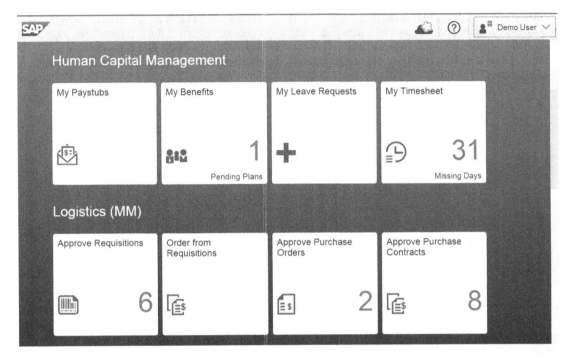

Figure 1-7. Fiori launchpad

When you click a tile, the app opens as master-detail page or as a full-screen app. In a master-detail view, the master page is on the left and the detail is on the right (see Figure 1-8).

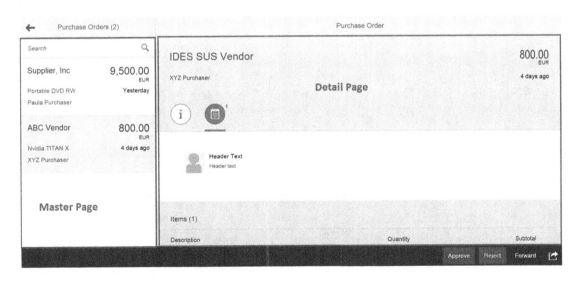

Figure 1-8. Master-detail view

Users can drill down into detail pages to navigate to other pages. For example, in Figure 1-9, additional details about a material are shown on a new page that loads in the same area as the previous detail page. This enables users to navigate to more detailed views while also letting the UI developer minimize the amount of data that must be shown on a single screen—too much data on a single screen leads to a complex, confusing UX.

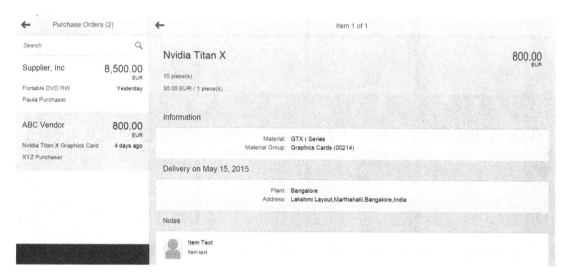

Figure 1-9. *Line-item page*

An app can also use the full screen, as shown in Figure 1-10. The choice of whether to use a master-detail app or a full-screen app is based on the scenario and the type of data that needs to be presented.

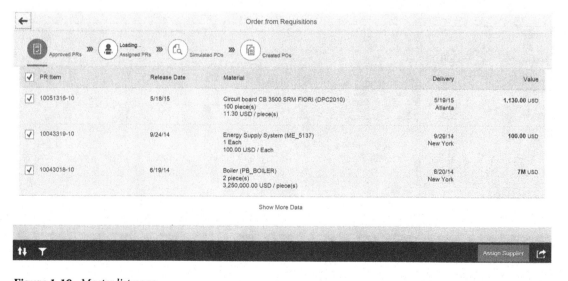

Figure 1-10. *Master list page*

In a full-screen app, unlike in the master-detail page design, the detail page is loaded as a new page (see Figure 1-11). Further drill-down pages—such as item details or additional information about items on the detail pages—are also loaded full-screen (see Figure 1-12).

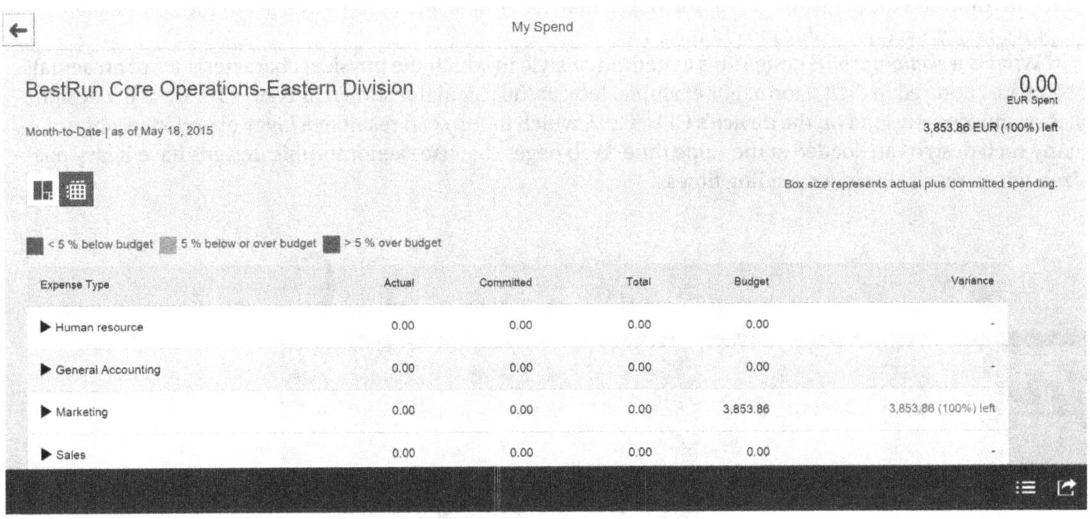

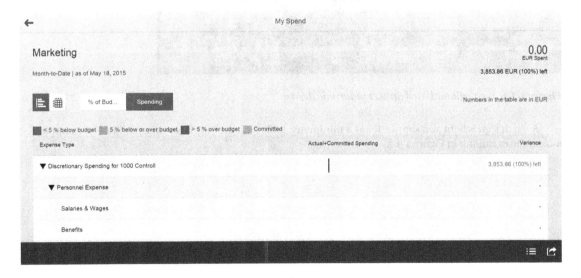

Figure 1-11. Detail page/list

Figure 1-12. Line item/detail

SAP Fiori Design Inspiration

The inspiration for the design of Fiori came from a web design and graphic design trend that is standard in most web-based applications today: *flat design*. You can see flat design everywhere, from the latest IOS 7 flat icons; to Android's material design; to web pages that use simple, flat designs and avoid the complicated, graphics-heavy, skeuomorphic look of the past.

What is a *skeuomorphic design*? It's a method or style in which the physical characteristics of an actual object are captured in digital form. For example, look at the calculator shown in Figure 1-13. Such a design places unnecessary load on the device's CPU/GPU, which in turn can result in a laggy experience when many such designs are loaded at the same time. Web pages that use skeuomorphic designs have heavy page sizes, which results in slower loading times.

Figure 1-13. *A calculator based on skeuomorphic design*

A flat design is light and simple. It has a minimalist look, with the emphasis on usability. For example, look at the calculator in Figure 1-14.

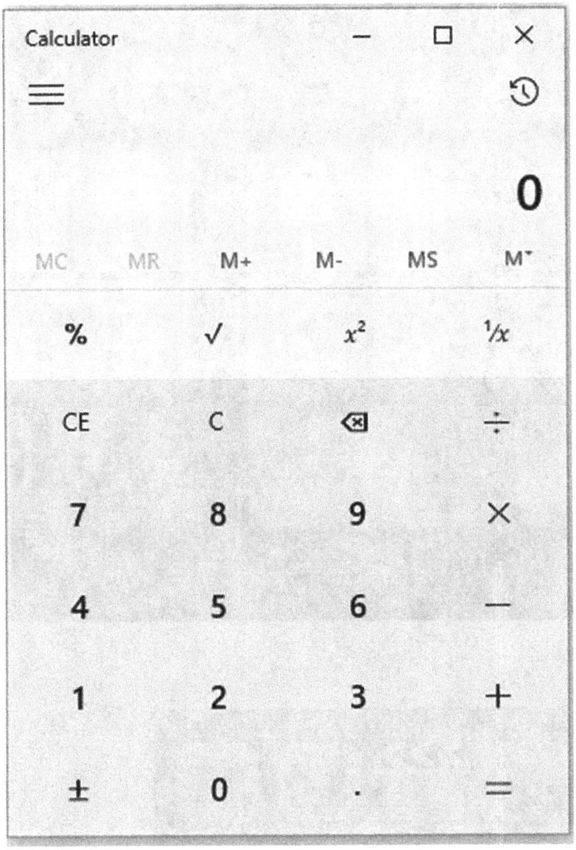

Figure 1-14. *A calculator based on flat design*

Microsoft was one of the first tech companies to adopt flat design, with its tile (formerly known as Metro UI) design in Windows 8 (see Figure 1-15). This design trend was quickly followed by other tech companies including Apple and Google. One of the main advantages of flat design in mobile devices is that it uses fewer resource such as battery life and GPU. And because the design is light in size, loading times and animations when navigating from one screen to another are smooth. No shadow effects on icons or in the apps tax the GPU. Figure 1-16 shows the transition of iOS from a skeuomorphic design to a flat design.

Figure 1-15. *Windows 8 flat design*

Figure 1-16. *Skeuomorphic design in iOS 6 (left) vs. flat design in iOS 7*

Here are the primary things customers associate with a flat design:

- Simple
- Clean
- Colorful
- Modern
- Trendy

And these are the advantages of flat design:

- Ease of use
- Modern appearance
- Responsive designs that are more efficient
- Faster loading times
- Straightforward design with no special effects that affect performance

Introduction to SAP Fiori

As mentioned earlier, Fiori was developed based on the HTML5 framework, with an emphasis on a flat UI design and user-centric apps. This helped SAP create a responsive UI that's compatible with all screen sizes and runs on any device that has an HTML5-compatible browser. Fiori was developed based on the design principles shown in Figure 1-17:

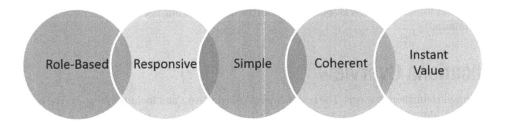

Figure 1-17. *Fiori design principles*

- *Role-based*
  - Each app is specific to a user's role: manager, employee, salesperson, and so on.
  - The role-based approach helps in developing user-centric apps.
  - A user may have multiple roles. Depending on the nature of their responsibilities, the same user may perform different tasks across multiple business domains. Apps that are developed to carry a specific task that belongs to different modules (HR, SRM, CRM, and so on) can be assigned to users based on their roles.
  - Developers can visualize a specific user's task and develop a UI that relates to the nature of the user's work.

- *Responsive*
    - Because it's HTML5-based, Fiori works seamlessly across all screen sizes and devices that have an HTML5-compatible browser.
    - Fiori apps adjust their layout based on the available screen real estate.
    - Fiori supports multiple interaction modes, such as keyboards, mice, and touch-based inputs.
    - Fiori works independently of platform or ecosystem (Windows, Android, or iOS). The apps work and respond the same across all platforms.
- *Simple*
    - The simple UI helps the user complete tasks quickly and easily.
    - Fiori apps emphasize a 1:1:3 approach: one user, one use case, and three screens (desktop, tablet, and mobile).
- *Coherent*
    - No matter how many apps Fiori has, they all have the same design footprint and thus the same look and feel.
    - This helps users become familiar with Fiori apps. After using one Fiori app, users feel comfortable with other Fiori apps, because every app speaks the same design language.
- *Instant value*
    - The time required to train users in the new UI is minimal for Fiori. The UI is simple and follows the same design pattern across apps, which makes it easier for users to adopt the new UI quickly. Hence the cost of training users is also minimized.

Fiori Applications Overview

The Fiori apps have been launched in waves. The first wave was called Wave 1 and included 25 apps. The next wave was called Wave 2, and so on.

Fiori Wave 1

The initial 25 Fiori apps were categorized as follows:

1. Manager
    - Approve Leave Requests (HR-based)
    - Approve Purchase Contracts (MM-based)
    - Approve Purchase Orders (MM-based)
    - Approve Requests (generic workflow application)
    - Approve Requisitions (MM-based)
    - Approve Shopping Cart (SRM-based)

- Approve Time Sheets(HR-based)
- Approve Travel Expenses (HR-based)
- Approve Travel Requests (HR-based)
- My Spend

2. Employee

- My Benefits (HR-based)
- My Leave Requests (HR-based)
- My Paystubs (HR-based)
- My Shopping Cart (SRM-based)
- My Timesheet (HR-based)
- My Travel Requests (HR-based)
- Track Shopping Carts (SRM-based)

3. Sales Representative

- Change Sales Order (SD-based)
- Check Price And Availability (SD-based)
- Create Sales Order (SD-based)
- Customer Invoices (SD-based)
- Track Sales Order (SD-based)
- Track Shipments (SD-based)

4. Purchasing Agent

- Order From Requisitions (MM-based)
- Track Purchase Order (SD-based)

Fiori Wave 2

As mentioned previously in the architecture section, from Fiori Wave 2 on, Fiori apps are primarily classified as follows:

- Transactional apps
- Analytical apps
- Fact sheets

Transactional Applications

Transactional applications are used for task-based access. Figure 1-18 shows a sample transactional app.

Figure 1-18. *Sample transactional app*

These apps give you access to transactions that let you create or change an entire functional process. Because the Fiori UI gives priority to simplifying tasks, such apps provide guidance on how to complete the tasks. Transactional apps are compatible with the SAP HANA database and any other database used by SAP ERP.

Analytical Applications

These apps give you insight into a particular area and provide reports that let you drill down into the app for further KPI analysis of the data (see Figure 1-19). The data used to generate these reports may be huge, ranging from several hundred megabytes to gigabytes. By using the processing power of HANA, these apps generates reports in seconds.

Figure 1-19. *Sample analytical application*

Fact Sheets

These apps are used for searching and exploring objects (see Figure 1-20). They're also used to navigate between related objects. For example, if you search in the Fiori search window for a certain material, Fiori displays the material's details in the search result. It searches the ERP back end for the material and shows you the result.

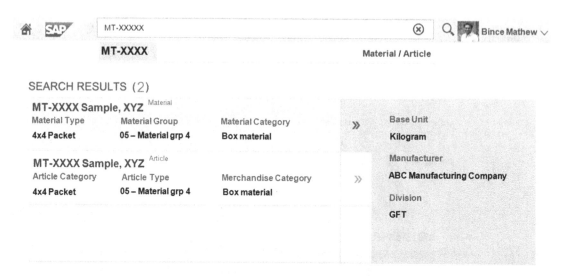

Figure 1-20. Search scenario in Fiori

When you click a result in the search window, you see a fact sheet app containing a summary of the material (see Figure 1-21).

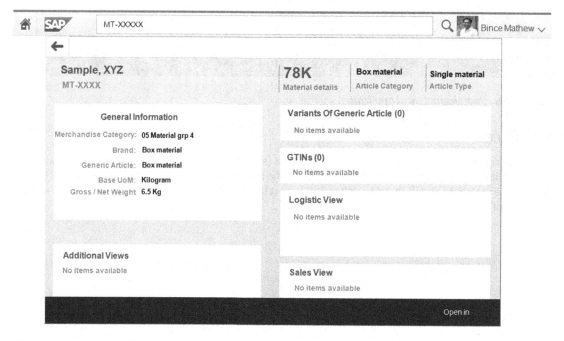

Figure 1-21. Fiori fact sheet

Fiori Architecture for Transactional Applications

Fiori transactional applications let users perform transactional tasks like creating leave requests, creating travel requests, approving purchase orders, and so on. Transactional apps support the HANA database and all other traditional databases that SAP ERP supports.

The architecture shown in Figure 1-22 gives a generic overview of how Fiori apps are deployed and consumed by end users. The first block shows the devices (desktops, tablets, and mobile devices) that access the Fiori launchpad (the entry point to all Fiori apps, covered in Chapter 2). When a user accesses the Fiori apps for the first time, the apps are downloaded into the web browser on the desktop, mobile device, or tablet, just as if a web page is being accessed.

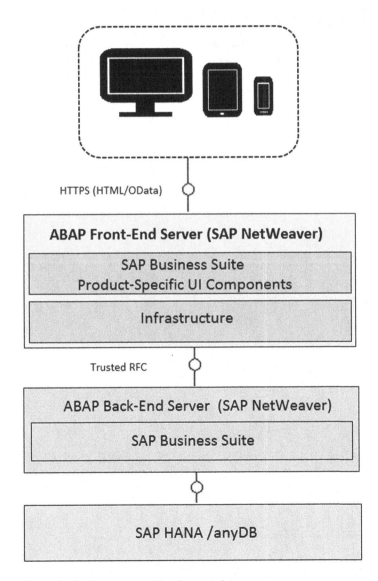

Figure 1-22. *Fiori transactional app architecture*

The ABAP front-end server contains the UI layer, which has product-specific UI components for the Fiori apps. For example, the UI add-ons can be for ERP-specific tasks (FI, MM, SD), customer relationship management (CRM), supplier relationship management (SRM), supply chain management (SCM), governance risk control (GRC), and so on. The infrastructure contains the SAP UI5 libraries (required to run UI5 apps), Fiori launchpad components (which come preinstalled from NetWeaver 7.4), and SAP Gateway with the OData service enabled.

The front-end components access and communicate with the ABAP back-end server through trusted RFC connections. Although it is recommended that you run Fiori transactional apps with the HANA database, they work with any database supported by SAP R/3.

Fiori Architecture for Analytical Applications

Analytical applications give users access to real-time data regarding the business. These apps collect and process a huge amount of data in a matter of seconds and present the results in a simplified format that the user can understand and relate to easily. Analytical apps use the huge data-processing and analytical power of SAP HANA. Figure 1-23 shows the architecture layout of a Fiori analytical app.

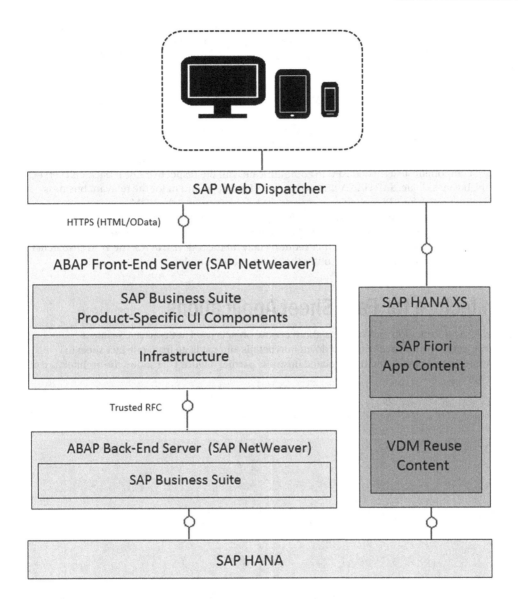

Figure 1-23. *Fiori analytical app architecture*

Monitoring options are also available by using key point indicators (KPIs) in real time. For example, users can keep track of stock values in the market or pressure gauge readings from instruments, and take action immediately in real time. To configure KPIs, SAP provides a set of KPI modeler tools (discussed later in this book).

Analytical apps run only on SAP HANA. They use virtual data models (VDMs): structured representations of SAP HANA database views. VDMs provide direct access to SAP business data by using standard SQL/OData requests.

Similar to transactional apps, the ABAP front-end server contains the UI layer, which holds product-specific UI components related to ERP (MM, SD, FI), SRM, CRM, SCM, and so on. The infrastructure layer contains the SAP UI libraries, Fiori launchpad, and SAP Gateway with the OData service enabled.

The front-end components use trusted RFC to communicate with the respective ABAP back-end server, which contains the business logic. SAP HANA XS also contains Fiori app content for the relevant business suite products, the framework for KPI modeling, a generic drill-down app, and the VDM.

The Web Dispatcher is the entry point for all HTTPS requests in the system. It basically reroutes incoming HTTPS requests to the appropriate servers. For example, some Fiori apps may send HTTPS requests to hit the ABAP front-end server, and other requests may hit the SAP HANA XS; the Web Dispatcher identifies the incoming requests' targets and reroutes the requests accordingly.

Fiori Architecture for Fact Sheet Applications

Fact sheet apps display information and key facts about central objects used in the user's business operations. From a fact sheet tile, users can drill down into details and navigate from one fact sheet to another: for example, from a document to the related business partner. Figure 1-24 shows the architecture of a Fiori fact sheet app.

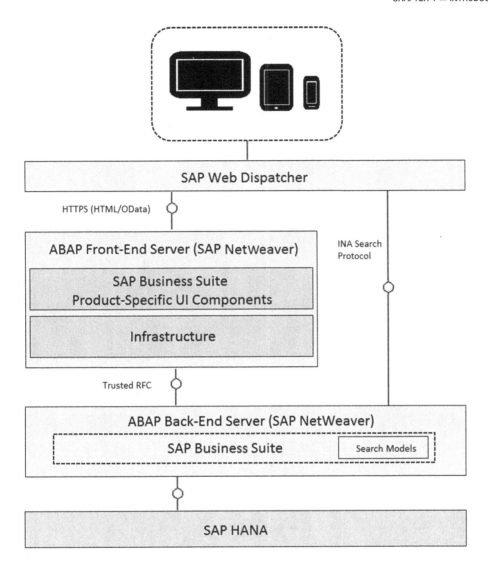

Figure 1-24. *Fiori fact sheet app architecture*

From a fact sheet app, users can start transactions by navigating into transactional apps, access back-end systems, and so on. Users can access fact sheets from the search bar in the Fiori launchpad, from other fact sheets, or from transactional and analytical apps. Fact sheet apps run only on SAP HANA.

The fact sheet's ABAP front-end server is the same as for transactional and analytical apps: it contains product-specific UI components, the SAP UI5 library, the Fiori launchpad, and SAP Gateway.

The front-end server has read access to the ABAP back-end server via trusted RFC connections. The back-end server contains the business suite with relevant business logic, OData services for the apps, and search models.

Web Dispatcher reroutes incoming HTTPS requests that hit the system. It selects the appropriate server for each request. For example, a fact sheet's INA protocol may request access to the search models that reside in the ABAP back-end server.

In the next chapter, you learn about the prerequisites for the Fiori landscape, how to set up the Fiori landscape, and how to configure the Fiori launchpad.

CHAPTER 2

Setting Up the Fiori Landscape

The latest version of the SAP software comes with the Fiori launchpad and Gateway services preinstalled. For older versions, you need to install Gateway and back-end Fiori components separately. This chapter covers this process, including the prerequisites and how to set up the Fiori landscape.

Fiori Prerequisites

Older versions of SAP (ECC6 with EHP version less than 7) require two primary types of add-ons before you can set up the Fiori landscape:

- SAP NetWeaver Gateway and user interface add-ons

  - The NetWeaver Gateway version for SAP ERP with NetWeaver 7.31 or less should be NetWeaver Gateway 2.0 SP 06 with add-on IW_DEP 200 and SAP Notes 1799722 and 1805831. (You can check this link to find out how to search for SAP Notes relevant to your system version: https://scn.sap.com/community/mobile/blog/2013/06/25/sap-fiori-ll03--apply-all-sap-notes-before-implementation.)

  - You should also have SAP NetWeaver AS ABAP 7.00 SPS21 or above with SAP Note 1774246 (prerequisites for this note are 1799549, 1805986, 1754533, and 1809628).

- Back-end system add-ons (for ECC, SRM, CRM, and so on).

You can configure the Fiori landscape as an embedded or hub-based system. SAP Gateway is on a separate system that is connected to the respective back-end system. This chapter covers the hub-based system configuration.

Prerequisites for the Front-End Server (SAP NetWeaver Gateway)

Table 2-1 shows the SAP NetWeaver Gateway 2.0 components for the SAP NetWeaver installation.

© Bince Mathew 2015
B. Mathew, *Beginning SAP Fiori*, DOI 10.1007/978-1-4842-1335-3_2

Table 2-1. *SAP Gateway Components*

Prerequisite	NetWeaver Product Version	Software Components
SAP NetWeaver 7.0 for SAP EhP1	Gateway Server Core NW 700/701	GW_CORE 190 SAP IWFND 240
	Gateway PGW	IW_PGW 100 IW_PGW 200
SAP NetWeaver 7.0 for SAP EhP2	Gateway Server Core NW 702	GW_CORE 200 SAP IW FND 250 SAP WEB UIF 7.01
	Gateway PGW	IW_PGW 100 IW_BEP 200
SAP NetWeaver 7.0 for SAP EhP3	Gateway Server Core NW 703/731	GW_CORE 200 SAP IW FND 250 SAP WEB UIF 7.31
	Gateway PGW	IW_PGW 100 IW_BEP 200
SAP NetWeaver 7.4	Gateway Server is a built-in part of NetWeaver 7.4.	GW_FND 740
	Gateway PGW	IW_PGW 100

User Interface Add-on Components

Table 2-2 lists user interface add-on components for the SAP NetWeaver installation. These components are relevant only for NetWeaver versions prior to SAP NetWeaver 7.4.

Table 2-2. *UI Add-On Components for SAP NetWeaver*

SAP NetWeaver Version	Required UI Software Components	Support Package Level
All installations prior to SAP NetWeaver 7.4	UI_INFRA 100 UI2_700 100 UI2_FND 100 UI2_SRVC 100 UISAPUI5 100	SP06
SAP EhP1 for SAP NetWeaver 7.0 or higher	UI2_701 100 UI2_702 100	SP06
SAP EhP3 for SAP NetWeaver 7.1 or higher SAP EhP1 for SAP NetWeaver 7.3 or higher	UI2_731 100	SP06

Prerequisites for the Back-End Server for SAP ERP

Table 2-3 lists the SAP NetWeaver Gateway 2.0 components for the SAP NetWeaver installation.

Table 2-3. *SAP NetWeaver Gateway 2.0 Components*

Prerequisites
SAP NetWeaver 7.0 SPS 21 or higher
For SAP Fiori apps based on SAP ERP:

For SAP Fiori apps based on SAP ERP:

- SAP Enterprise Resource Planning (ERP) 6.0 SPS 15 or higher
- SAP ERP 6.0 SPS 15 or higher
- SAP ERP 6.0 EhP2 SPS 06 or higher
- SAP ERP 6.0 EhP3 SPS 05 or higher
- SAP ERP 6.0 EhP4 SPS 05 or higher
- SAP ERP 6.0 EhP5 SPS 03 or higher
- SAP ERP 6.0 EhP6 SPS 01 or higher

ERP installations prior to SAP NetWeaver 7.4:

- Back-end event provider: software component IW_BEP 200 SP 07

Initial Configuration

After you set up the SAP Gateway, UI add-ons, and the back-end server add-ons, you can begin your Fiori configuration:

1. Create Fiori users, and assign authorizations.

2. Connect the SAP NetWeaver Gateway with the back-end SAP suite.

3. Configure Web Dispatcher (required only for fact sheets and analytical apps).

4. Set up the Fiori launchpad and the launchpad designer.

Creating Fiori Users and Assigning Authorizations

Before you can start using Fiori, you need to set up two primary types of users: admin users and end users. These users must be created in both the front-end server and the respective back-end SAP suite. Follow these steps:

1. Log in to the front-end server (SAP Gateway server).

2. Execute the following transaction: SU01.

3. In this example, you create two users named FIORI_ADMIN (see Figure 2-1) and FIORI_USER. Log in to the SAP back-end suite (SAP ECC, SRM, CRM, and so on), and create these users.

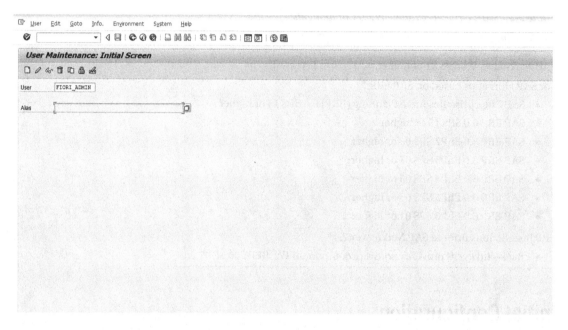

Figure 2-1. *SAP transaction User Maintenance SU01*

Once you've created the users, you need to give them the authorizations that make them admin and end users:

4. Log in to the front-end server (SAP Gateway server).

5. Execute the transaction PFCG (see Figure 2-2).

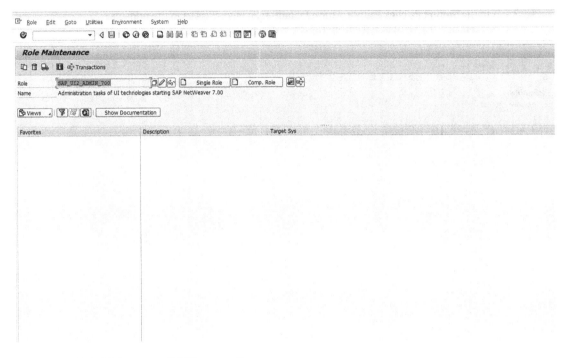

Figure 2-2. *Role Maintenance PFCG transaction*

6. Under Role Maintenance, make a copy of the role SAP_UI2_ADMIN_700 (see Figure 2-3).

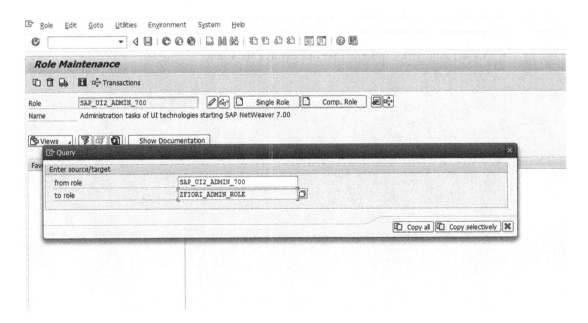

Figure 2-3. *Making a custom role for the admin user*

7. On the Menu tab, click Authorization Default (see Figure 2-4). On the pop-up screen, select TADIR Service from the drop-down list.

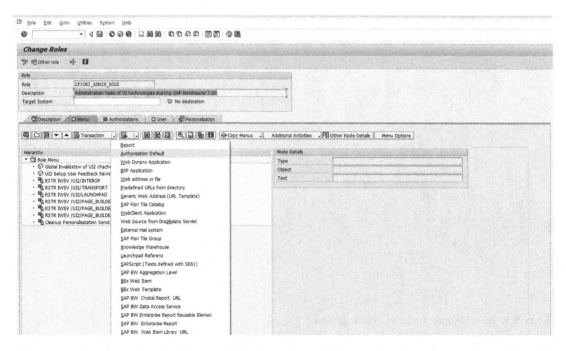

Figure 2-4. *Click Authorization Default*

8. Make the following entries, as shown in Figure 2-5:

- Program ID: **R3TR**

- Object Type: **IWSG Gateway: Service Groups Metadata**

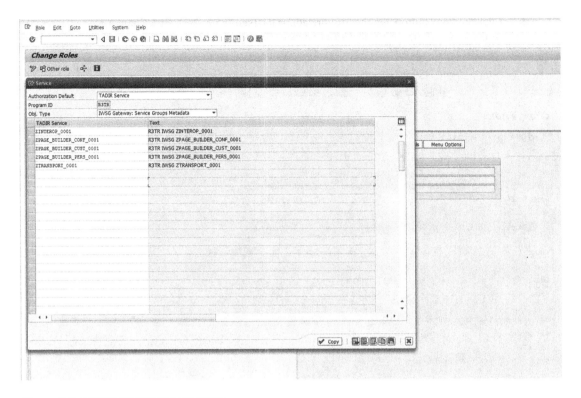

Figure 2-5. *TADIR Service pop-up screen*

Add the following TADIR service values:

- ZINTEROP_0001

- ZPAGE_BUILDER_CUST_0001

- ZPAGE_BUILDER_PERS_0001

- ZPAGE_BUILDER_CONF_0001

- ZTRANSPORT_0001

9. Click the Copy button. On the Authorizations tab (see Figure 2-6), click Change Authorization Data. Then, click Generate (see Figure 2-7).

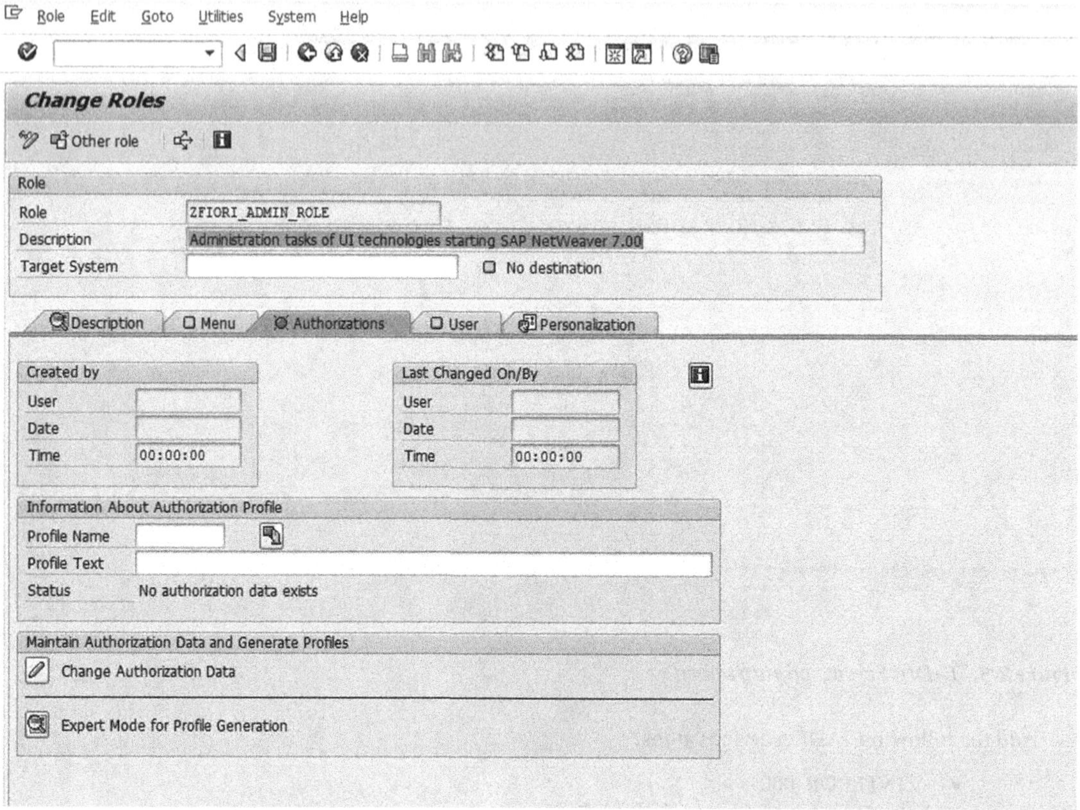

Figure 2-6. *Authorizations tab*

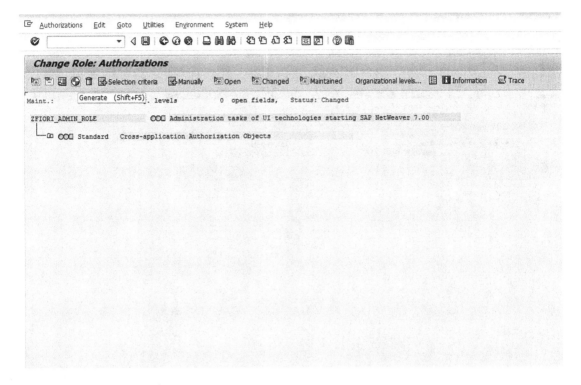

Figure 2-7. *Generating authorizations*

10. Similarly, for the end user, copy the SAP_UI2_USER_700 role and add the TADIR service with the following values (see Figure 2-8):

- ZINTEROP_0001

- ZPAGE_BUILDER_PERS_0001

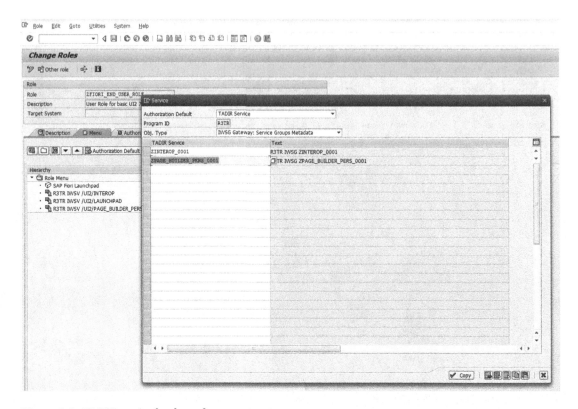

Figure 2-8. *TADIR service for the end user*

Once you've created these roles, you need to assign them to FIORI_ADMIN and FIORI_USER:

11.   Execute the transaction PFCG.

12.   Under Role Maintenance, give the custom role name you created:
       ZFIORI_ADMIN_ROLE.

13.   Go to the User tab, add the FIORI_ADMIN user to the list, and click Save
       (see Figure 2-9).

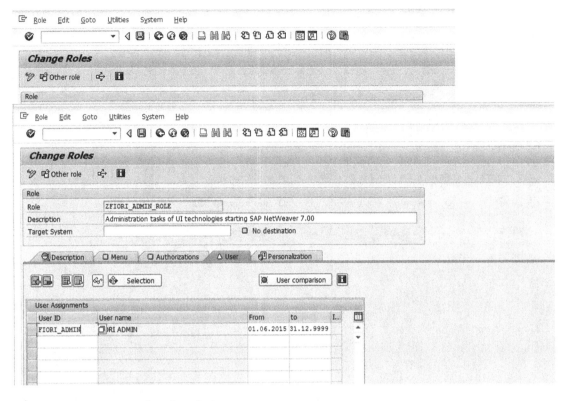

Figure 2-9. *Assigning a role to the admin user*

14. Follow the same steps to assign ZFIORI_END_USER_ROLE to FIORI_USER (see Figure 2-10).

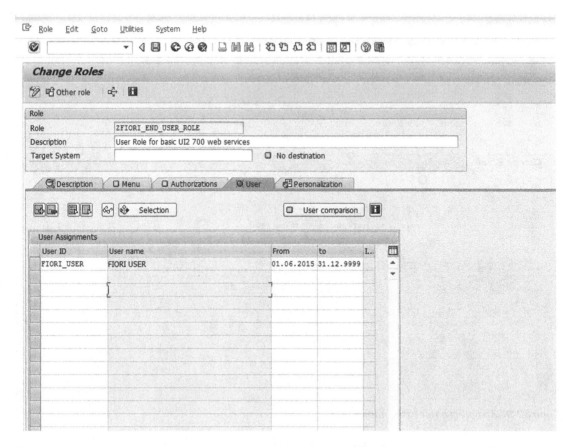

Figure 2-10. *Assigning a role to the end user*

Connecting SAP NetWeaver Gateway with the Back-End SAP Suite

In order to make SAP Gateway communicate with your back-end SAP system, you need to assign a few roles and set up a trusted RFC connection between the two systems.

Assigning a Role Template for Administrators (SAP Gateway System)

Here are the steps:

1.   Execute the transaction PFCG.

2.   Create a new custom role: in this example, Z_TMPL_ADMIN.

3.   Click Single Role.

4.   On the Authorizations tab, click Change Authorization Data.

5.   In the dialog box, select /IWFND/RT_ADMIN, and click the Adopt Reference button (see Figure 2-11).

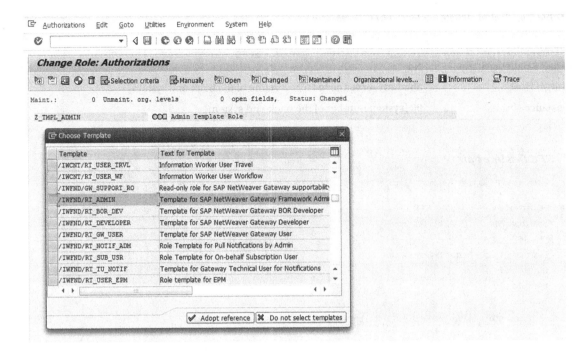

Figure 2-11. *Creating an admin role template*

6. Click the Generate button.

7. On the Users tab, add the administrative user ID.

Creating Trusted RFCs in SAP Gateway to Connect with the SAP Back-End System

In order for Fiori apps to communicate between SAP Gateway and SAP back-end systems, a trust relationship must be maintained between the systems. You can do this by configuring the SAP Gateway system as the trusting system and the SAP back-end system as the trusted system. Here are the steps:

1. Execute the transaction SM59.

2. Click the Create button.

3. Under RFC Destination, give the destination name (preferably in the format **<system id>CLNT<client>**).

4. In the Connection Type field, enter the value **3**.

5. Enter a description for the connection in the Description 1 field.

6. Click Save.

7. On the Technical Settings tab (see Figure 2-12), enter the values listed in Table 2-4.

Table 2-4. *Technical Settings for the RFC Destination*

Name	Value
Load Balancing Status	No
Target Host	**abcd.myserver.corp** (server name of the back-end system)
Instance No.	**00** (system number of the back-end system)

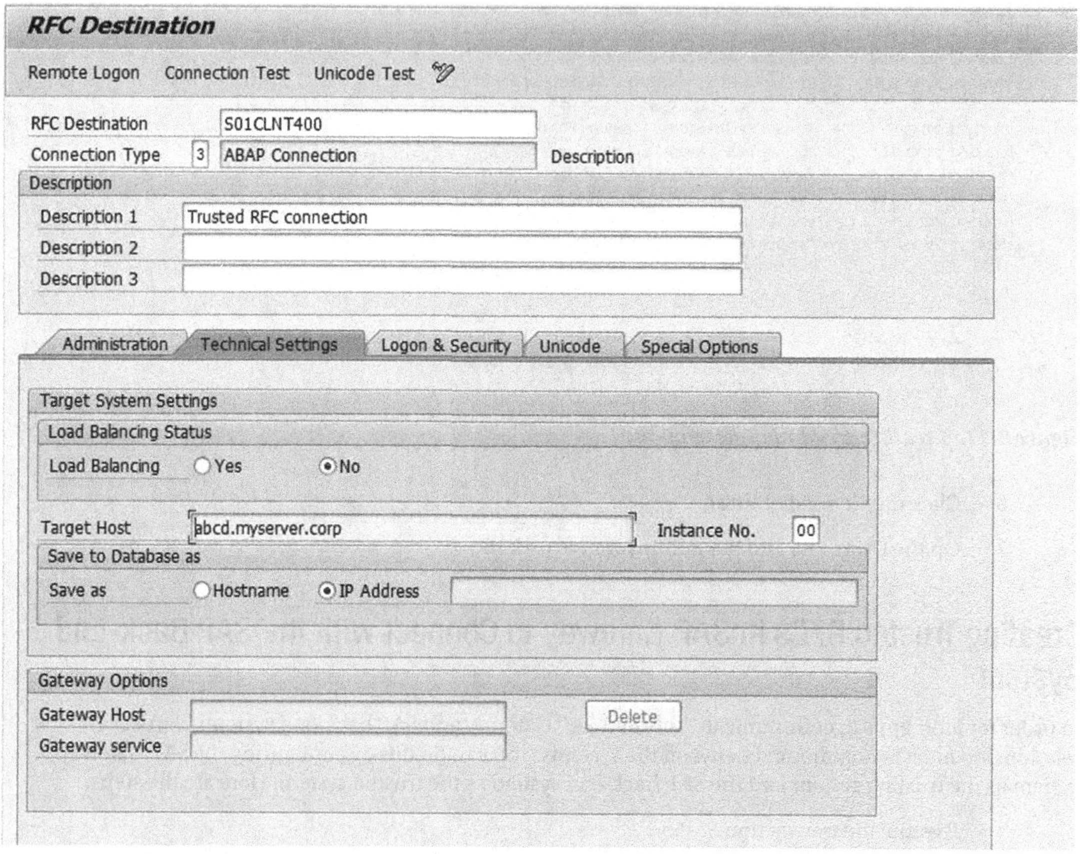

Figure 2-12. *Trusted RFC technical settings*

On the Logon & Security tab (see Figure 2-13), enter the values listed in Table 2-5, and then click Save.

Table 2-5. *Logon & Security Settings for the RFC Destination*

Name	Value
Language	**EN**
Client	**400** (client of the back-end system)
User	Select the Current User check box.
Trust Relationship	Yes

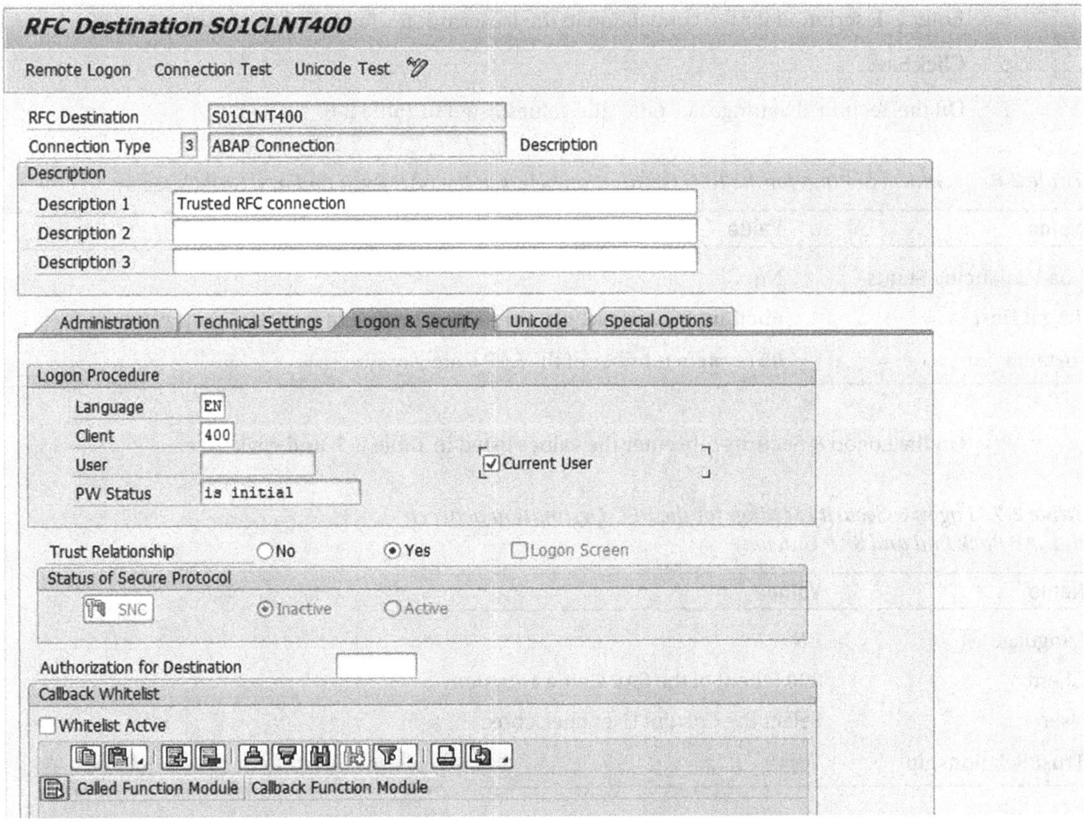

Figure 2-13. *Trusted RFC Logon & Security settings*

Defining a Trusted Connection between the SAP Back-End System and the SAP Gateway System

Similar to the previous step, a trusted connection must be maintained in the opposite direction. In this case, you have to configure the SAP back-end system to be the trusting system and SAP Gateway as the trusted system:

1. Execute the transaction SM59.

2. Click Create.

3. Under RFC Destination, give the destination name (preferably in the format **<system id>CLNT<client>**).

4. In the Connection Type field, enter the value **3**.

5. Enter a description for the connection in the Description 1 field.

6. Click Save.

7. On the Technical Settings tab, enter the values listed in Table 2-6.

Table 2-6. *Technical Settings for the RFC Destination between the SAP Back End and SAP Gateway*

Name	Value
Load Balancing Status	No
Target Host	**abcd.mygatewayserver.corp** (server name of the SAP Gateway system)
Instance No.	**00** (system number of the SAP Gateway system)

8. On the Logon & Security tab, enter the values listed in Table 2-7, and click Save.

Table 2-7. *Logon & Security Settings for the RFC Destination between the SAP Back End and SAP Gateway*

Name	Value
Language	**EN**
Client	**200** (client of the SAP Gateway system)
User	Select the Current User check box.
Trust Relationship	Yes

Now do the following in the SAP back-end system:

1. Execute the transaction SMT1.

2. Click Create.

3. Proceed with the wizard (see Figure 2-14), and give the RFC destination name that you created to connect to the SAP gateway system. An RFC logon occurs, and the required information is exchanged between the two systems.

4. Click Save.

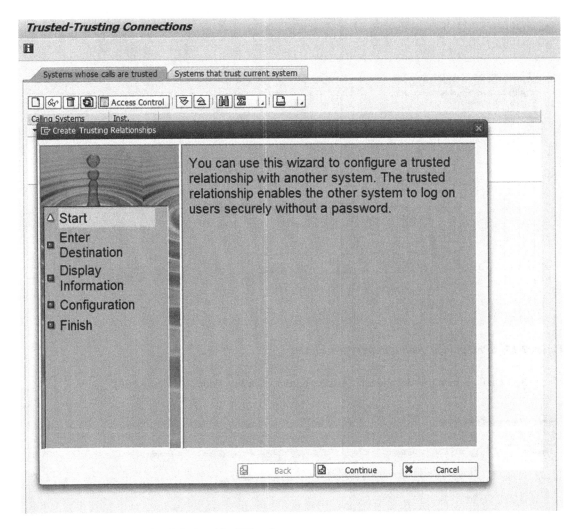

Figure 2-14. *Create Trusting Relationships Wizard*

Creating a System Alias

A *system alias* is a unique name you give a system that points to other systems. You're required to maintain system aliases so you can activate a service that resides on another system by connecting to the system based on its system alias. Follow these steps:

1. Execute the transaction SPRO.

2. Go to the path SAP NetWeaver ➤ Gateway ➤ OData Channel ➤ Configuration ➤ Connection Settings ➤ SAP NetWeaver Gateway to SAP System ➤ Manage SAP System Aliases, as shown in Figure 2-15.

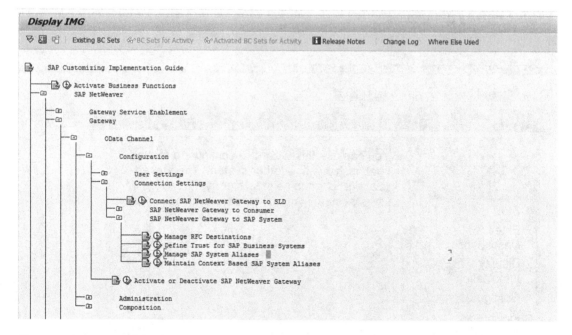

Figure 2-15. *SPRO path for maintaining system aliases*

3. On the screen showing the list of existing entries, click New Entry (see Figure 2-16).

Figure 2-16. *Creating a system alias*

4. Add the entry shown in Table 2-8.

Table 2-8. *System Alias Settings on the SAP Gateway System to Connect with the SAP ERP System*

Setting	Value
SAP System Alias	**ECCCLNT201** (RFC destination name)
Description	Description of the RFC destination
RFC Destination	**ECCCLNT201** (RFC destination name)
Software Version	**DEFAULT**

If the Local system alias for SAP Gateway does not exist, add the entry shown in Table 2-9 (see Figure 2-17).

Table 2-9. *Settings for the Local System Alias*

Name	Value
SAP System Alias	**LOCAL**
Description	**Local System Alias**
Local GW	Select the Local GW check box.
RFC Destination	**NONE**
Software Version	**DEFAULT**

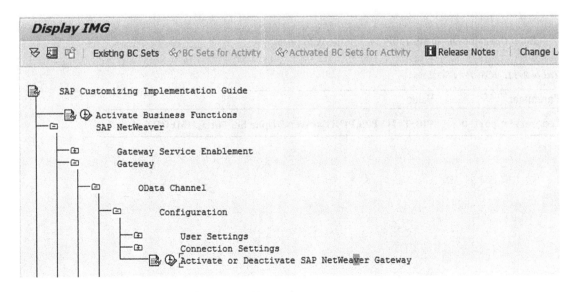

Figure 2-17. *Creating a default local system alias*

Activating SAP Gateway

In the Gateway front-end server, you need to activate Gateway. Follow these steps:

1. Execute the transaction SPRO.

2. Go to path SAP NetWeaver ➤ Gateway ➤ OData Channel ➤ Configuration ➤ Connection Settings ➤ Activate or Deactivate SAP NetWeaver Gateway (see Figure 2-18).

Figure 2-18. *Activating SAP Gateway*

Configuring SAP Web Dispatcher

SAP Fiori apps connect to multiple SAP back-end systems. But these apps are based on the HTML5 framework and JavaScript. When they access multiple back-end systems, the apps are blocked by a same-origin-policy error. To overcome this issue, you can use SAP Web Dispatcher to combine all the back-end hostnames/IPs, ports, and so on in a single origin. Doing so also provides a certain level of security. SAP Web Dispatcher is not mandatory for Fiori transactional apps, but it is mandatory for fact sheets and analytical apps. Web Dispatcher must be configured as an SSL client.

Because Web Dispatcher is a big topic, this section covers only the parts of the configuration that are related to Fiori. Follow these steps:

1. Edit the instance profile of the Web Dispatcher:
   WDP_W<InstanceNumber>_<hostname>.

2. To enable the HTTPS protocol for Web Dispatcher, install the `sapcrypto.dll` file. Make the entries listed in Table 2-10 in the Web Dispatcher instance profile.

Table 2-10. *Settings for Web Dispatcher*

Parameter	Value
DIR_INSTANCE	<SECUDIR_Directory>
ssl/ssl_lib	<Location_of_SAP_Cryptographic_Library>
ssl/client_pse	<Location_of_SSL_server_PSE>
ssl/server_pse	< Location_of_SSL_client_PSE >
wdisp/ssl_encrypt	**1**
wdisp/ssl_auth	**1**
wdisp/add_client_protocol_header	**1**
wdisp/ping_protocol	**https**
icm/HTTPS/verify_client	**1**

Enter the values listing in Table 2-11 in the ICM ports.

Table 2-11. *ICM Port Settings*

Parameter	Value
icm/server_port_0	**PROT=HTTPS,PORT**=<Web Dispatcher Port>**,TIMEOUT=120**

Include the parameters from Table 2-12 in the Web Dispatcher routes profile.

Table 2-12. *Routes Profile Settings*

Parameter	Value
wdisp/system_0	**SID**=<Front-End SID>, **MSHOST**=<Front-End Hostname>, **MSPORT**=<Front-End Messaging Port>, **SRCSRV**=*:<Web Dispatcher Port>,**SRCURL**=/sap/**opu**/;/sap/**public**/;/sap/**bc**/;/sap/**saml2**/;/**ui2/nwbc**/, **CLIENT**=<Front-End client>
wdisp/system_1	**SID**=<Back-End SID>, **MSHOST**=<Back-End Hostname>, **MSPORT**=<Back-End Messaging Port>, **SRCSRV**=*:<Web Dispatcher Port>,**SRCURL**=/sap/**es**/, **CLIENT**= <Back-End client>
wdisp/system_2	**SID**=<HANA SID>, **EXTSRV**=<HANA XS URL>,**SRCSRV**=*:<Web Dispatcher Port>,**SRCURL**=/sap/**hba**/;/sap/**hana**/;/sap/**bi**/;/sap/**viz**/;/sap/**vi**/;/sap/**ui5**/

After making these changes, you can test the Web Dispatcher using the following URL in your browser: https://<Web Dispatcher Hostname> :<Web Dispatcher Port>/sap/admin/public/default.html.

Setting Up the Fiori Launchpad, Fiori Launchpad Designer, and Fiori Admin Page

You need to activate the OData services required for the launchpad to communicate with and fetch business data from the SAP back-end servers. Follow these steps:

1. Log on to the SAP Gateway Server (front-end server).

2. Execute the transaction SPRO.

3. Go to the path SAP NetWeaver ➤ Gateway ➤ OData Channel ➤ Administration ➤ General Settings ➤ Activate and Maintain Services (see Figure 2-19).

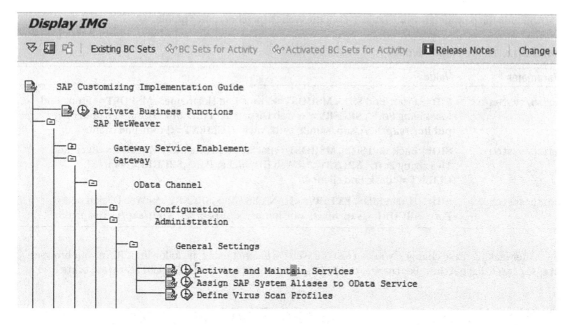

Figure 2-19. *Activating OData services for the launchpad*

4. Click the Add Service button.

5. Select Local as the System Alias.

6. From the list of services displayed, select the technical service /UI2/LAUNCHPAD.

7. In the Add Service dialog box, enter the package name and choose ICF Node as Standard Mode.

8. Add the technical services listed in Table 2-13.

Table 2-13. *Settings for the ICF Node*

Technical Service Name	Description
/UI2/PAGE_BUILDER_CONF	Page Builder - Configuration Level
/UI2/PAGE_BUILDER_CUST	Page Builder - Customizing Level
/UI2/PAGE_BUILDER_PERS	Page Builder - Personalization Level
/UI2/INTEROP	Gateway Service of Interoperability
/UI2/TRANSPORT	UI2: Transport Service

Activating ICF Nodes

You need to activate the ICF nodes related to Fiori in order to access the relevant Fiori URLs. Here are the steps:

1. Execute the Transaction SICF.

2. Select the services in Tables 2-14, 2-15, and 2-16; click Maintain Service; and activate each of those services (see Figure 2-20).

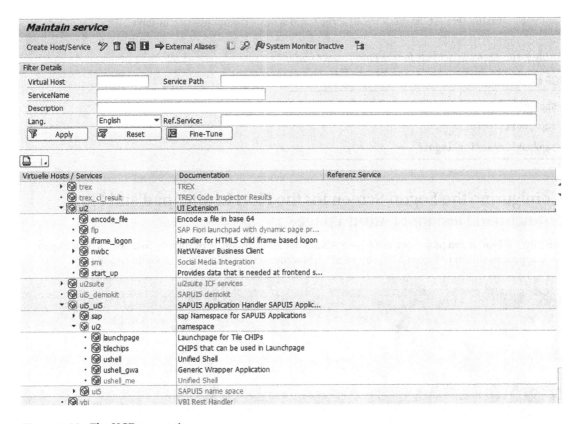

Figure 2-20. *The SICF transaction*

3. Go to /default_host/sap/bc/, and activate the nodes listed in Table 2-14.

Table 2-14. *Nodes to Activate for the Fiori Launchpad*

ICF Node Path
/sap/bc/ui2/start_up
/sap/bc/ui2/nwbc/

4. Go to /default_host/sap/bc/ui5_ui5/, and activate the nodes listed in Table 2-15.

Table 2-15. *Nodes to Activate for the Fiori Launchpad*

ICF Node Path
/sap/bc/ui5_ui5/ui2/ushell
/sap/bc/ui5_ui5/sap/arsrvc_upb_admn
/sap/bc/ui5_ui5/sap/ar_srvc_news
/sap/bc/ui5_ui5/sap/ar_srvc_launch

5. Go to /default_host/sap/public/bc/, and activate the nodes listed in Table 2-16.

Table 2-16. *Nodes to Activate for the Fiori Launchpad*

ICF Node Path
/sap/public/bc/ui5_ui5/
/sap/public/bc/ui2/
/sap/public/bc/icf/logoff

Configuring the Logon Screen for the Fiori Launchpad and Fiori Launchpad Designer (Admin page)

Initially, the Fiori logon page does not have a default background image or theme. To make the Fiori logon page appear as shown in Figure 2-21, you need to do some configuration in SICF. Follow these steps:

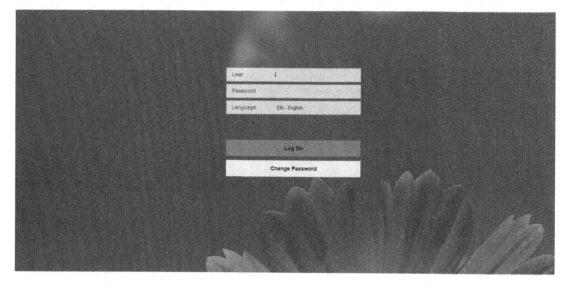

Figure 2-21. *Fiori logon screen*

1. Log in to SAP Gateway (front-end server).

2. Execute the transaction SICF.

3. Go to the path /sap/bc/ui5_ui5/ui2/ushell, and double-click ushell.

4. Click the Error Pages tab (see Figure 2-22).

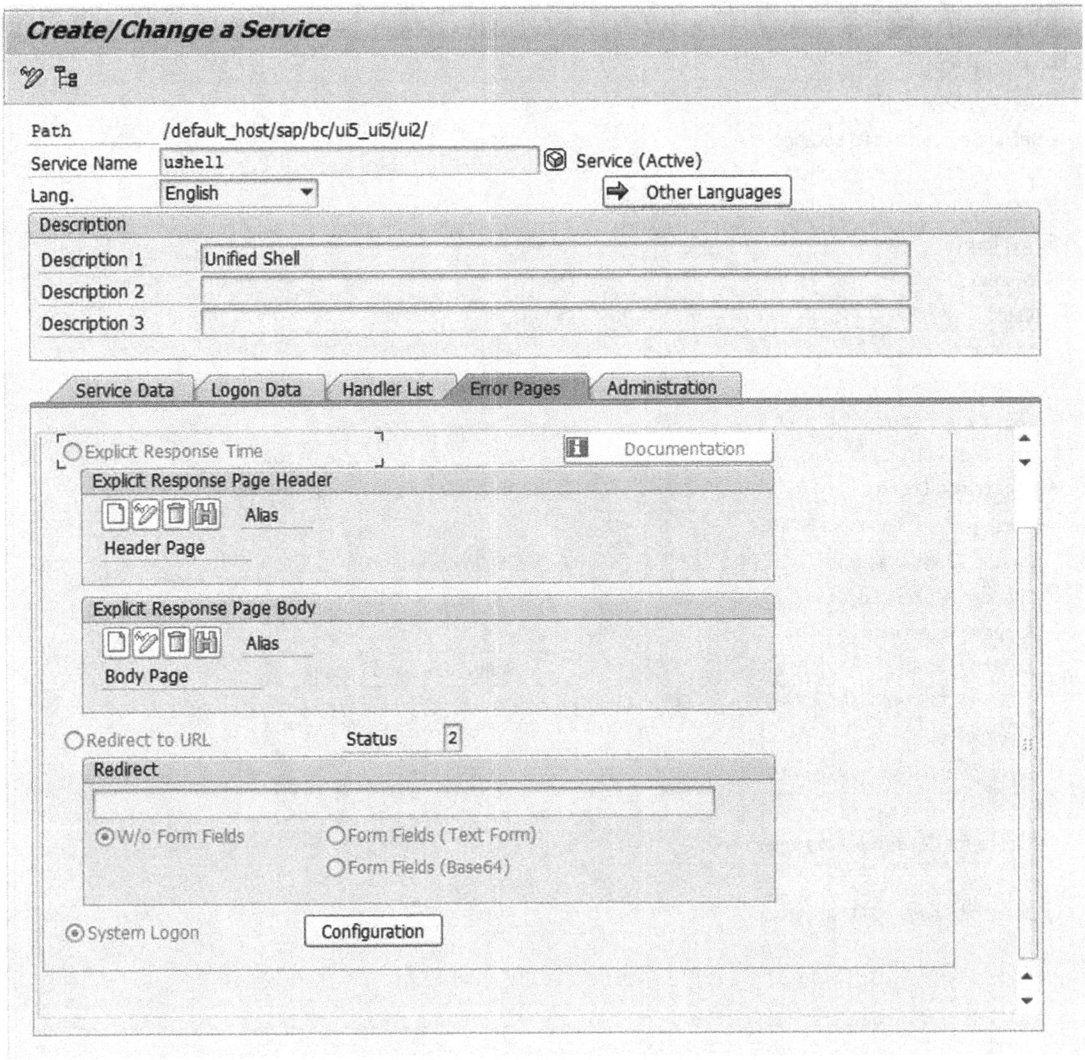

Create/Change a Service

Path   /default_host/sap/bc/ui5_ui5/ui2/
Service Name ushell   Service (Active)
Lang.   English ▼   ⇒   Other Languages

Description

Description 1   Unified Shell
Description 2
Description 3

| Service Data | Logon Data | Handler List | Error Pages | Administration |

○ Explicit Response Time   ℹ️   Documentation

Explicit Response Page Header

▢ ✎ 🗑 🔍 Alias
Header Page

Explicit Response Page Body

▢ ✎ 🗑 🔍 Alias
Body Page

○ Redirect to URL   Status   2

Redirect

◉ W/o Form Fields   ○ Form Fields (Text Form)
                           ○ Form Fields (Base64)

◉ System Logon   Configuration

Figure 2-22. *Fiori launchpad page configuration*

5. Choose System Logon, and then click the Configuration button.

6. In the dialog box, select Custom Implementation. In the ABAP Class field, enter
    the value **/UI2/CL_SRALOGIN** (see Figure 2-23).

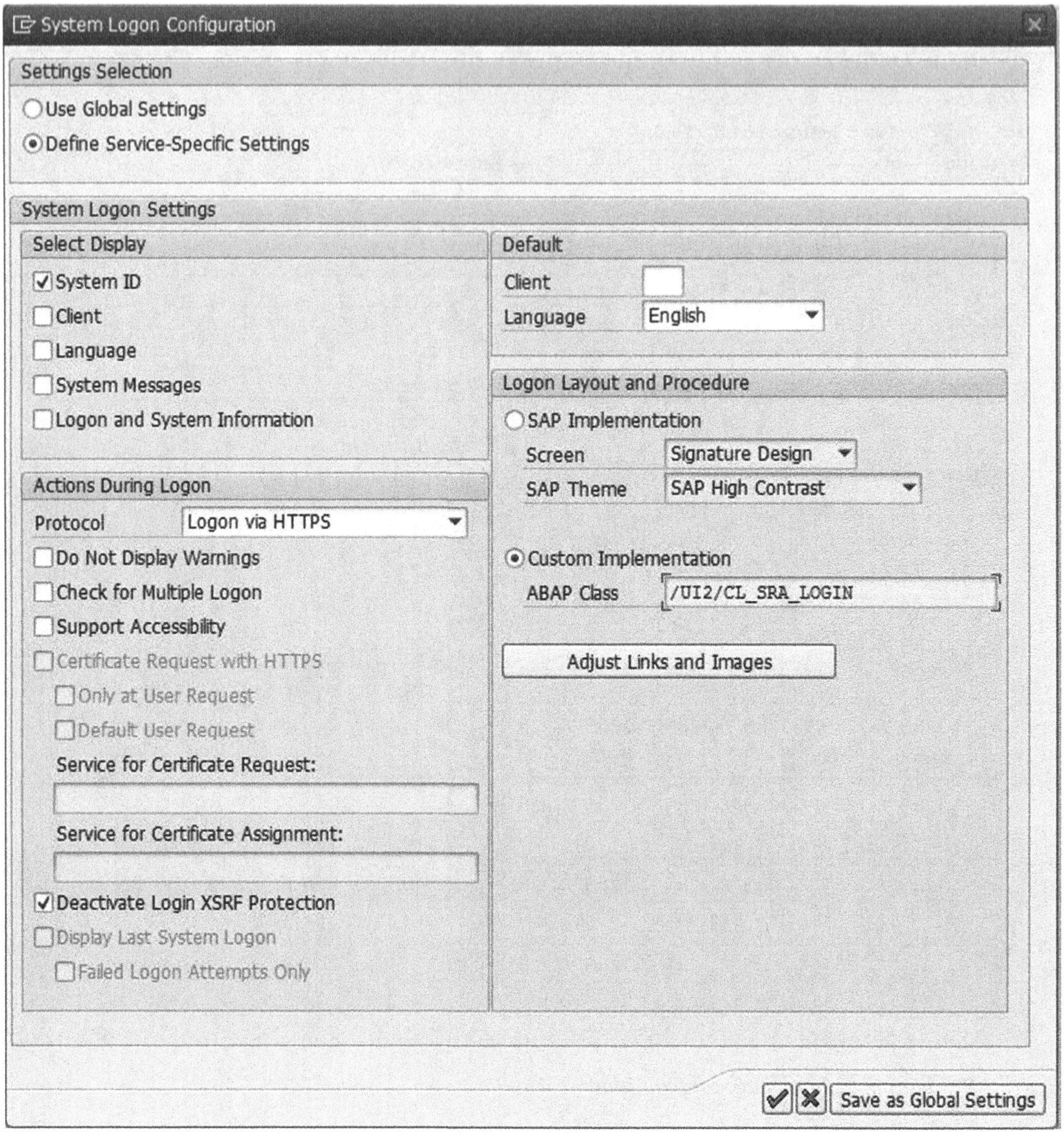

Figure 2-23. *Fiori launchpad logon configuration*

    7.   Click Save.

    8.   For the Admin page and Fiori Launchpad Designer page, go to the path /sap/bc/ ui5_ui5/sap/arsrvc_upb_admn and perform the same configuration steps.

Configuring the Logout Screen

When a user logs out from the Fiori launchpad, a logoff page is displayed. This particular page can be replaced with any custom page you wish. Here are the steps:

1. Execute the transaction SICF.

2. Go to the path /default_host/sap/public/bc/icf/logoff.

3. Double-click the logoff service.

4. Click the Change icon.

5. On the Error Pages tab, select the Logoff Page tab.

6. Select the option Redirect to URL, and enter the custom logoff page URL (see Figure 2-24).

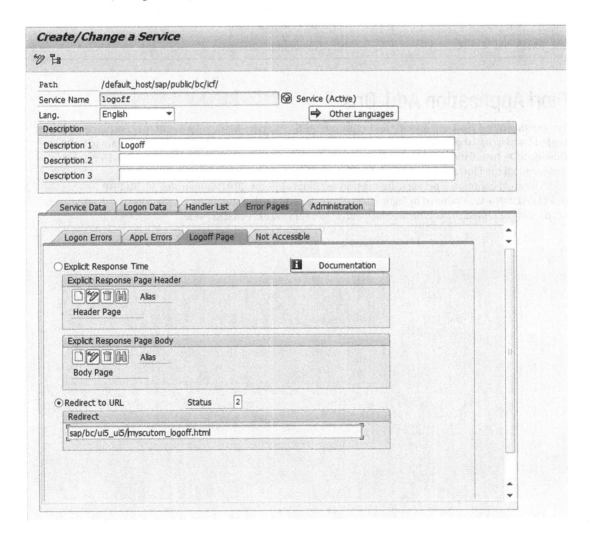

Figure 2-24. *Customizing the Fiori logoff page*

In NetWeaver 7.4, you can automate some of the manual configuration steps by using a predefined task list. The task list must be carried out in the order shown in Table 2-17.

Table 2-17. *Predefined Task List for NetWeaver 7.4*

Task List	Manual Configuration Steps Automated Using the Task List
SAP_GATEWAY_BASIC_CONFIG	Activating SAP NetWeaver Gateway
SAP_FIORI_LAUNCHPAD_INIT_SETUP	Activating the launchpad OData services
	Configuring ICF nodes
SAP_SAP2GATEWAY_TRUSTED_CONFIG	Creating trusted RFCs in NetWeaver Gateway to the SAP business suite
	Defining trust RFCs between the SAP business suite and SAP NetWeaver Gateway
SAP_GATEWAY_ADD_SYSTEM	Creating system aliases
SAP_BASIS_SSL_CHECK	No equivalent manual step

Fiori Application Add-Ons

You can download Fiori app-specific add-ons from the SAP Service Marketplace at http://service.sap.com/support and install them using the SAINT t-code. From the SAP Service Marketplace, navigate to Software Download ➤ Installation and Upgrades ➤ A-Z Index ➤ F ➤ SAP Fiori ➤ SAP Fiori for Suite. Here, you can download all the Fiori apps for ERP, CRM, SRM, EHS, and so on.

The most common Fiori apps are the transactional apps for ERP (found under FIORI ERP APPLICATIONS X2, as shown in Figure 2-25). You can find further details for configuring these add-ons at https://fioriappslibrary.hana.ondemand.com/sap/fix/externalViewer/.

INSTALLATIONS AND UPGRADES - F

Installations and Upgrades - F° SAP Fiori

SAP FIORI

- **SAP Fiori app implementation foundation**
- **SAP Fiori for Suite**
  - FIORI APPROVE REQUESTS X1
    SAP Fiori for request approvals
  - FIORI CRM APPLICATIONS X2
    SAP Fiori transactional apps for SAP CRM
  - FIORI ERP APPLICATIONS X1
    SAP Fiori principal apps for SAP ERP
  - FIORI ERP APPLICATIONS X2
    SAP Fiori transactional apps for SAP ERP
  - FIORI SRM APPLICATIONS X1
    SAP Fiori principal apps for SAP SRM
  - SAP FIORI FOR SAP CARAB
    SAP Fiori for SAP Customer Activity Repository retail applications bundle
  - SAP FIORI FOR SAP CPM
    SAP Fiori for SAP Commercial Project Management
  - SAP FIORI FOR SAP CRM
    SAP Fiori for SAP CRM
  - SAP FIORI FOR SAP DSIM
    SAP Fiori for SAP Demand Signal Management
  - SAP FIORI FOR SAP EHSM
    SAP Fiori for SAP EHS Management
  - SAP FIORI FOR SAP EM
    SAP Fiori for SAP Event Management
  - SAP FIORI FOR SAP ERP
    SAP Fiori for SAP ERP
  - SAP FIORI FOR SAP ERP HCM
    SAP Fiori for SAP ERP HCM
  - SAP FIORI FOR SAP FM
    SAP Fiori for SAP Fashion Management
  - SAP FIORI FOR SAP FND
    SAP Fiori for SAP Business Suite foundation component
  - SAP FIORI FOR SAP GRC
    SAP Fiori for SAP solutions for GRC

Figure 2-25. *Fiori app-specific add-ons*

The next chapter discusses the Fiori launchpad and Fiori app configuration in detail.

CHAPTER 3

Fiori Launchpad and Applications

After setting up Fiori Landscape, now we can customize the Fiori Launchpad and set up the standard applications. In this chapter you will learn about different applications available for Fiori, Fiori Launchpad basics, Fiori Launchpad administration, Configuring Tiles, assigning roles to users, End user launchpad customizations and Fiori Approval workflow application configurations.

The Fiori Launchpad and Launchpad Designer

The Fiori launchpad is the single point of entry for end users to access Fiori apps. Fiori has a launchpad designer for the use of Fiori administrators.

End users can access the apps assigned to them based on their roles. For example, if you are a manager, when you log in to the Fiori launchpad, you see manager-related apps in addition to the default apps.

Fiori administrators can do the following:

- Create catalogs and groups

- Assign catalogs and groups to end users

- Create custom tiles

- Configure and modify standard tiles

- Edit launchpad settings, configure target mappings, and so on

The default URL for the Fiori launchpad is as follows:

```
http://<host>.<domain>:<port>/sap/bc/ui5_ui5/ui2/ushell/shells/abap/Fiorilaunchpad.html?
sap-client=<client>&sap-language=EN
```

The default URL for the Fiori launchpad designer is as follows:

```
http://<host>.<domain>:<port>/sap/bc/ui5_ui5/sap/arsrvc_upb_admn/main.html?
sap-client=<client>?scope=CUST
```

Fiori Launchpad

In the Fiori launchpad, each app is represented as a tile. Figure 3-1 shows an example of what end users see when they log in to their Fiori home page.

Figure 3-1. *Fiori launchpad for end users*

Fiori Launchpad Basics

You need to be familiar with a few concepts about the Fiori launchpad. First, the launchpad has different types of tiles:

- *Static tiles:* Display predefined contents that are static in nature, such as text and icons (see Figure 3-2).

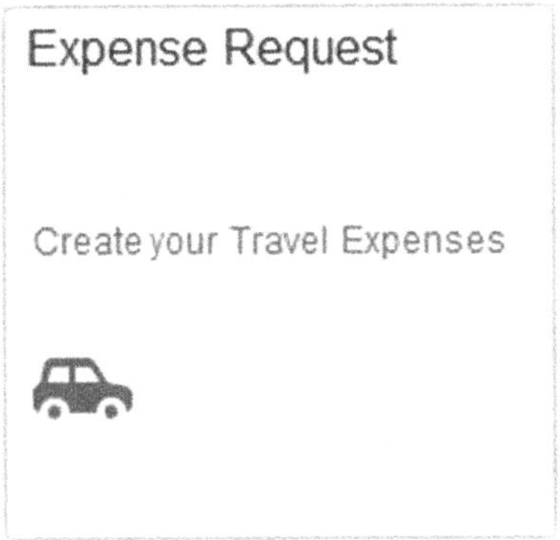

Expense Request

Create your Travel Expenses

Figure 3-2. *Static tile*

- *Dynamic tiles:* Show dynamic number values such as pending purchase order approvals, travel requests, and so on (see Figure 3-3).

Approve Travel
Request

 1

Request

Figure 3-3. *Dynamic tile*

- *KPI tiles:* Key performance indicator tiles, which display alerts or reports. The tile gives a short summary of the data in the form of a micro chart (see Figure 3-4).

Comparative Annual
Totals

Country 1	234 M
Country 2	97 M
Country 3	197 M

USD, By Region

Figure 3-4. *KPI tile*

- *News tiles:* Bring RSS feeds into the Fiori launchpad. You can configure these tiles to display photos and live feeds from multiple RSS feeds. You can also configure the refresh rate for each feed (see Figure 3-5).

Figure 3-5. *News tile*

- *Jam tiles:* Display SAP Jam content. Jam is a social collaboration platform that connects across all SAP technologies such as ABAP, SAPUI5, and Web Dynpro.

Groups and Catalogs

Another concept in the Fiori launchpad are groups and catalogs. Catalogs are like books with a variety of contents, as shown in Figure 3-6:

- Tiles are the contents that go in each catalog.

- Each tile can represent a particular Fiori app or point to another page containing a group of tiles.

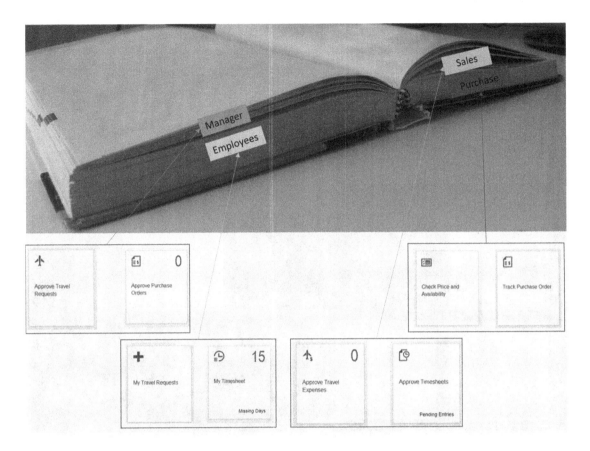

Figure 3-6. *Different tiles that go into catalogs*

Groups are similar to favorites. Users can create them in the Fiori launchpad, or a Fiori administrator can create a group and pin it to the user's home page for easy access (see Figure 3-7).

Figure 3-7. *Fiori launchpad groups*

Fiori Launchpad Designer

Fiori launchpad administrators have access to the Fiori launchpad designer (the Fiori administrator consoler), where they can control and assign roles, catalogs, and tiles to end users. The tiles a user sees on their launchpad are assigned to their ID by the launchpad admin.

Before making any changes in the Fiori launchpad designer, the Fiori admin needs a transport request that lets them transport the changes made in the development system to the QA and production systems later:

1. To assign a transport request, click the settings icon on the upper-right corner of the Fiori launchpad designer (see Figure 3-8).

Figure 3-8. *Click the Settings icon*

2. Deselect the None (Local Object) check box, and assign your new transport request for the launchpad designer from the drop-down list (see Figure 3-9).

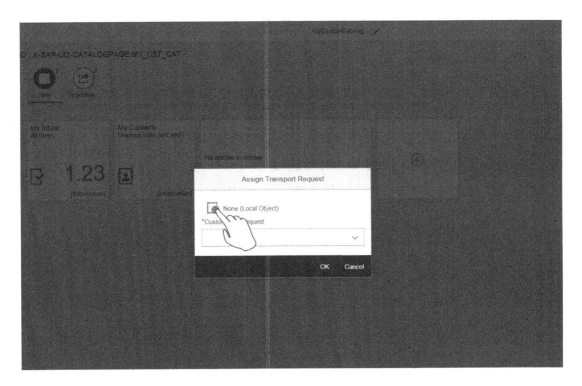

Figure 3-9. *Assign your transport request*

Every tile an end users accesses on their Fiori home page has an invisible target mapping tile linked to it (see Figure 3-10). The target mapping carries out the navigation of the tile to the Fiori app the user wants to access.

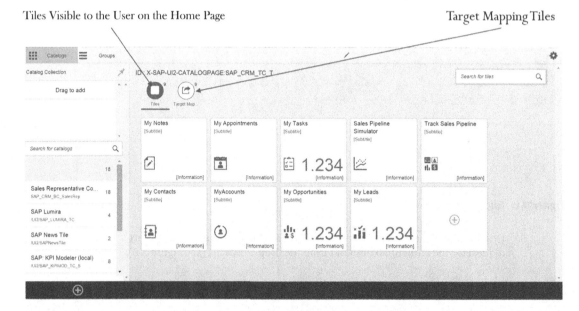

Figure 3-10. *Fiori launchpad designer tiles and target mappings*

The administrator can modify the target mappings of any standard apps and also create custom tiles with the corresponding target mapping for custom apps. You learn in detail about target mapping in the next section.

Assigning Catalogs and Tiles to End Users

In order for end users to see and access tiles, a Fiori administrator must configure the catalog and assign it to the end users in the Fiori launchpad designer. Here are the steps:

1. In the launchpad designer, click the + icon at lower-left (see Figure 3-11).

Figure 3-11. *Click + in the launchpad designer*

2. Give the catalog a title and a unique ID, as shown in Figure 3-12. This ID will be later used in the back-end system to assign the catalog to the users.

Figure 3-12. *Give the catalog a title and ID*

3. Click the + icon to add a new tile (see Figure 3-13).

Figure 3-13. *Add a tile*

4. You see a set of tile types that you can choose from. Click Dynamic (see Figure 3-14). You can also add static and news tiles.

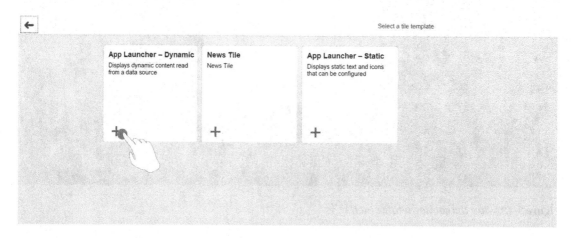

Figure 3-14. *Choosing the dynamic tile type*

5. After creating tiles, you need to configure their properties. To begin, click the new dynamic tile (see Figure 3-15).

Figure 3-15. *Click the new tile*

6. In this example, you configure the dynamic tile with one of the standard Fiori apps (see Figure 3-16):

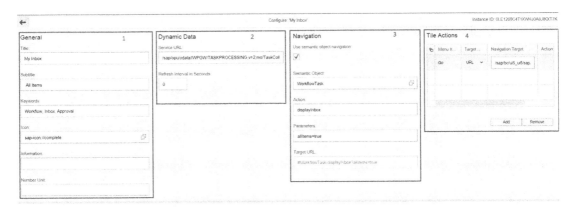

Figure 3-16. *Configure the dynamic tile*

a. In the General section, give the tile a title, subtitle, keywords (which help Fiori know where to show the app in search results in the launchpad), and icon.

b. Because this is a dynamic tile, you must provide a OData service URL in order to show dynamic data.

    c.   The Navigation section is where you indicate whether users can open the app via semantic object-based navigation or directly provide the URL of the app they want to launch. The semantic object is the link between the tile and the target-mapping tile that opens the app. The Action option specifies the type of action the user will carry out with the app: Display, Create, and so on.

    d.   The Tile Actions feature lets the tile execute additional actions.

7.   You configure the same settings for a static tile, with the exception of the Dynamic Data field (see Figure 3-17).

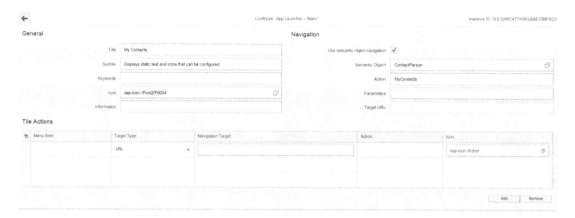

Figure 3-17. *Configuring a static tile*

8.   You can configure a news tile with multiple RSS feeds and set the refresh interval for each feed (see Figure 3-18).

Figure 3-18. *Configuring a news tile*

9. You need to configure the target mappings for dynamic and static tiles. (News tiles don't require a target mapping.) To do so, click the Create Target Mapping button at lower-right (see Figure 3-19).

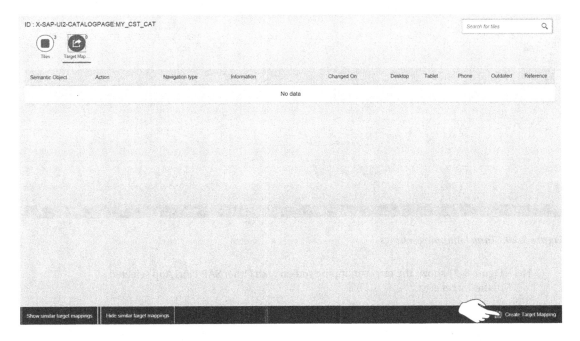

Figure 3-19. *Click Create Target Mapping*

10. Give the target mapping settings for the dynamic tile (see Figure 3-20):

- In the Intent area, you link the tile and the target-mapping tile. If you check Figure 3-16, you see a semantic object and an action in the Navigation area. This is how semantic objects are linked between tiles and target mappings.

- The Target area has two options for the navigation source. The SAPUI5 Fiori App option has a direct URL and a component name, which is maintained in component.js in the Fiori app source code. The Other SAP Fiori App option specifies an app in the LPD_CUST transaction with a launchpad role and launchpad instance.

- The General area is used to specify device types supported by the app and to enter additional parameters.

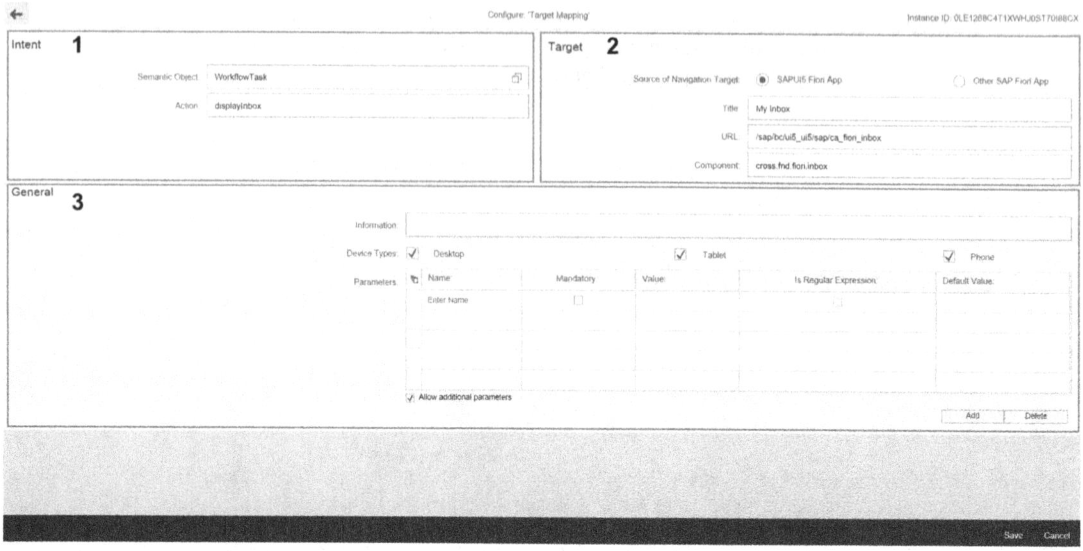

Figure 3-20. *Target mapping settings*

11. Figure 3-21 shows the target-mapping screen with Other SAP Fiori App selected in the Target area.

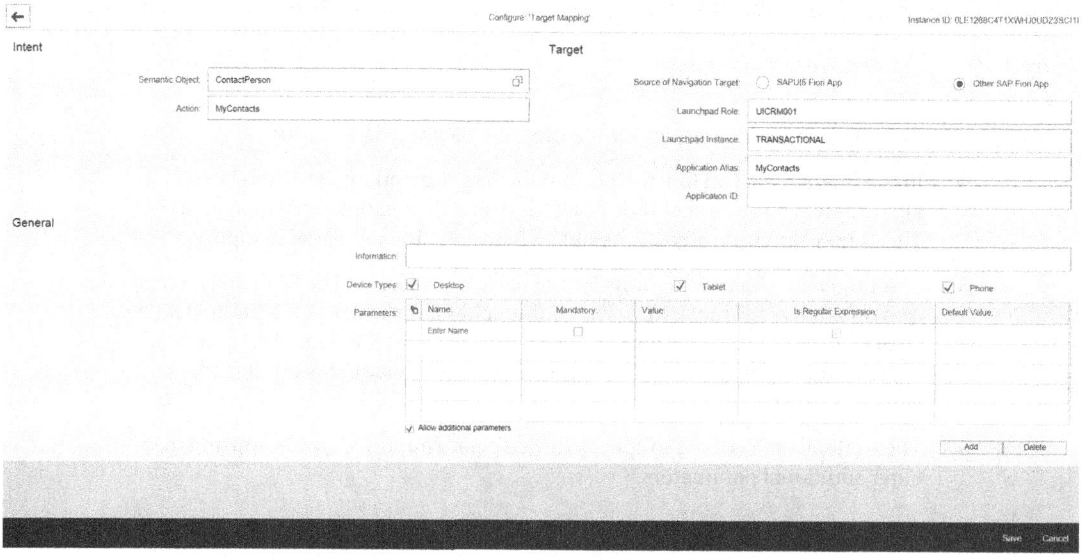

Figure 3-21. *Target mapping with the Other SAP Fiori App option selected*

Assigning and Maintaining Roles for End Users

Once you've configured tiles, you need to log in to the SAP Gateway server and assign the catalog to the end user's ID:

1. Go to transaction PFCG in the SAP Gateway system (see Figure 3-22).

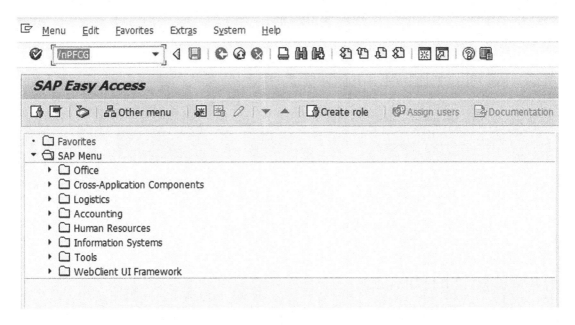

Figure 3-22. *Go to transaction PFCG*

2. Create a new role for the user (see Figure 3-23).

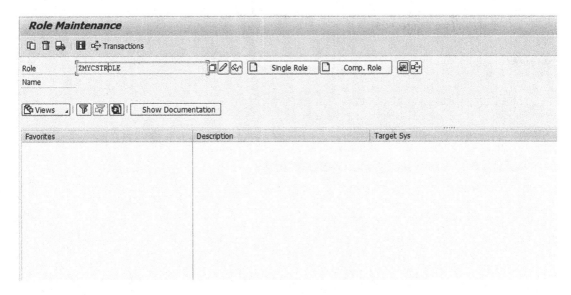

Figure 3-23. *Create a user role*

3. Switch to edit mode, and click the Menu tab. Click the Transaction button, and select SAP Fiori Tile Catalog (see Figure 3-24).

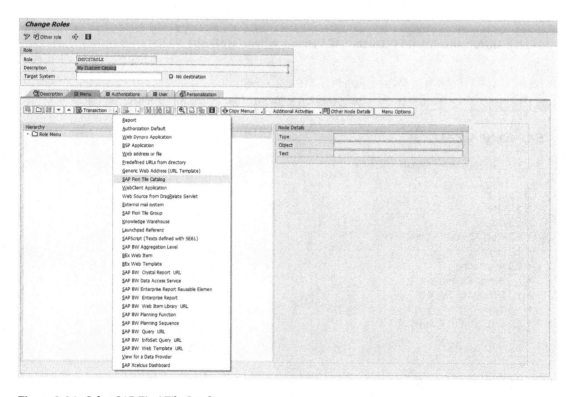

Figure 3-24. *Select SAP Fiori Tile Catalog*

4. In the pop-up, give the catalog ID that you created earlier in the launchpad designer (see Figure 3-25).

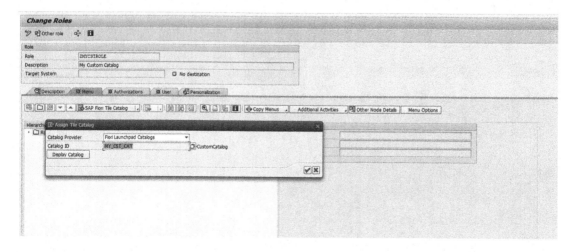

Figure 3-25. *Enter the catalog ID*

5. On the User tab, give the end user's ID to assign the role to the user (see Figure 3-26). Now the user has access to the tiles in the custom catalog you created in the launchpad designer.

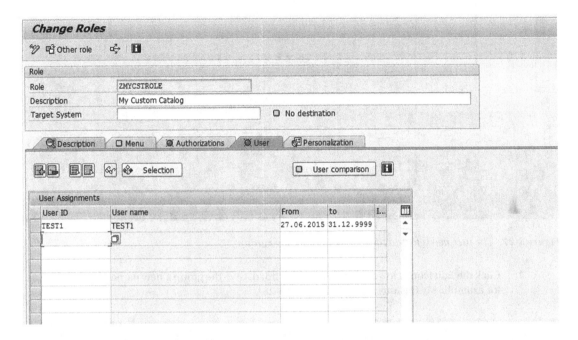

Figure 3-26. *Assign the role to the user*

Configuring the Fiori Home Page

Even though the app is accessible to the end user, it isn't visible when they log in to the launchpad. To see the app on the home page, the user must assign the app to an existing group or create a custom group and add the app to it (see Figure 3-27). Here are the steps:

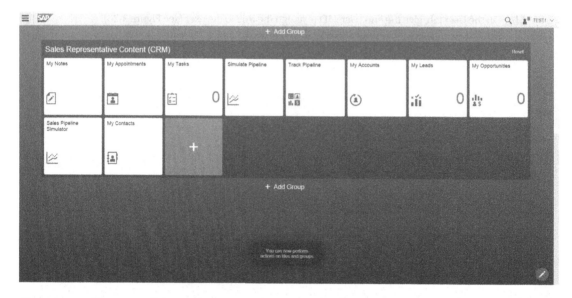

Figure 3-27. *The user needs to add the app to a home-page group*

1. Click the Edit icon at lower-right in the launchpad. Give the group a new name: for example, My Custom Group (see Figure 3-28).

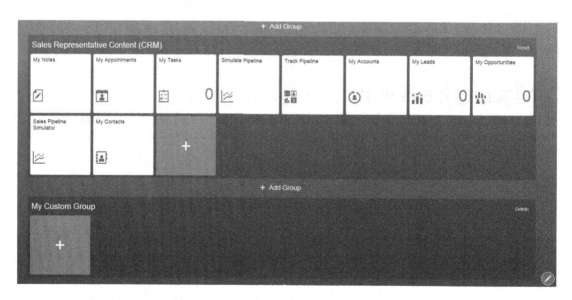

Figure 3-28. *Name the new group*

2. Click the + icon and add the app assigned. Then, in the catalog list, click the + icon to add the app to your custom group (see Figure 3-29).

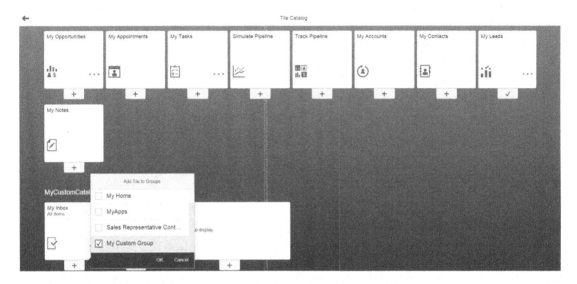

Figure 3-29. *Add the app to the group*

3. The new tile now appears in the custom group (see Figure 3-30).

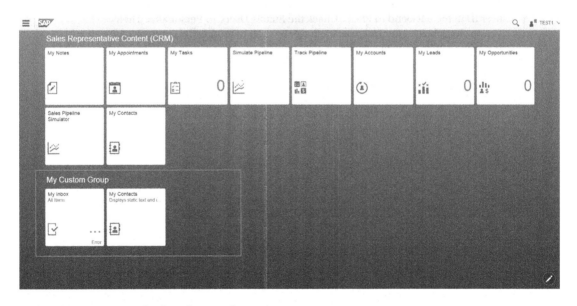

Figure 3-30. *The group displays the new tile*

Creating Groups in Fiori Launchpad Designer

This process of creating a custom group and adding apps to it may be confusing or frustrating for some users. To avoid this, Fiori launchpad admins can create groups in the Fiori launchpad designer the same way you create a catalog:

1. Click the Groups tab in the launchpad designer, and then click the + icon at lower-left (see Figure 3-31).

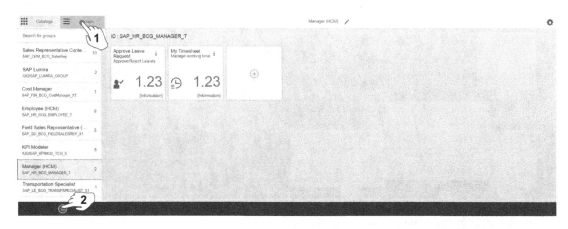

Figure 3-31. *Add a new group*

2. Give the group a title and a unique ID. This group ID will be assigned to the user ID in the back end in PFCG. Check the Enable Users To Personalize Their Group check box if you want users to have the right to modify the contents of this predefined group (see Figure 3-32).

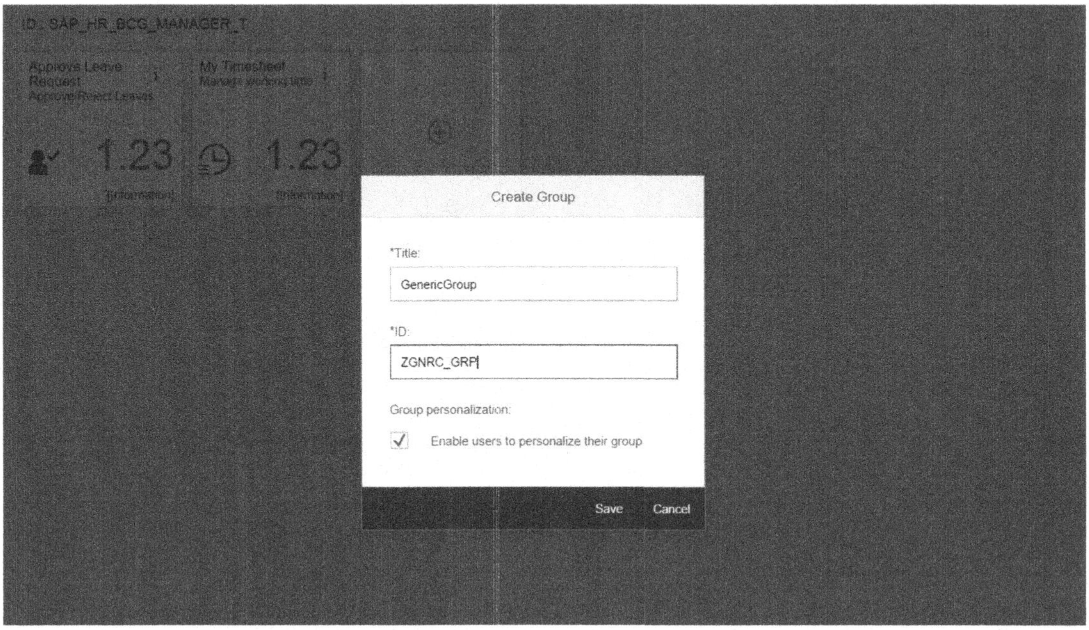

Figure 3-32. Letting users modify the group

3. Click the + icon to start adding tiles to the group (see Figure 3-33).

Figure 3-33. The empty group

4. Select the tiles for the group (see Figure 3-34).

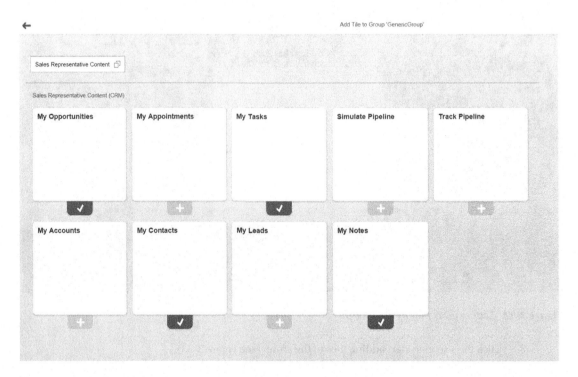

Figure 3-34. *Select tiles for the group*

5. The selected tiles are added to the new group (see Figure 3-35).

Figure 3-35. *The completed group*

Assigning Groups to End Users

Similar to assigning catalog IDs to user IDs, the Fiori admin must assign group IDs to user IDs in the Gateway system. Follow these steps:

1. Open the SAP Gateway system, execute transaction PFCG, and create a new role (see Figure 3-36).

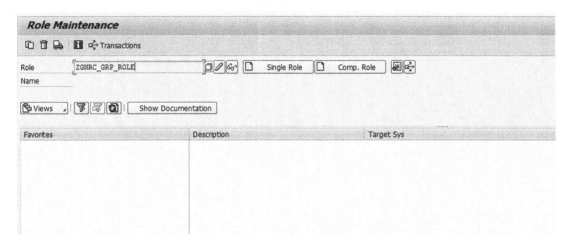

Figure 3-36. Create a new role

2. On the Menu tab, click Transaction, and select SAP Fiori Tile Group (see Figure 3-37).

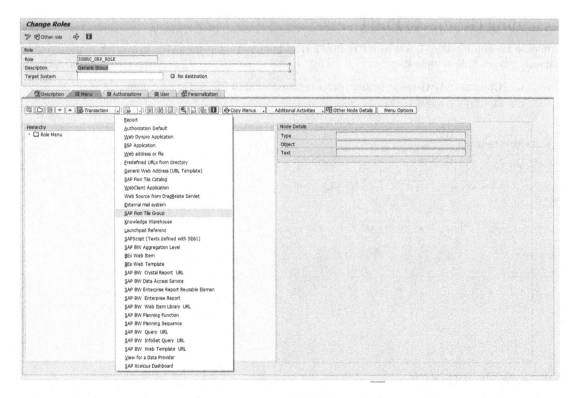

Figure 3-37. *Select SAP Fiori Tile Group*

3. In the pop-up, select the group ID you created in the launchpad designer (see Figure 3-38).

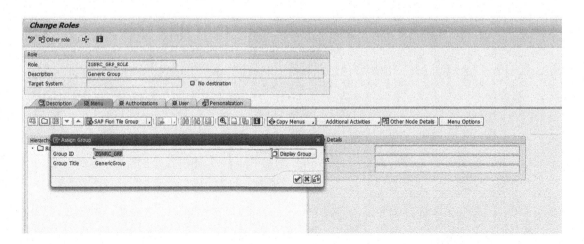

Figure 3-38. *Select the group ID*

4. Go to the User tab, and assign the end user to the group (see Figure 3-39).

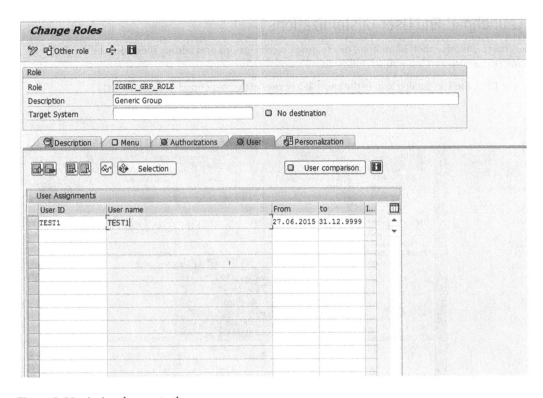

Figure 3-39. *Assign the user to the group*

5. When the user logs in to their home page, they see the predefined group (see Figure 3-40).

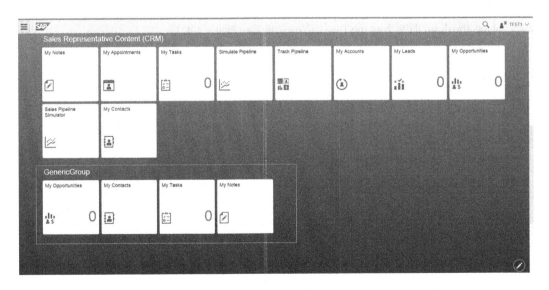

Figure 3-40. *The group appears on the user's home page*

Fiori Launchpad End User Customizations

End users can customize their launchpad by creating custom groups and adding tiles from the catalog. To customize the end-user launchpad, follow these steps:

1. Click the Tile Catalog icon in the lower-left corner of the launchpad (see Figure 3-41).

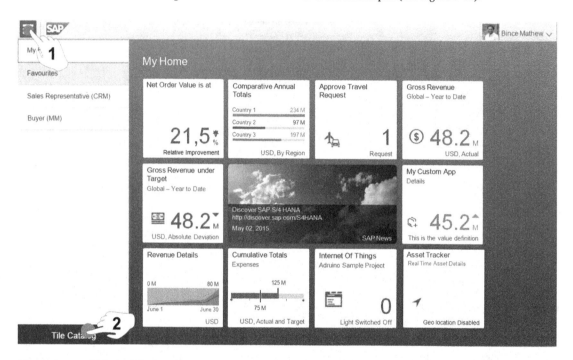

Figure 3-41. *Click the Tile Catalog icon*

2. Select the desired tile from the Tile Catalog page (see Figure 3-42).

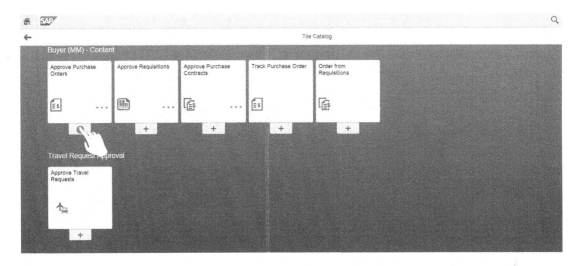

Figure 3-42. *Select a tile*

3. Click New Group to add the tile to your custom group (see Figure 3-43).

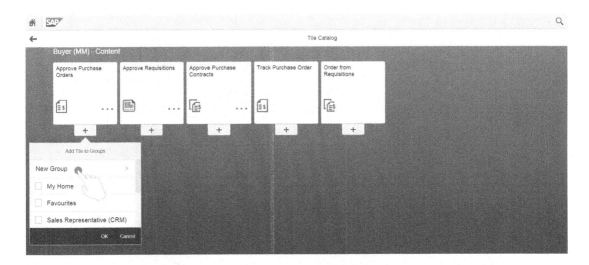

Figure 3-43. *Click New Group*

4. Give the group a name (see Figure 3-44).

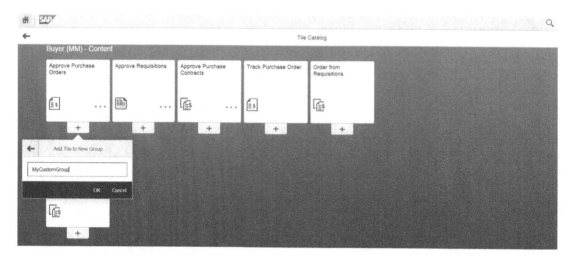

Figure 3-44. *Name the group*

On the launchpad, you can see the new group with the tile selected from the catalog, as shown in Figure 3-45.

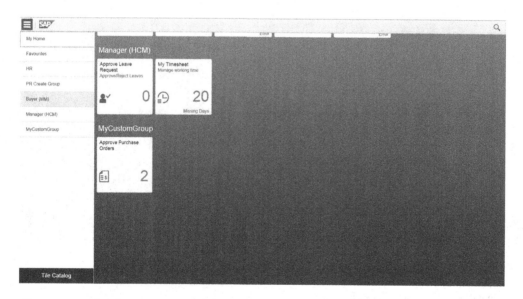

Figure 3-45. *The tile appears on the launchpad*

In the latest version of Fiori launchpad, you can alternatively add new tiles and create groups by clicking the Edit icon at lower-right (see Figure 3-46). Then follow these steps:

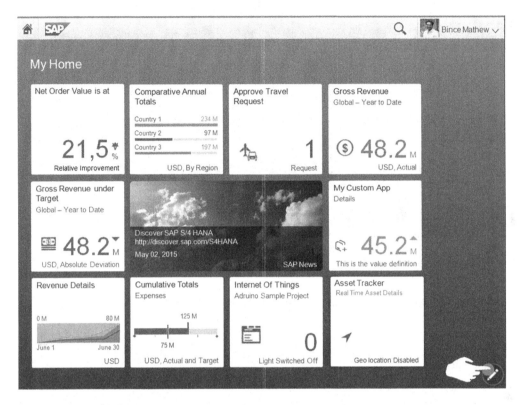

Figure 3-46. *Click the Edit icon*

1. In Edit mode, create a new group by entering a name for the group (see Figure 3-47).

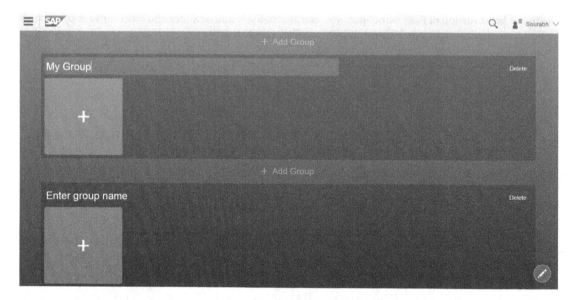

Figure 3-47. *Enter a group name*

2. To navigate to the Tile Catalog page, click the + icon (see Figure 3-48).

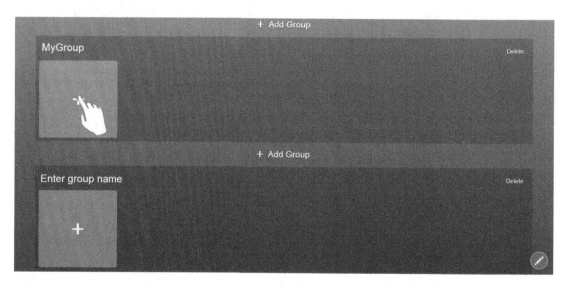

Figure 3-48. *Click + to go to the Tile Catalog page*

3. On the Tile Catalog page, select the tiles you want to add to the group (see Figure 3-49).

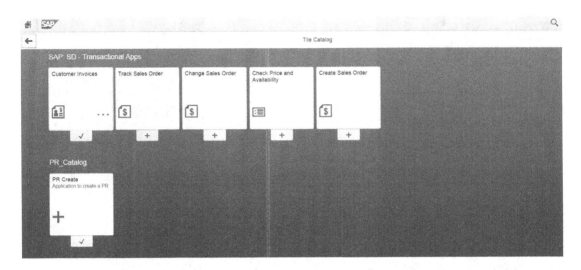

Figure 3-49. *Select tiles to add*

4. Once a tile has been added, you can edit its properties by right-clicking it and choosing Settings (see Figure 3-50).

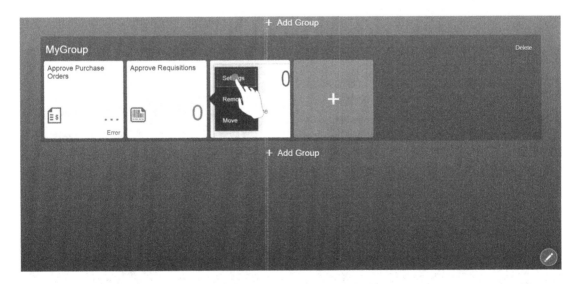

Figure 3-50. *Right-click the tile to edit its properties*

5.   You can change the tile's title, subtitle, and info text (see Figure 3-51).

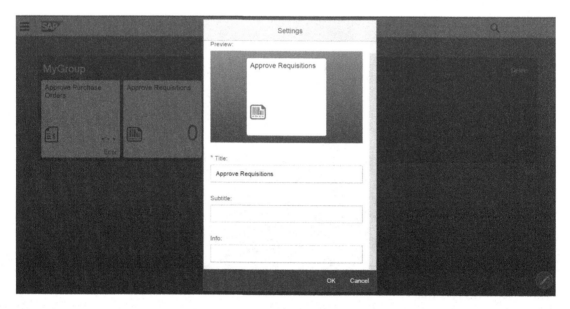

Figure 3-51.   *Editing a tile's properties*

6.   You can also move tiles from one group to the other by selecting Move
     (see Figure 3-52).

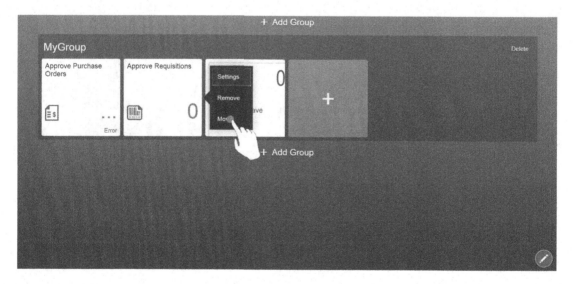

Figure 3-52.   *Moving a tile*

7. From the list, select the group to which you want to move the tile (see Figure 3-53).

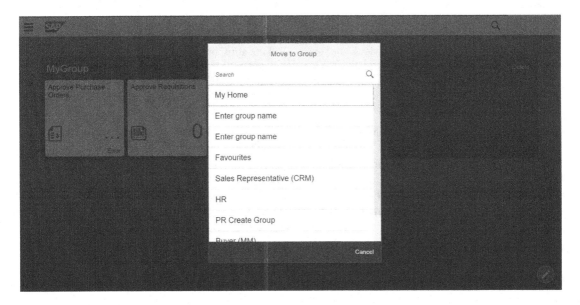

Figure 3-53. *Choose the group to move a tile to*

Configuring the Fiori Approval Application Workflow

Approval apps are a set of standard apps from Fiori that integrate with the standard approval workflows in the SAP system, such as leave approval, timesheet approval, PO approval, and so on (the next section gives a full list of these apps). Although these are standard apps, the standard workflows may be different for each customer in each scenario; and some customers may use a custom workflow for a specific scenario. You can configure Fiori approval apps in order to integrate them with the workflows customers use.

There are some differences in the way you configure approval apps in Wave 1 and Wave 2. So, first let's look at the differences between Wave 1 and Wave 2 apps (see Table 3-1).

Table 3-1. *Wave 1 vs. Wave 2 Apps*

Wave 1	Wave 2
Released in May 2013 (ola Architecture)	Released in November 2013 (new architecture)
All the apps were coded using HTML views, and every app had an index.html page like a normal web page.	All the apps, including the Wave 1 apps, were ported to XML views, and the index.html pages were replaced by shells. Wave 2 apps no longer require an index.html page while running in the Fiori launchpad.
Navigation between apps was not possible.	Cross-app navigation was introduced in the new architecture of the Wave 2 apps.
Extensibility options for the UI were not available. Developers had to download the app's original source code, modify the app, and upload it to the server.	UI extension points were introduced, enabling developers to enhance, replace, or modify the UI of any Fiori app.
Every app had a separate UI package that needed to be installed.	UI packages were grouped based on modules like CRM, GRC, MRP, and so on.
Wave 1 packages are no longer supported by SAP. These packages are valid only for customers that went live before November 2013.	Wave 2 packages are valid for all customers and are supported by SAP.

Configuring Wave 1 Approval Applications

The Wave 1 approval apps are as follows:

- Approve Requests (a generic approval app that can be configured with any custom approval workflows)
- Approve Leave Requests
- Approve Timesheets
- Approve Travel Requests
- Approve Travel Expenses
- Approve Shopping Carts
- Approve Purchase Orders
- Approve Requisitions
- Approve Purchase Contracts

Each standard approval app must be configured initially to link it with the standard/custom workflow the customer is using in their SAP landscape for that scenario. To configure the apps, follow these steps:

1. Execute the transaction SPRO, and navigate to SAP Reference IMG ➤ SAP NetWeaver ➤ Gateway Service Enablement ➤ Content ➤ Task Gateway ➤ Task Gateway Service ➤ Scenario Definition (see Figure 3-54).

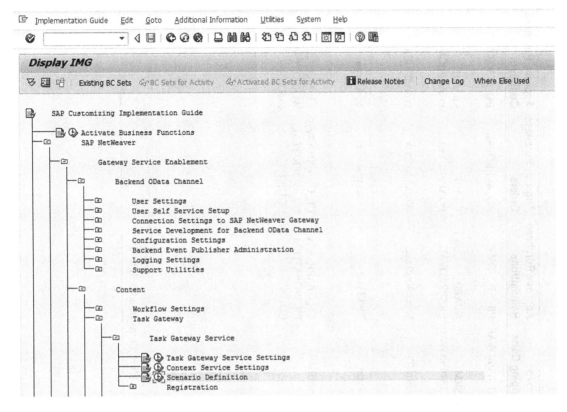

Figure 3-54. *Defining a scenario*

2. Click the scenario definition at left, and enter the details for the approval app you want to configure (see Figure 3-55). These values are provided in Table 3-2.

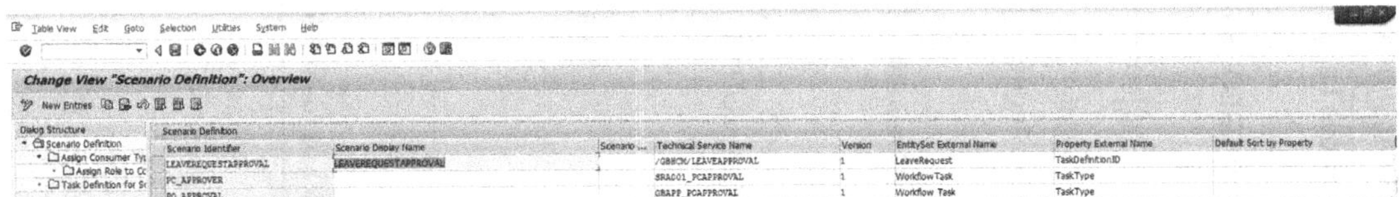

Figure 3-55. *Enter the app details*

Table 3-2. Fiori Wave 1 Approval App Configuration Chart

Field	Approve Requests (Custom Workflow)	Approve Leave Requests	Approve Shopping Carts	Approve Purchase Requisitions	Approve Purchase Orders	Approve Purchase Contracts
Scenario Identifier	<Custom_ID>	LEAVEREQUESTAPPROVAL	CARTAPPROVAL	PR_APPROVAL	PO_APPROVAL	PC_APPROVAL
Technical Service Name	/IWPGW/ TASKPROCESSING	/GBHCM/LEAVEAPPROVAL	/GBSRM/ CARTAPPROVAL	GBAPP_ PRAPPROVAL	GBAPP_ POAPPROVAL	SRA001_ PCAPPROVAL
EntitySet External Name	Task	LeaveRequest	WorkflowTask	WorkflowTask	WorkflowTask	WorkflowTask
Property External Name	TaskDefinitionID	TaskDefinitionID	TaskType	TaskType	TaskType	TaskType
Class for Scenario Count	If the scenario is not part of the Business Workflow engine, and you want to see the number of tasks pending for this scenario, enter the name of the class that implements the /IWWRK/IF_TGW_ SCENARIO interface in the SAP system.	/GBHCM/CL_APPROVAL_ ITEM_COUNT	Not available	CL_GBAPP_APV_ PR_WORKITEM_ COUNT	CL_GBAPP_APV_ PO_WORKITEM_ COUNT	CL_SRA001_PC_ WORKITEM_ COUNT
Quick Act	Select the Quick Act check box to enable quick approval of workflow items (iPad only).					

3. Click Assign Consumer Type, and enter the device types on which you want the app to be supported (see Figure 3-56).

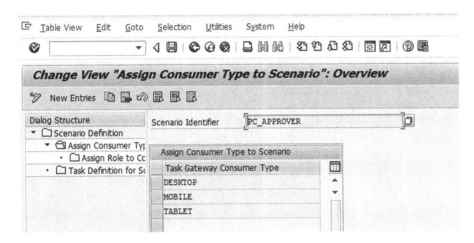

Figure 3-56. *Specify device types*

4. Assign the role to the consumer type (see Figure 3-57).

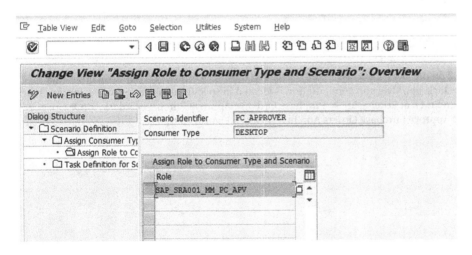

Figure 3-57. *Assign the role*

5. In the Task Definition For Scenario dialog, enter the task ID of the standard/ custom workflow used for that scenario in the back-end system (see Figure 3-58). For example, for purchase-order approval, enter the task ID of the workflow configured for PO approval in the back end.

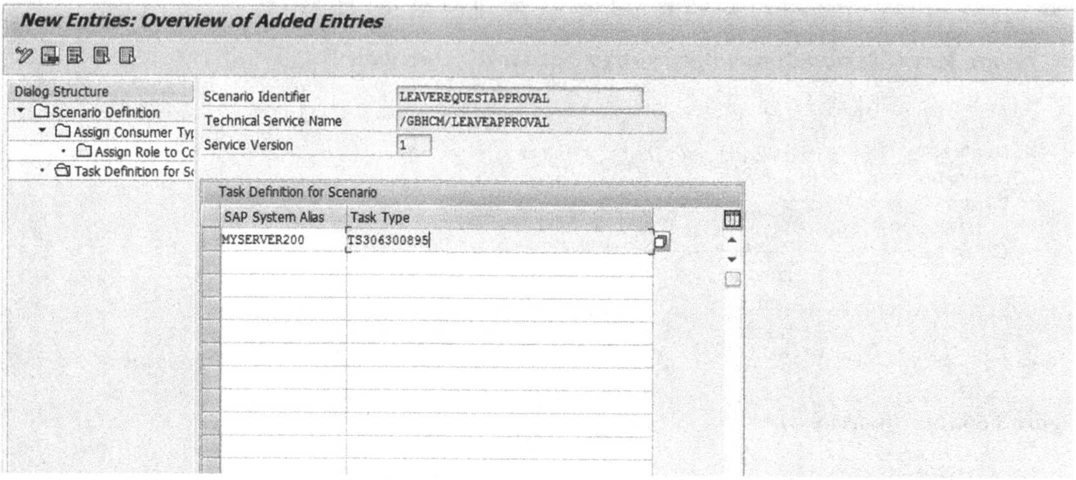

Figure 3-58. *Enter the task ID*

Configuring Wave 2 Approval Apps

Beginning with Wave 2 on the latest ECC EHP7 NetWeaver 7.4, the SPRO settings for approval apps have changed. In the latest stack, approval app configuration is located in specific areas: for example, for purchase order approval, you can find it at Purchasing ➤ Purchase Order ➤ Approve Purchase Orders App ➤ Specify Workflow Task IDs for Approve Purchase Orders App in SPRO (see Figure 3-59).

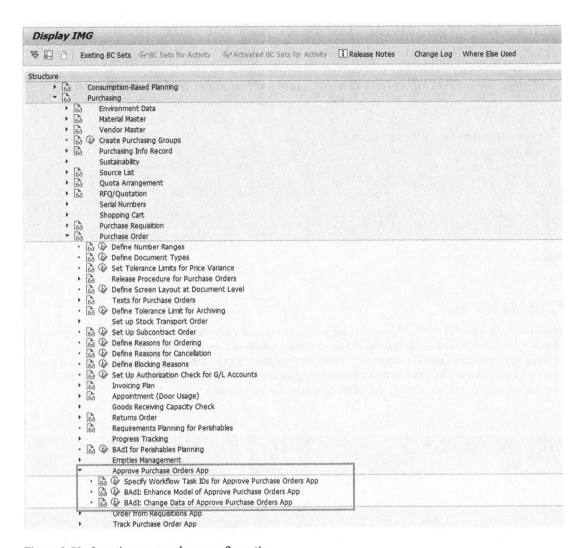

Figure 3-59. *Locating approval app configuration*

Enter the task ID for the workflow app as shown in Figure 3-60.

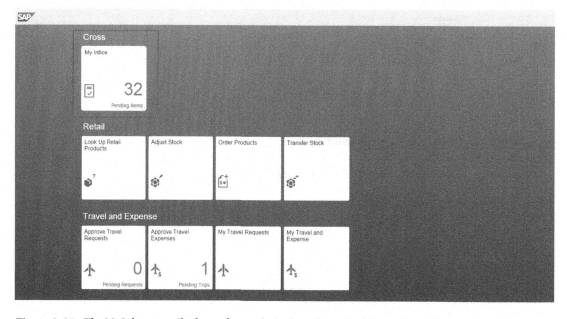

Figure 3-60. *Enter the task ID*

Fiori My Inbox

In addition to the workflow-based approval apps, Fiori has recently added the My Inbox app. This app is basically a unified inbox that can handle all the approval workflows a user receives. Users can now view all pending approvals and tasks in a single app. The My Inbox app tile shows the total number of pending items (see Figure 3-61) for the user rather than only the pending items for a specific approval app (for instance, Approve Leave Requests shows only the number of pending leave approvals).

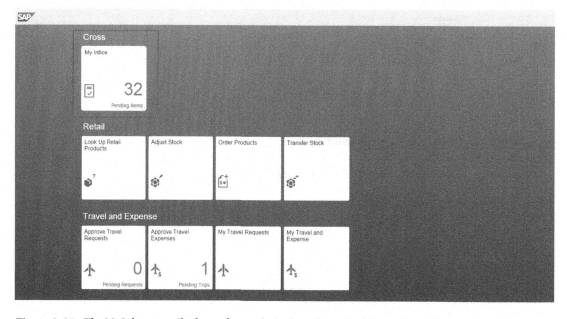

Figure 3-61. *The My Inbox app tile shows the total number of pending requests*

Figure 3-62 shows the different types of approval workflows that appear in the My Inbox app.

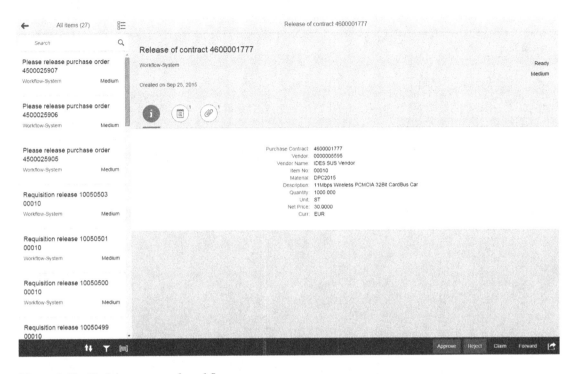

Figure 3-62. *My Inbox approval workflows*

Users can enter comments on the workflow before approving or rejecting, as in a chat window. Thus if one of the approvers has a comment, they can post it in the app, and the appropriate user can reply (see Figure 3-63).

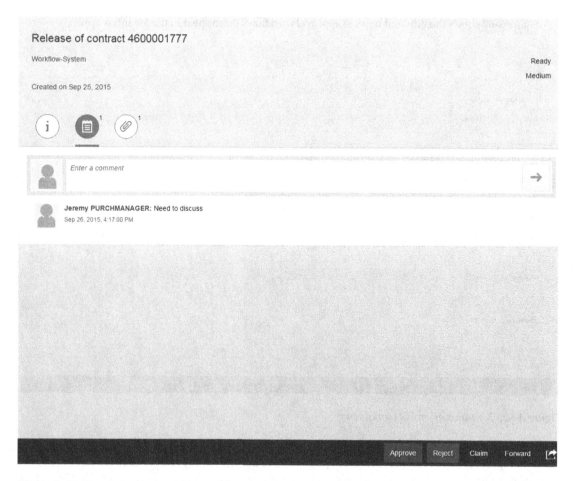

Figure 3-63. *Posting comments on a workflow task from in My Inbox*

You can find details about installing My Inbox in the Fiori apps reference library at
`https://fioriappslibrary.hana.ondemand.com/sap/fix/externalViewer/#/detail/Apps('F0862')`.
Because the app is a new addition, it has a dedicated SCN page for discussing issues, installation steps, the
latest feature updates, and so on: `http://scn.sap.com/docs/DOC-62602`.

The next chapter discusses how to customize and extend a standard Fiori app.

■ ■ ■

CHAPTER 4

Customizing and Extending Standard Fiori Applications

Fiori standard apps are not always accepted by customers as is. Sometimes developers need to extend or modify an application according to meet the customer's requirements. SAP Fiori has an enhancement framework that makes this task easier. In this chapter, you learn how to customize and extend the standard Fiori apps.

Installing Eclipse and UI5 Add-Ons

This chapter looks at the steps involved in extending and customizing a standard SAP Fiori app. The two primary IDEs currently used for Fiori development and customization are as follows:

- Eclipse-based IDEs (Juno, Kepler, or Luna)

- Web IDEs (on premises or cloud-based)

To extend a standard app, you need to use the Eclipse Juno 32-bit or 64-bit version. You can go to this web page to download Eclipse:

`www.eclipse.org/downloads/packages/eclipse-ide-java-ee-developers/marsr`

After installing Eclipse, you need to install the SAP UI5 add-ons to Eclipse. To do so, open Eclipse and then follow these steps.

1. Go to Help ➤ Install New software, and enter the URL `https://tools.hana` `.ondemand.com/juno` to install the UI add-on as shown in Figure 4-1.

2. Select the UI Development Toolkit For HTML5 check box.

3. Click Next, and install the add-on.

4. Eclipse prompts you to restart after installing the add-ons. Restart Eclipse, and the add-ons will be successfully added.

Electronic supplementary material The online version of this chapter (doi:10.1007/978-1-4842-1335-3_4) contains supplementary material, which is available to authorized users.

© Bince Mathew 2015
B. Mathew, *Beginning SAP Fiori*, DOI 10.1007/978-1-4842-1335-3_4

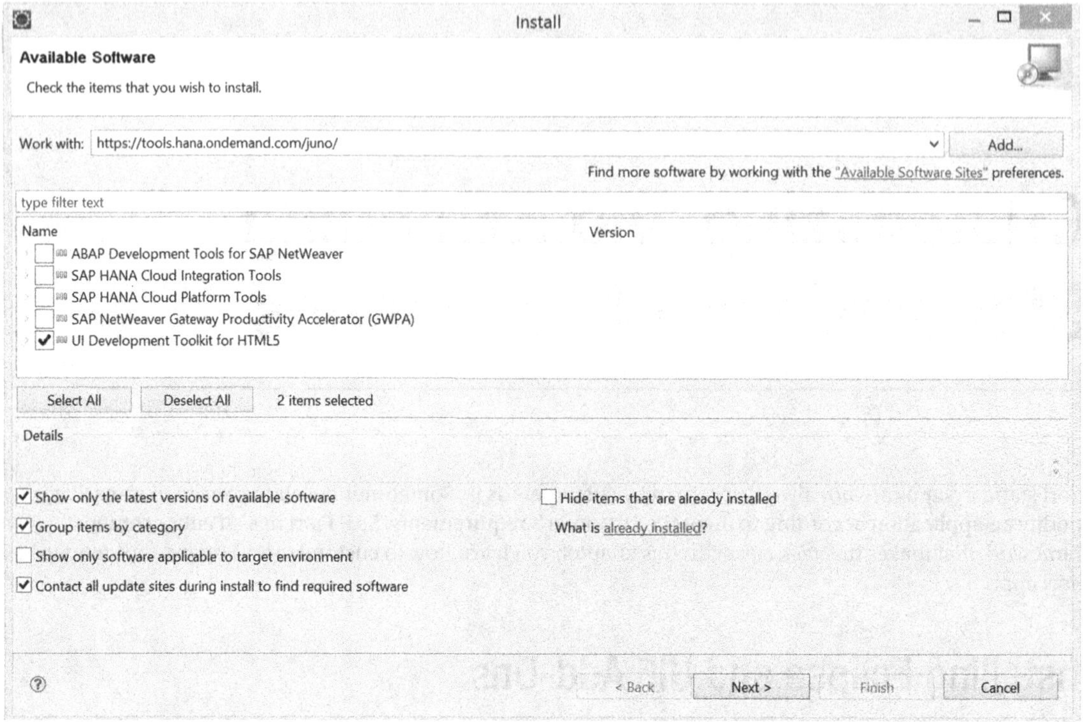

Figure 4-1. UI5 add-on screen in Eclipse

To extend the Fiori applications, we need to add the Fiori Toolkit plugin into eclipse. The fiori toolkit can be downloaded from the below site `http://scn.sap.com/docs/DOC-50114`. (Click on the "I Agree & Download" link on the page to start the download). Once the plugin has been downloaded open the eclipse and do the following steps to install it :

1. Go to Help ➤ Install New Software.

2. Click the Add button, and then click Archive.

3. Navigate to the folder where you downloaded the Fiori toolkit, and click OK.

4. Select the SAP Fiori Toolkit check box.

5. Click Next, accept the warning and license agreement, and click Finish.

6. Restart Eclipse to complete the installation

Since SAP released Web IDE, the Fiori toolkit add-on version 1.1.4 for Eclipse is no longer being updated. Currently, Eclipse Luna gets the latest Fiori UI5 library add-ons. Detailed steps for downloading and configuring Eclipse and Web IDE are presented in Chapter 6.

Downloading the Standard Fiori Application Code

This scenario uses the Track Purchase Orders standard app, as shown in Figure 4-2.

Figure 4-2. *Screenshot of the standard Track Purchase Orders app*

First you need to find the BSP app of the Track Purchase Order app to extend it. There are two ways to find the app source code in the system.

First, you can execute the transaction SICF, navigate to `/default_host/sap/bc/ui5_ui5/sap`, and search for the app manually. In this scenario, the BSP app name is mm_purord_tpo (see Figure 4-3).

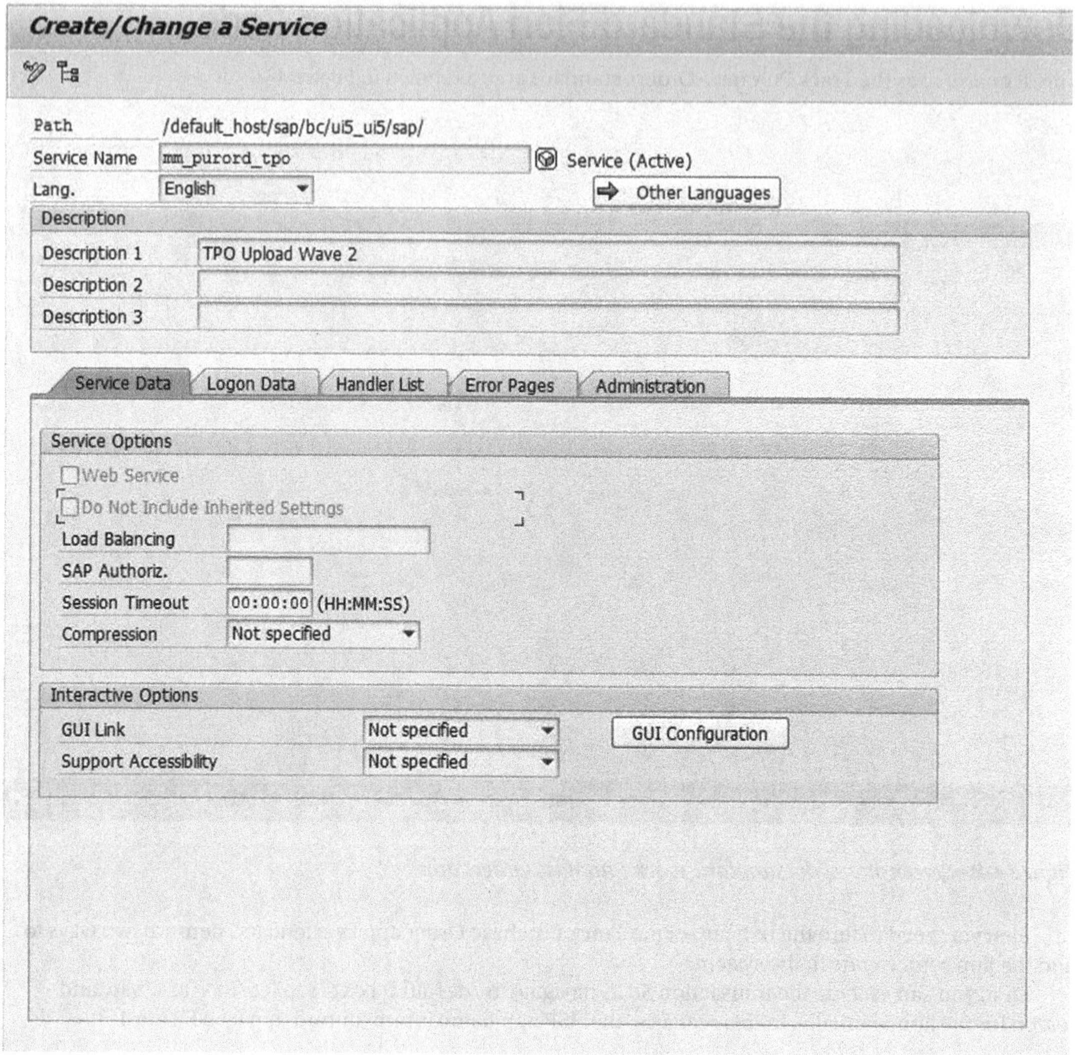

Figure 4-3. Manually searching for the BSP app

Or second, you can open the launchpad designer, and search for the Track Purchase Order app in the business catalog (see Figure 4-4). Then follow these steps:

Figure 4-4. *Launchpad designer catalog tiles*

1. Click the target-mapping icon, select the relevant target mapping, and click Configure at the bottom of the launchpad designer (see Figure 4-5).

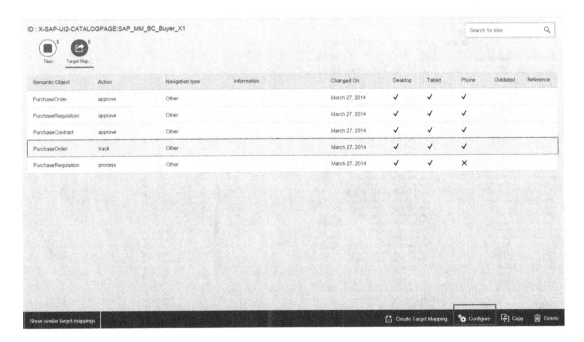

Figure 4-5. *Select the target mapping*

2. On the target mapping configuration page, you can find the launchpad role (see Figure 4-6).

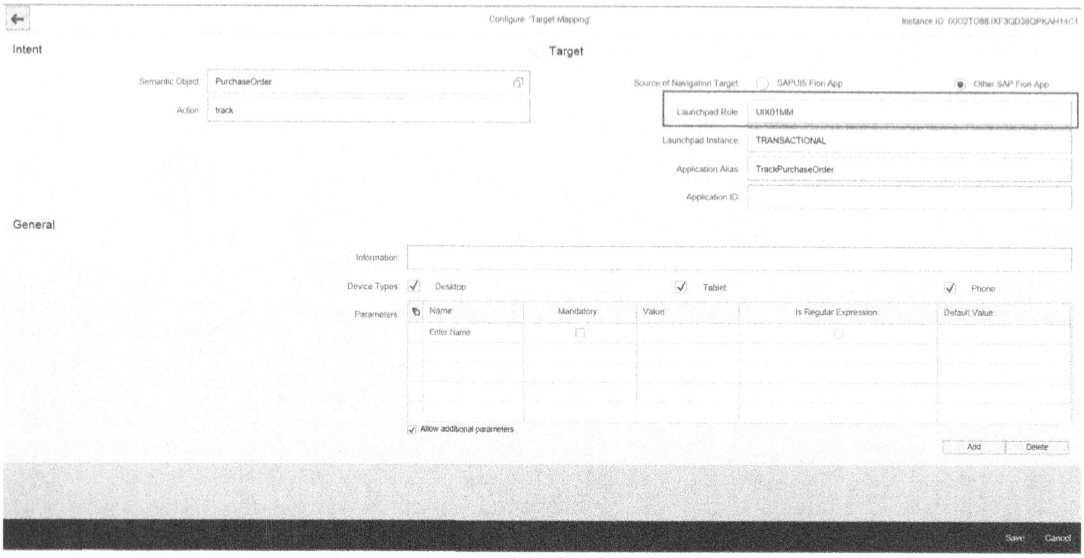

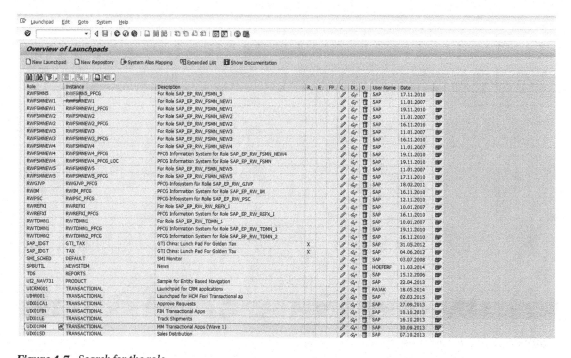

Figure 4-6. Find the launchpad role

3. Go to the Gateway system, execute the transaction LPD_CUST, and search for the launchpad role (see Figure 4-7).

Role	Instance	Description	R.	E.	FP.	User Name	Date
RWFSMN5	RWFSMN5_PFCG	For Role SAP_EP_RW_FSMN_5				SAP	17.11.2010
RWFSMNEW1	RWFSMNEW1	For Role SAP_EP_RW_FSMN_NEW1				SAP	11.01.2007
RWFSMNEW1	RWFSMNEW1_PFCG	For Role SAP_EP_RW_FSMN_NEW1				SAP	19.11.2010
RWFSMNEW2	RWFSMNEW2	For Role SAP_EP_RW_FSMN_NEW2				SAP	11.01.2007
RWFSMNEW2	RWFSMNEW2_PFCG	For Role SAP_EP_RW_FSMN_NEW2				SAP	16.11.2010
RWFSMNEW3	RWFSMNEW3	For Role SAP_EP_RW_FSMN_NEW3				SAP	11.01.2007
RWFSMNEW3	RWFSMNEW3_PFCG	For Role SAP_EP_RW_FSMN_NEW3				SAP	16.11.2010
RWFSMNEW4	RWFSMNEW4	For Role SAP_EP_RW_FSMN_NEW4				SAP	11.01.2007
RWFSMNEW4	RWFSMNEW4_PFCG	PFCG Information System for Role SAP_EP_RW_FSMN_NEW4				SAP	19.11.2010
RWFSMNEW4	RWFSMNEW4_PFCG_LOC	PFCG Information System for Role SAP_EP_RW_FSMN				SAP	19.11.2010
RWFSMNEW5	RWFSMNEW5	For Role SAP_EP_RW_FSMN_NEW5				SAP	11.01.2007
RWFSMNEW5	RWFSMNEW5_PFCG	For Role SAP_EP_RW_FSMN_NEW5				SAP	17.11.2010
RWGJVP	RWGJVP_PFCG	PFCG-Infosystem für Rolle SAP_EP_RW_GJVP				SAP	18.02.2011
RWIM	RWIM_PFCG	PFCG Information System for Role SAP_EP_RW_IM				SAP	16.11.2010
RWPSC	RWPSC_PFCG	PFCG-Infosystem für Rolle SAP_EP_RW_PSC				SAP	12.11.2010
RWREFXI	RWREFXI	For Role SAP_EP_RW_RW_REFX_I				SAP	10.01.2007
RWREFXI	RWREFXI_PFCG	PFCG Information System for Role SAP_EP_RW_REFX_I				SAP	16.11.2010
RWTDMN1	RWTDMN1	For Role SAP_EP_RW_TDMN_1				SAP	10.01.2007
RWTDMN1	RWTDMN1_PFCG	PFCG Information System for Role SAP_EP_RW_TDMN_1				SAP	19.11.2010
RWTDMN2	RWTDMN2_PFCG	PFCG Information System for Role SAP_EP_RW_TDMN_2				SAP	16.11.2010
SAP_IDGT	GTI_TAX	GTI China: Lunch Pad For Golden Tax	X			SAP	31.05.2012
SAP_IDGT	TAX	GTI China: Lunch Pad For Golden Tax	X			SAP	04.06.2012
SMI_SCHED	DEFAULT	SMI Monitor				SAP	03.07.2008
SPBUTIL	NEWSITEM	News				HOEFERF	11.03.2014
TDS	REPORTS					SAP	15.12.2006
UI2_NAV731	PRODUCT	Sample for Entity Based Navigation				SAP	22.04.2013
UICRM001	TRANSACTIONAL	Launchpad for CRM applications				RAJAK	18.05.2014
UIHR001	TRANSACTIONAL	Launchpad for HCM Fiori Transactional ap				SAP	02.03.2015
UIX01CA1	TRANSACTIONAL	Approve Requests				SAP	27.09.2013
UIX01FIN	TRANSACTIONAL	FIN Transactional Apps				SAP	10.10.2013
UIX01LE	TRANSACTIONAL	Track Shipments				SAP	16.10.2013
UIX01MM	TRANSACTIONAL	MM Transactional Apps (Wave 1)				SAP	30.09.2013
UIX01SD	TRANSACTIONAL	Sales Distribution				SAP	07.10.2013

Figure 4-7. Search for the role

4. Open the launchpad. In the right pane, under Application Parameter, you see the full path of the app (see Figure 4-8).

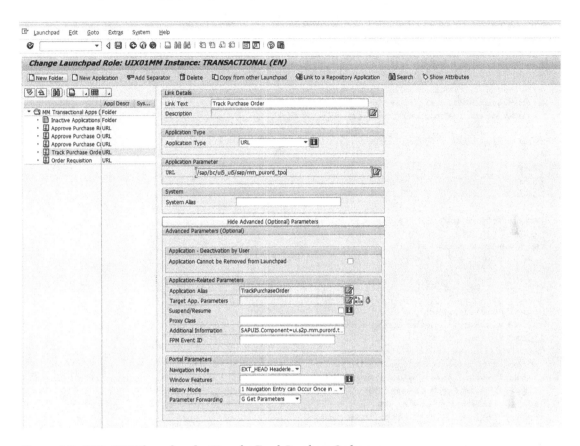

Figure 4-8. *LPD_CUST launchpad settings for Track Purchase Order app*

After you've found the app name, you need to download the app's source code into Eclipse. SAP provides the app /UI5/UI5_REPOSITORY_LOAD to download and upload Fiori apps (both standard and custom). Follow these steps:

1. Go to transaction SE38, and execute the app /UI5/UI5_REPOSITORY_LOAD (see Figure 4-9). Give your UI5 app name in the input field, select Download, and execute the app.

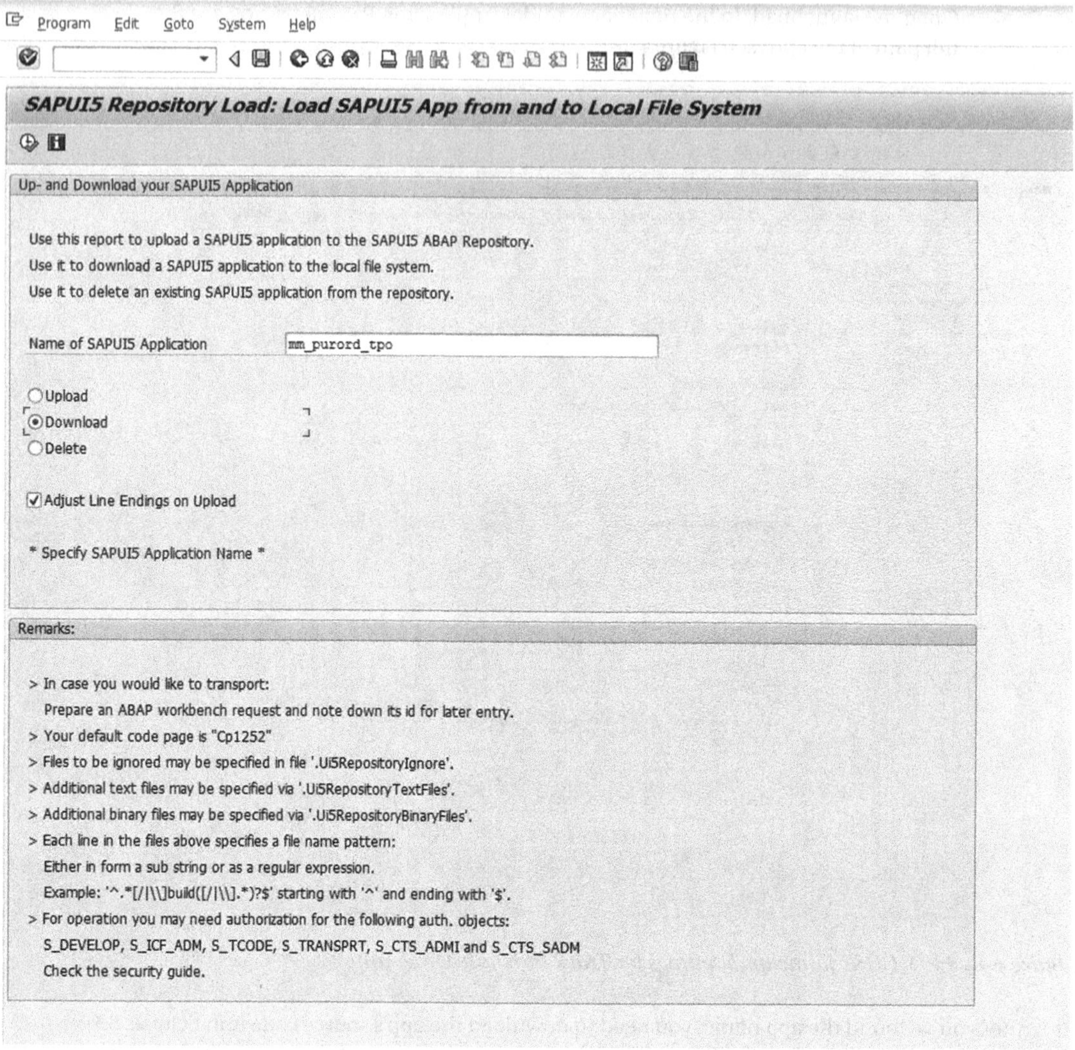

Figure 4-9. *Downloading the Track Purchase Order app source code*

2. Select a folder on your system where you want to download the code, as shown in Figure 4-10.

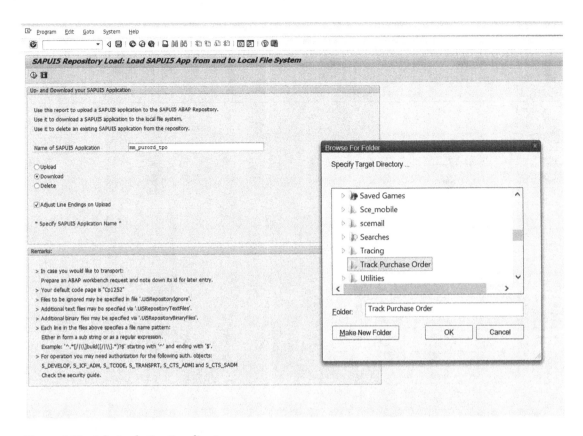

Figure 4-10. *Select a destination directory*

3. The system asks for permission to access the folder; click Yes to allow access (see Figure 4-11). The system lists all the files that will be downloaded. Click the Click Here To Download link at the bottom of the page.

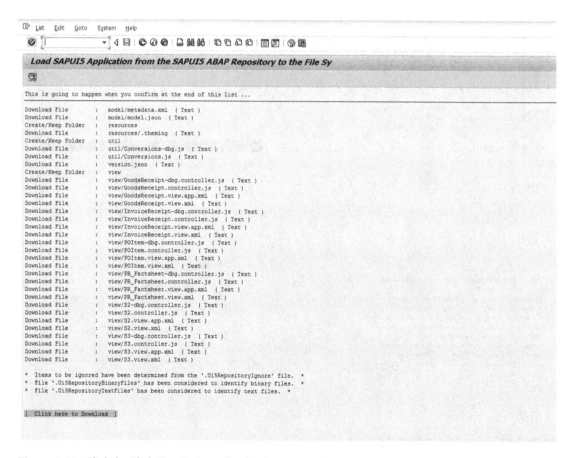

Figure 4-11. *Click the Click Here To Download link*

4. In the pop-up, leave the External Codepage field blank, and click the checkmark button (see Figure 4-12).

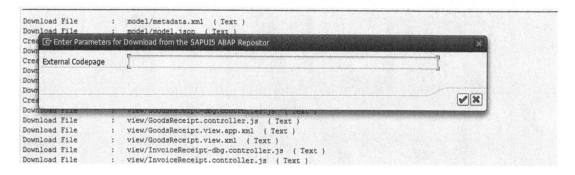

Figure 4-12. *Leave this field blank*

5. You get a confirmation after the source code has been downloaded, as shown in Figure 4-13.

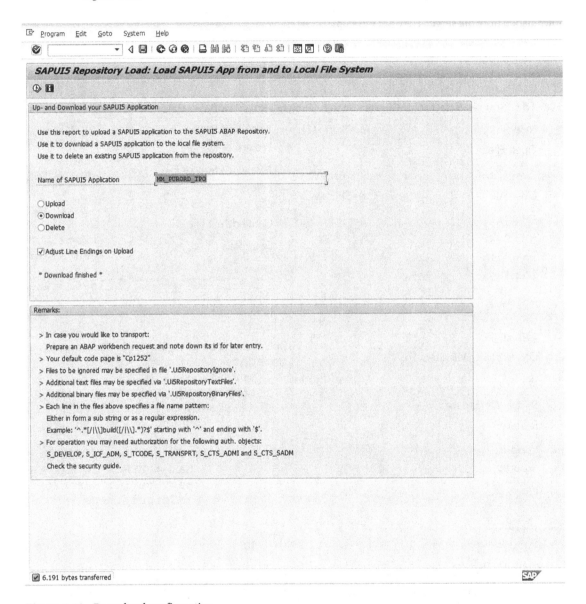

Figure 4-13. Download confirmation

Now that the app has been downloaded to your local PC, you need to import the source code into Eclipse.

Importing Fiori Standard Application Code into Eclipse

Before creating an extension Fiori extension project, you have to import into Eclipse the standard code you downloaded from the server. Here are the steps:

1. Open Eclipse, and click New ➤ Other (see Figure 4-14).

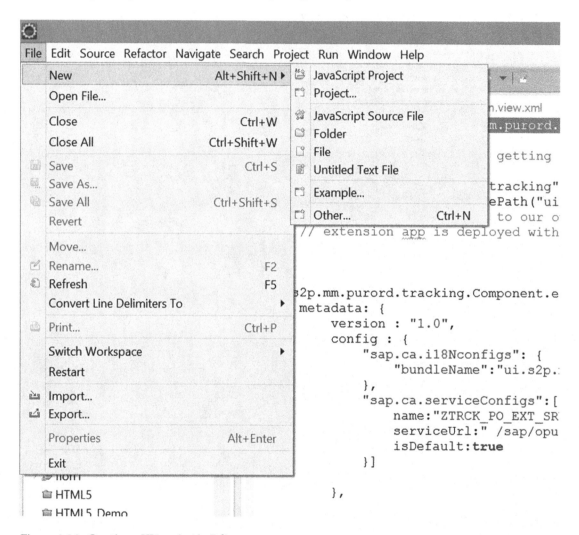

Figure 4-14. *Creating a UI5 project in Eclipse*

2. Select Application Project in the SAPUI5 Application Development folder (see Figure 4-15).

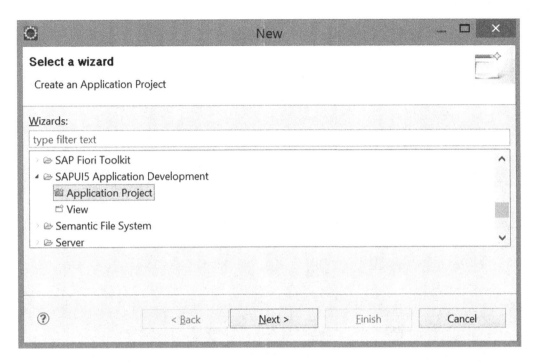

Figure 4-15. *Select Application Project*

3. Click "Next", on the second screen give a name for your project and uncheck the "Create an Initial View" check box and click on Finish (Refer Figure 4-16).

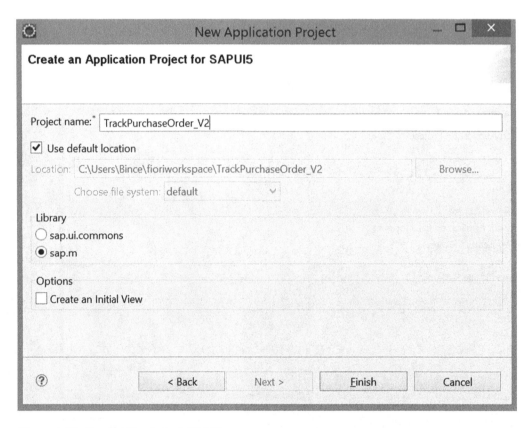

Figure 4-16. *Deselect Create An Initial View*

4. The new project is created on the left side of Eclipse in the project explorer pane (see Figure 4-17).

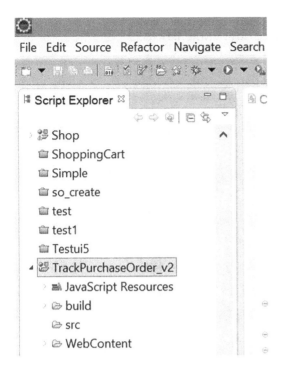

Figure 4-17. *Project Explorer*

5. Copy the contents of the WebContent folder of the source code for the standard Fiori Track Purchase Order app you downloaded earlier (see Figure 4-18).

Name	Date modified	Type	Size
i18n	7/11/2015 10:32 PM	File folder	
META-INF	7/11/2015 10:32 PM	File folder	
view	7/11/2015 10:32 PM	File folder	
WEB-INF	7/11/2015 10:32 PM	File folder	
Component.js	7/11/2015 10:29 PM	JS File	2 KB
index.html	7/11/2015 9:56 PM	HTML File	2 KB

Po Tracking Extended ▸ WebContent

Figure 4-18. *Standard Track Purchase Order UI5 source code*

6. In Eclipse, right-click the WebContent folder, and paste in the copied code (see Figure 4-19). Select Yes to All in the pop-up screen to overwrite the folder's contents.

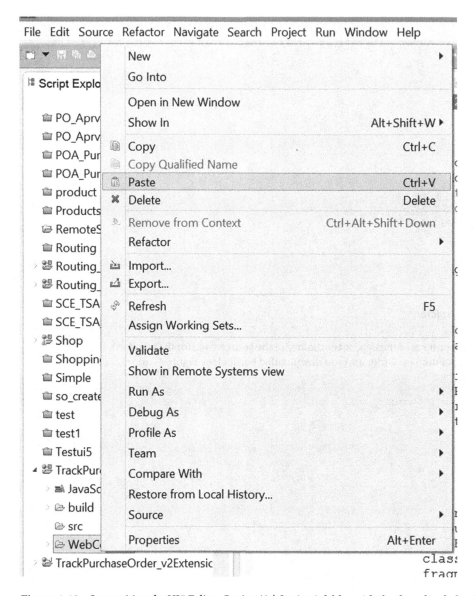

Figure 4-19. Overwriting the UI5 Eclipse Project WebContent folder with the downloaded code

7. The standard app is imported into Eclipse. You can see the source code in the WebContent folder (see Figure 4-20).

- ▲ 🗝 TrackPurchaseOrder_v2
  - › 🗏 JavaScript Resources
  - › 🗁 build
  - 🗁 src
  - ▲ 🗁 WebContent
    - › 🗁 i18n
    - › 🗁 META-INF
    - › 🗁 model
    - 🗁 resources
    - › 🗁 util
    - › 🗁 view
    - › 🗁 WEB-INF
    - 📄 Component-dbg.js
    - › 📄 Component-preload-dbg.js
    - › 📄 Component-preload.js
    - 📄 Component.js
    - 📄 Configuration-dbg.js
    - 📄 Configuration.js
    - 📄 index.html
    - › 📄 Main-dbg.controller.js
    - 📄 Main.controller.js
    - 📄 Main.view.xml
    - 📄 version.json

Figure 4-20. *Eclipse project with the standard code*

If you check one of the standard code's views, such as S2.view.xml, you see a <core:ExtensionPoint/> tag (see Figure 4-21). This is basically a flag for the Fiori toolkit or Web IDE to find extension points where you can insert custom code into the standard code. Usually, extension points are available for Header, Maint Content, and Footer, but they may differ from view to view. Some views don't have extension points, in which case you have the option to replace the entire view with custom code.

Figure 4-21. *Extension points in the standard code*

Similarly, you can see the `*.controller.js` and a `*.-dbg.controller.js` files for every controller of each view (see Figure 4-22). Files ending with `*-dbg.controller.js` are the expanded versions of the same code in the `*.controller.js` files. At runtime, the Fiori apps only load `*.controller.js`, unless you change the debugger settings to load `*.-dbg.controller.js` manually.

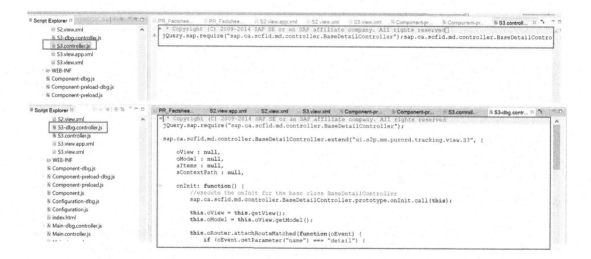

Figure 4-22. *Standard app code*

Also, you see `Component-preload.js` as well as a `-dbg` version (see Figure 4-23). `Component-preload.j` is basically a summary of all the code in `controller.js` for each view, `configuration.js`, and the component controller in the standard app project. This feature is extremely useful for Fiori client apps running on mobile devices, where space and loading time are critical.

Figure 4-23. Component-preload.js

Before you create an extension project, you need a custom OData service to help bring your custom data from the back end into the extended app. To check the standard OData service that is being used by the standard app, open the `Configuration-dbg.js` file: the OData service name is in the service list (see Figure 4-24).

```
 * Copyright (C) 2009-2014 SAP SE or an SAP affiliate company. All rights reserved
jQuery.sap.declare("ui.s2p.mm.purord.tracking.Configuration");
jQuery.sap.require("sap.ca.scfld.md.ConfigurationBase");
jQuery.sap.require("sap.ca.scfld.md.app.Application");

sap.ca.scfld.md.ConfigurationBase.extend("ui.s2p.mm.purord.tracking.Configuration", {

    oServiceParams: {
        serviceList: [
            {
                name: "SRA020_PO_TRACKING_SRV",
                masterCollection: "POLists",
                serviceUrl: "/sap/opu/odata/sap/SRA020_PO_TRACKING_SRV;mo/",
                isDefault: true,
                mockedDataSource: "/ui.s2p.mm.purord.tracking/model/metadata.xml"
            }
        ]
    },

    getServiceParams: function () {
        return this.oServiceParams;
    },
```

Figure 4-24. OData service name

You need to create a custom OData service for the extended app. There are two ways to do it. First, you can create a completely custom OData service for the extended app, but this is not recommended because you have to adapt all the UI code to work with the new OData service entity fields. Second, you can create a new OData project, redefine the standard OData service that's being used by the app you want to extend, and add custom entities or add fields to existing entities.

Redefining a Standard OData Service

In this example, you redefine a standard OData service and add custom fields to the existing entity:

1. Log on to the Gateway server, and execute the transaction SEGW. OData service definitions may reside on the Gateway server, but the actual class implementation for fetching the back-end business data is implemented in the respective back-end system: ECC, SRM, CRM, and so on. Click the New icon to create a new project. Name the project: in this case, name it ZTRCK_PO_EXT. Click the check mark button to create the project (see Figure 4-25).

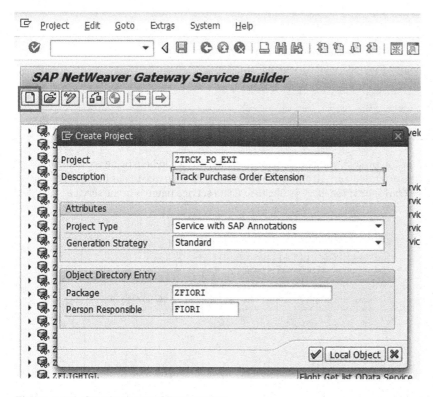

Figure 4-25. *Creating a new OData project*

2. Right-click the data model, and navigate to Redefine ➤ OData Service (GW) (see Figure 4-26).

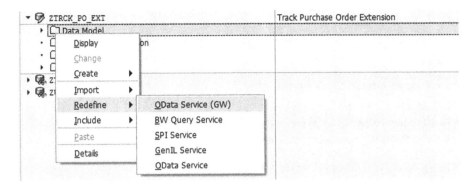

Figure 4-26. *Redefining the standard OData service*

3. Enter the OData service name that you found in the standard app source code (see Figure 4-27). (Alternatively, you can check for OData services in /IWFND/ MAINT_SERVICE).

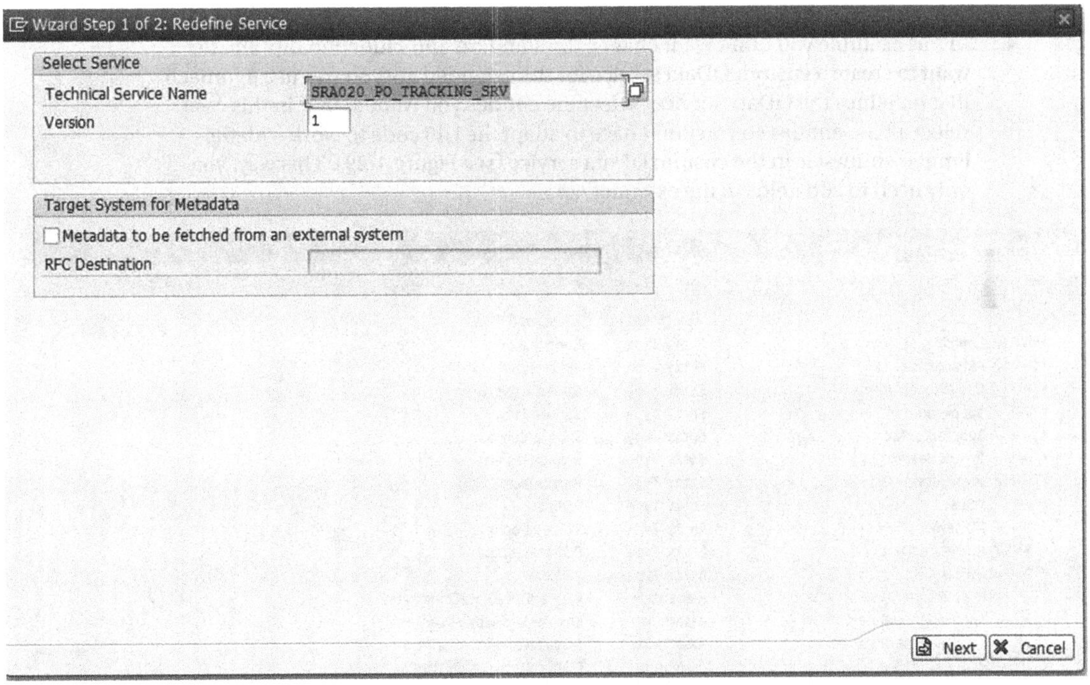

Figure 4-27. *Enter the OData service name*

Instead of creating a completely new OData service, you can append additional fields onto the DDIC structure the entities are using. Then use the BAdIs to update the OData model provider and data provider classes to add the fields to the standard OData service (see Figure 4-28).

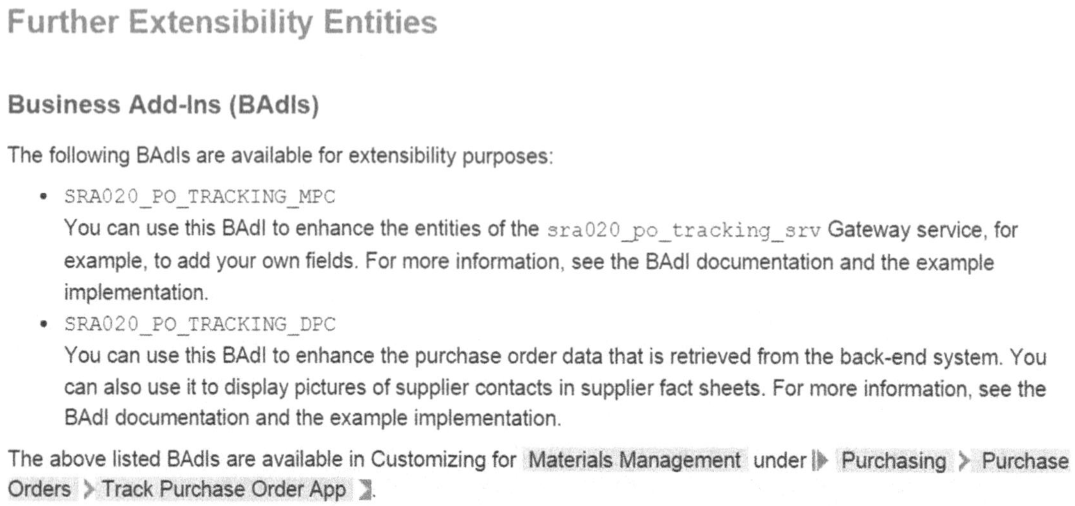

Further Extensibility Entities

Business Add-Ins (BAdIs)

The following BAdIs are available for extensibility purposes:

- `SRA020_PO_TRACKING_MPC`
  You can use this BAdI to enhance the entities of the `sra020_po_tracking_srv` Gateway service, for example, to add your own fields. For more information, see the BAdI documentation and the example implementation.
- `SRA020_PO_TRACKING_DPC`
  You can use this BAdI to enhance the purchase order data that is retrieved from the back-end system. You can also use it to display pictures of supplier contacts in supplier fact sheets. For more information, see the BAdI documentation and the example implementation.

The above listed BAdIs are available in Customizing for Materials Management under Purchasing > Purchase Orders > Track Purchase Order App.

Figure 4-28. *Standard BAdIs for extending OData model provider and data provider classes*

4. In this example you don't want change the standard app's functionality and do want to create a custom OData service for the extended app, so you use approach that redefines the OData service. Select the entities you want to use; in this case, select all the entities so you don't have to adapt the UI5 code to work with the limited entity sets in the custom OData service (see Figure 4-29). This way, you only need to add fields to the extended app.

Service	OData Artifacts	Description
Confirmation	Entity Type	Confirmation
PRFactsheet	Entity Type	PRFactsheet
GoodsReceiptItem	Entity Type	GoodsReceiptItem
SupplierInfo	Entity Type	SupplierInfo
SupplierContact	Entity Type	SupplierContact
InvoiceHeader	Entity Type	InvoiceHeader
InvoiceItem	Entity Type	InvoiceItem
POList	Entity Type	POList
POItemDocFlow	Entity Type	POItemDocFlow
PODetailedData	Entity Type	PODetailedData
POItem	Entity Type	POItem
POItemDetailDataConfirmation	Association	POItemDetailDataConfirmation
SupplierInfoSupplierContact	Association	SupplierInfoSupplierContact
InvoiceHeaderInvoiceItem	Association	InvoiceHeaderInvoiceItem
POItemDetailDataPricingConditions	Association	POItemDetailDataPricingConditions
PODetailedDataPOItemDetailData	Association	PODetailedDataPOItemDetailData
POListPODetailedData	Association	POListPODetailedData
PODetailedDataPOItem	Association	PODetailedDataPOItem
POItemDetailDataAccounting	Association	POItemDetailDataAccounting
POItemDetailDataPOItemDocFlow	Association	POItemDetailDataPOItemDocFlow
GoodsReceiptHeaderGoodsReceiptItem	Association	GoodsReceiptHeaderGoodsReceip...

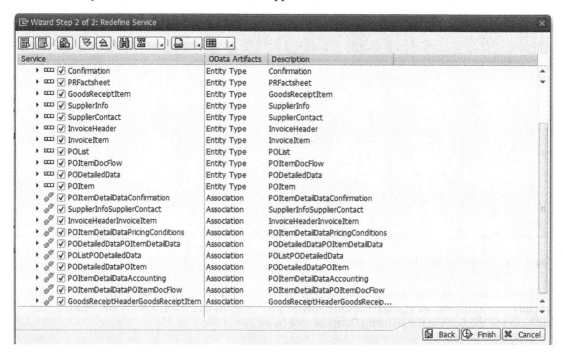

Figure 4-29. *Importing entity sets from the standard OData service*

5. For this example, you add your custom fields to the POList entity. To find the DDIC structure associated with the entity, go to SE80, and, under Package, enter the package name P_SRA020_ODATA. In the Structures folder, you see the SRA20_S_PO_LIST structure. Double-click the structure, click the GoTo button, and select Append Structure, as shown in Figure 4-30.

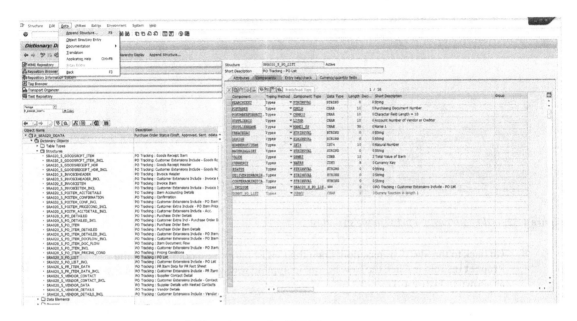

Figure 4-30. *Appending custom fields to the standard DDIC structure*

6. In the pop-up, give a name for the structure to append (see Figure 4-31).

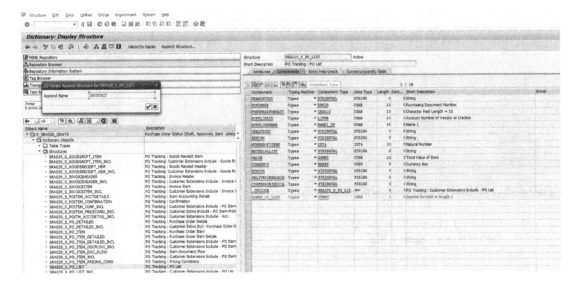

Figure 4-31. *Give a name for the structure to append*

7. Create two fields in which to add your custom data. Save and activate the structure (see Figure 4-32).

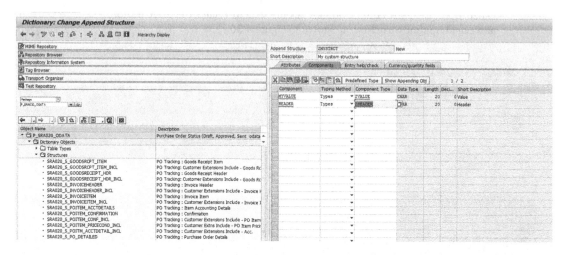

Figure 4-32. *Add your custom fields to the structure*

8. Go back to the SEGW transaction, open the POList entity, and double-click the Properties folder. Click the New button to append rows for your custom fields, as shown in Figure 4-33.

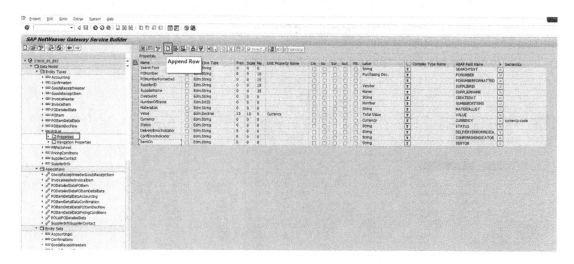

Figure 4-33. *Add your custom fields to the OData entity*

9. Click the F4 help icon in the ABAP Field Name column of your new row, and add the fields (see Figure 4-34).

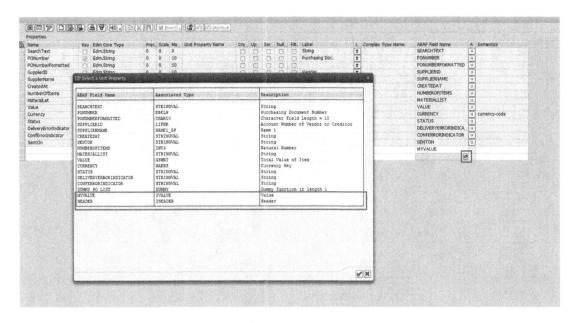

Figure 4-34. *Fields are now available in the property list*

Now you can see the two new fields appended to your entity (see Figure 4-35).

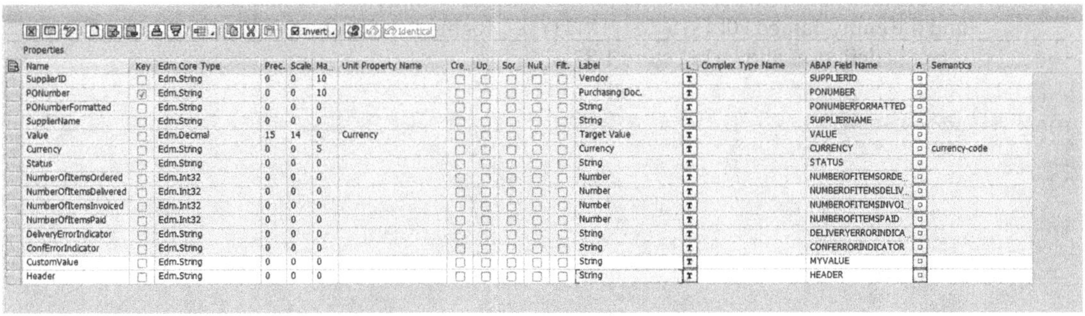

Figure 4-35. *The new fields are appended to the entity*

10. Click the Generate button to commit the changes to the OData service. Open the Runtime Artifacts folder, double-click ZCL_ZTRCK_PO_EXT_DPC_EXT, and then double-click the same class name in the right pane (see Figure 4-36).

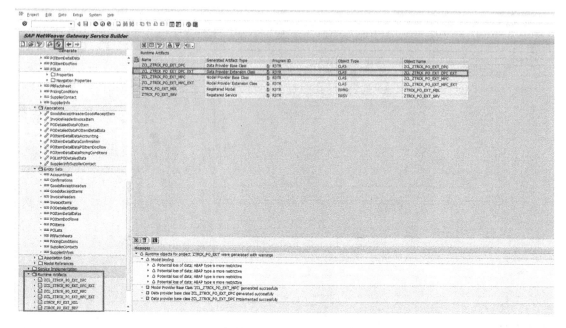

Figure 4-36. *You can see the data provider and model provider class on the right*

11. You need to write the logic to fill the two additional fields in the entity to add your custom data to the OData stream. Choose Methods ➤ Inherited Method, and find the entity named POLISTS_GET_ENTITYSET. Right-click the entity set, and select Redefine, as shown in Figure 4-37.

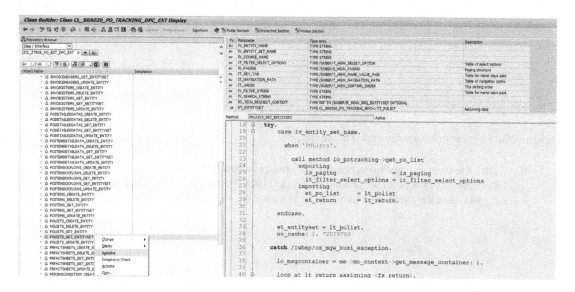

Figure 4-37. *Redefining the inherited method*

12. You can see the redefined method in the Redefinitions folder. Copy and paste the original code in the POLISTS_GET_ENTITYSET method (see Figure 4-38).

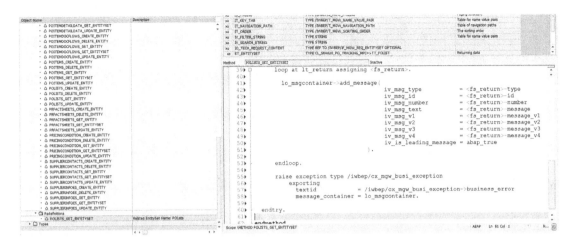

Figure 4-38. *Redefined method POLIST_GET_ENTITYSET*

13. Add your custom code to append the two new fields. Here you are just appending two hard-coded values into the internal table that is returned to the OData stream when the Track Purchase Order app calls the entity to retrieve the list of all purchase orders for the list control on the main page. You can see ET_ENTITYSET on the signature tab, which returns the table to the OData stream (see Figure 4-39).

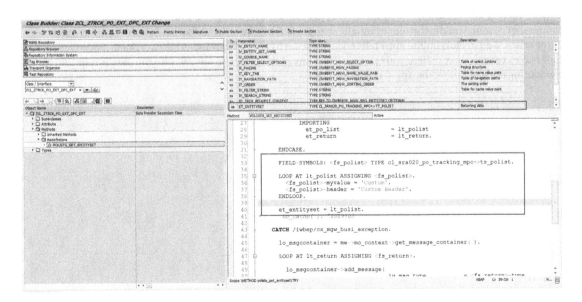

Figure 4-39. *Custom code to fill the additional fields in the OData service*

123

Test the OData service either from /IWFND/MAINT_SERVICE or directly in the browser (see Figure 4-40). Your code has appended the two new fields to the entity, and the data is updated in the response.

Figure 4-40. *OData service response with the new fields and values*

Fiori Apps Reference Library

To learn more about standard Fiori apps such as packages, OData services, BAdI implementations, and UI5 component names, you must either manually search SICF, SEGW, /IWFND/MAINT_SERVICE, and so o n or—the easy way—go to Fiori online apps reference library at https://fioriappslibrary.hana.ondemand.com/sap/fix/externalViewer. Here you can search for any of the Fiori UI5 apps to find the details required for configuring and extending the app (see Figure 4-41).

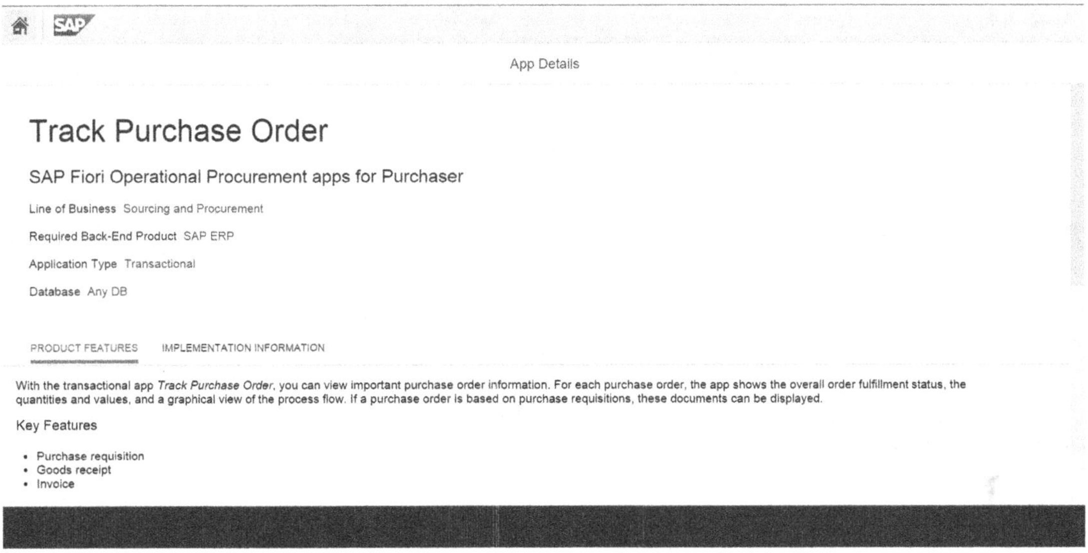

Figure 4-41. *Fiori reference library entry for Track Purchase Order*

On the Configuration tab, you can see the BSP name for Track Purchase Order (see Figure 4-42).

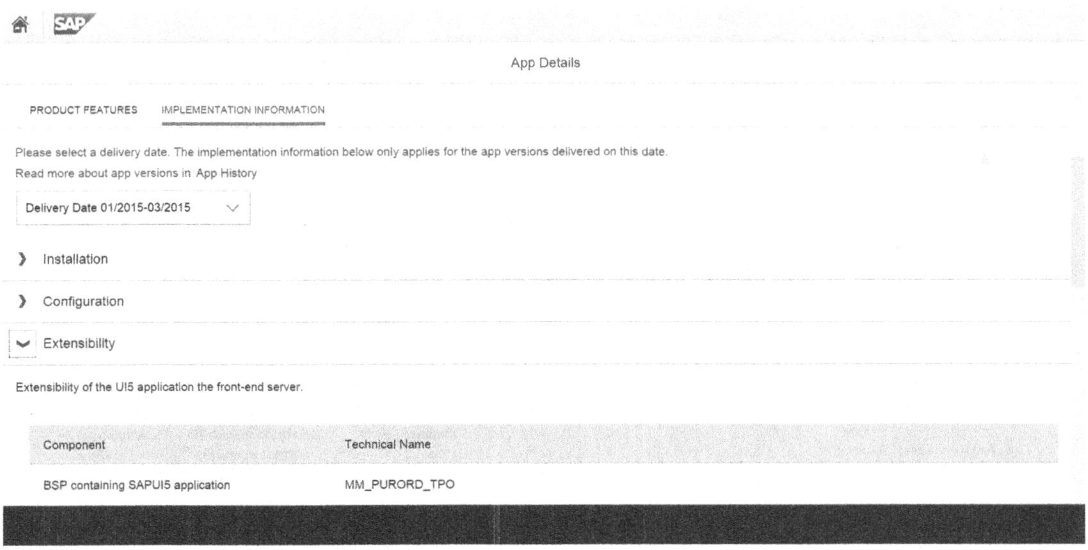

Figure 4-42. *BSP name*

Similarly, you can see all the extension point names for the app. To view the extensibility documentation, click the Read More link (see Figure 4-43).

Extension Points in Views

View	Extension Point	Use
GoodReceipt view app.xml	goodsReceiptInformation	Add fields to the Information area of the goods receipt details
InvoiceReceipt view app.xml	invoiceReceiptInformation	Add fields to the Information area of the invoice receipt details
POItem view app.xml	itemDetailsInformation	Add fields to the Information area of the purchase order item details
PR_Factsheet view app.xml	factSheetInformation	Add fields to the Information area of the purchase requisition details
S3 view app.xml	detailsHeader	Add fields to the purchase order details header

UI Controller Extensions

To plug in and execute custom code, the following hooks are available in the controller code

Controller	Hook Name	Hook Use
S2 controller.js	extHookOnPOListReceived	Allows you to check and change the data in the list of purchase orders

Read more in Extensibility Documentation

Figure 4-43. *Extension details for the Track Purchase Order app*

Here you find even more detailed information about the BAdIs, extension points, and so on (see Figure 4-44). Basically, the Fiori reference library is a combination of the SAP Help page and the generic information about each standard Fiori app, all in one place. Because the total number the Fiori apps is growing every month, manually searching for the details of each app's configuration in the Gateway and back-end server is no longer an easy task.

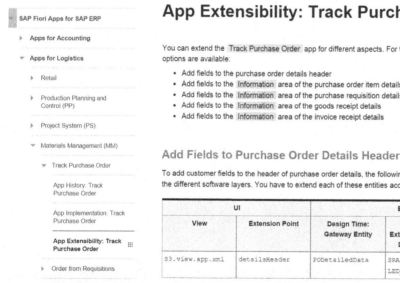

App Extensibility: Track Purchase Order

SAP Fiori Apps for SAP ERP

▶ Apps for Accounting

▼ Apps for Logistics

  ▶ Retail

  ▶ Production Planning and Control (PP)

  ▶ Project System (PS)

  ▼ Materials Management (MM)

    ▼ Track Purchase Order

      App History: Track Purchase Order

      App Implementation: Track Purchase Order

      App Extensibility: Track Purchase Order

    ▶ Order from Requisitions

    ▶ Approve Purchase Orders

You can extend the Track Purchase Order app for different aspects. For this purpose, the following extensibility options are available:

- Add fields to the purchase order details header
- Add fields to the Information area of the purchase order item details
- Add fields to the Information area of the purchase requisition details
- Add fields to the Information area of the goods receipt details
- Add fields to the Information area of the invoice receipt details

Add Fields to Purchase Order Details Header

To add customer fields to the header of purchase order details, the following extensibility entities are available on the different software layers. You have to extend each of these entities according to your specific business needs:

UI		Back End/ABAP		
View	Extension Point	Design Time: Gateway Entity	Design Time: Extension Include (in DDIC Structure)	Runtime: Data Structure to Be Redefined
S3.view.app.xml	detailsHeader	PODetailedData	SRA020_S_PO_DETAILED_INCL	SRA020_S_PO_DETAILED

Figure 4-44. *Detailed extension document*

Extending the Fiori Standard Application UI in Eclipse

Now that you have a custom OData service, it's time to create a Fiori extension project from your previously imported standard app. Wave 1 of the Fiori apps did not include the extension project concept. So, in Wave 1, you had to modify the standard code according to your needs and then upload it—a tedious task. From Wave 2 on, SAP Fiori has an enhancement framework implemented in the app source code that lets you enhance, modify or replace any view or controller of the standard app. Here are the steps:

Creating a Fiori Extension Project

1. Open Eclipse, right-click on the project which we imported earlier in this chapter, and click Create SAP Fiori Extension Project (see Figure 4-45). You do not see this option if the Fiori toolkit plug-in has not been added to Eclipse.

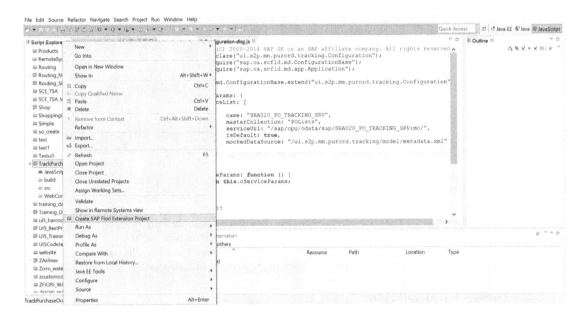

Figure 4-45. *Creating an extension project*

2. Give the extension project a new name, and click Next. You can also replace the standard OData service using this wizard by selecting the check box (see Figure 4-46). But if your OData service is not on the same network, you may want to maintain some certificates so you can access it. In this example, you manually add the new OData URL directly in the extension project after it is created.

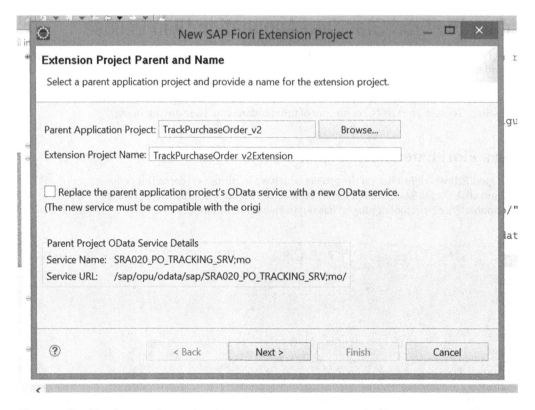

Figure 4-46. *Give the extension project a name*

3. Click Component.js. The code extends the i18n files that contain the language
    support. If you examine the code, you can recognize a JSON structure starting
    with metadata: (see Listing 4-1 and Figure 4-47). This structure basically tells the
    app at runtime what customizations you have made to the standard apps.

Listing 4-1. Metadata Syntax

```
metadata: {
    version : "1.0",
    config : {
        "sap.ca.i18Nconfigs": {
            "bundleName":"ui.s2p.mm.purord.tracking.TrackPurchaseOrder_
            v2Extension.i18n.i18n"
        },
    },

    customizing: {
    }
}
```

```
jQuery.sap.declare("ui.s2p.mm.purord.tracking.TrackPurchaseOrder_v2Extension.Component");

// use the load function for getting the optimized preload file if present
sap.ui.component.load({
    name: "ui.s2p.mm.purord.tracking",
    url: jQuery.sap.getModulePath("ui.s2p.mm.purord.tracking.TrackPurchaseOrder_v2Extension") + "/../(parent proj
    // we use a URL relative to our own component; might be different if
    // extension app is deployed with customer namespace
});

ui.s2p.mm.purord.tracking.Component.extend("ui.s2p.mm.purord.tracking.TrackPurchaseOrder_v2Extension.Component",
    metadata: {
        version : "1.0",
        config : {
            "sap.ca.i18Nconfigs": {
                "bundleName":"ui.s2p.mm.purord.tracking.TrackPurchaseOrder_v2Extension.i18n.i18n"
            },

        },

        customizing: {
        }
    }
});
```

Figure 4-47. *Metadata structure*

At runtime, how does an extended app recognize its parent app? If you look closely at the extended app's folders, you don't see any of the standard app's views or code. The idea behind the extended app is that at runtime, it loads the parent app's source code; and wherever you have extended the app with custom code, it adds that custom code to the <Core:ExtensionPoint/> tag in the standard code or replaces the entire view with your custom view. In order for the extension app to get the parent app's source code, you need to specify the path of the standard app in the extended app's Component.js file under jQuery.sap.getModulePath. For example, the name of the BSP app of your standard app is mm_purord_tpo (see Listing 4-2); you must include that name so the extended app can load the parent app at runtime.

Listing 4-2. Referencing the Standard App Path in the Extended App

```
jQuery.sap.declare("ui.s2p.mm.purord.tracking.TrackPurchaseOrder_v2Extension.Component");

// use the load function for getting the optimized preload file if present
sap.ui.component.load({
    name: "ui.s2p.mm.purord.tracking",
    url: jQuery.sap.getModulePath("ui.s2p.mm.purord.tracking.TrackPurchaseOrder_
    v2Extension") + "/../mm_purord_tpo" // provide parent project url

});
```

4. You have to add your custom OData URL to the extended app. You specify the custom OData URL in the same metadata JSON structure under sap.ca.serviceConfigs (see Figure 4-48).

```
jQuery.sap.declare("ui.s2p.mm.purord.tracking.TrackPurchaseOrder_v2Extension.Component");

// use the load function for getting the optimized preload file if present
sap.ui.component.load({
    name: "ui.s2p.mm.purord.tracking",
    url: jQuery.sap.getModulePath("ui.s2p.mm.purord.tracking.TrackPurchaseOrder_v2Extension") + "/../mm_purord
    // we use a URL relative to our own component; might be different if
    // extension app is deployed with customer namespace
});


ui.s2p.mm.purord.tracking.Component.extend("ui.s2p.mm.purord.tracking.TrackPurchaseOrder_v2Extension.Component
    metadata: {
        version : "1.0",
        config : {
            "sap.ca.i18Nconfigs": {
                "bundleName":"ui.s2p.mm.purord.tracking.TrackPurchaseOrder_v2Extension.i18n.i18n"
            },
            "sap.ca.serviceConfigs":[{
                name:"ZTRCK_PO_EXT_SRV",
                serviceUrl:" /sap/opu/odata/sap/ZTRCK_PO_EXT_SRV",
                isDefault:true
            }]

        },

        customizing: {


        }
    }
});
```

Figure 4-48. OData service configuration

Adding Extensions to the Project

1. To add extensions to the views where you want to make changes, right-click the newly created extended app and choose Add SAP Fiori Extension (see Figure 4-49).

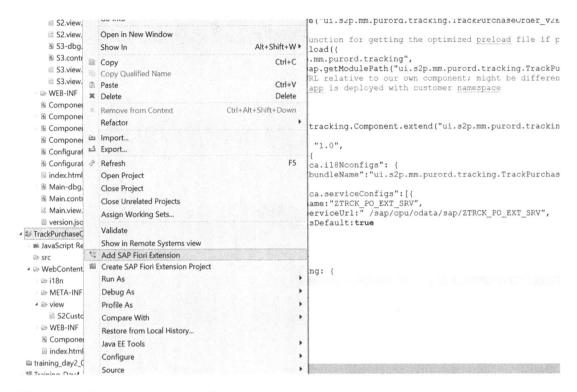

Figure 4-49. *Creating an extension in the project*

2.　From the drop-down, select which view to extend. In this case, select S2.view (see Figure 4-50).

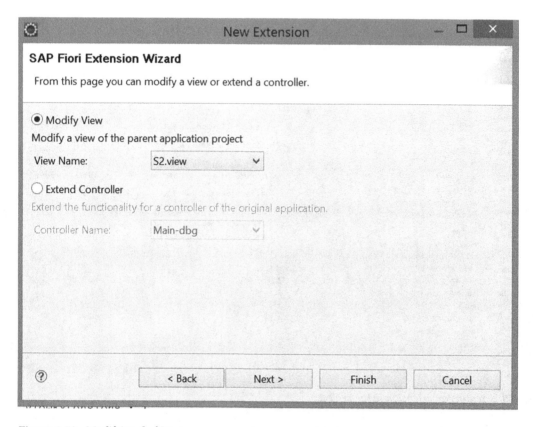

Figure 4-50. *Modifying thef S2 view*

3. On the next page, select whether to replace the view, extend the view, or modify the view (Hide Control). In this case, select Replace View (see Figure 4-51).

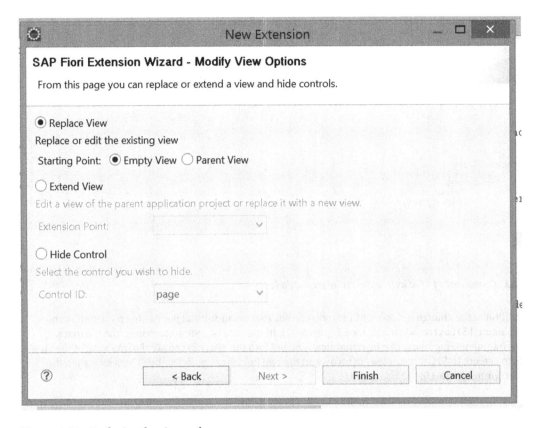

Figure 4-51. *Replacing the view code*

4. After the extension is created, in Component.js, you'll notice a change in the metadata: JSON structure: an addition under Customizing:. The name sap.ui.viewReplacements indicates that it's a view replacement, not a modification. If it were a modification, the name would be something like sap.ui.viewModifications; and in the case of an extension, the name would be sap.ui.ViewExtensions (see Figure 4-52). You can also make these changes manually rather than using the wizard.

```
        // we use a URL relative to our own component; might be different if
        // extension app is deployed with customer namespace
    }));


ui.s2p.mm.purord.tracking.Component.extend("ui.s2p.mm.purord.tracking.TrackPurchaseOrder_v2Extension.Component
    metadata: {
        version : "1.0",
        config : {
            "sap.ca.i18Nconfigs": {
                "bundleName":"ui.s2p.mm.purord.tracking.TrackPurchaseOrder_v2Extension.i18n.i18n"
            },

        },

        customizing: {
            "sap.ui.viewReplacements": {
                "ui.s2p.mm.purord.tracking.view.S2": {
                    viewName: "ui.s2p.mm.purord.tracking.TrackPurchaseOrder_v2Extension.view.S2Custom",
                    type: "XML",
                },
            },

        }
    }
}));
```

Figure 4-52. *Component.js file with view-replacement code*

In addition to the change in Compnent.js, you can see that an additional file has been created in the view folder, named S2Custom.view.xml (see Figure 4-53). In the case of a view extension, the file that's created is a fragment. Fragments can be dynamically called into the <CoreExtensionPoint/> tag of the view you wants to extend. In S2Custom.view.xml, you add the two fields you get from the OData stream to the existing List control in the UI.

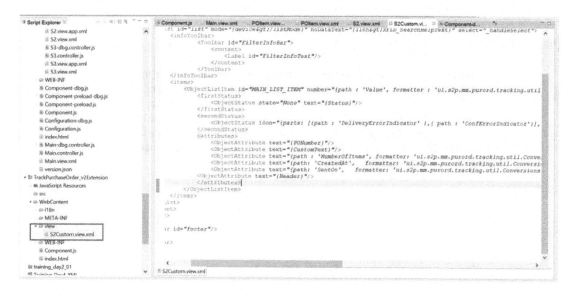

Figure 4-53. *Extended a view for the standard S2 view*

5.   Now you modify a view—in this case, POItem.view, as shown in Figure 4-54.

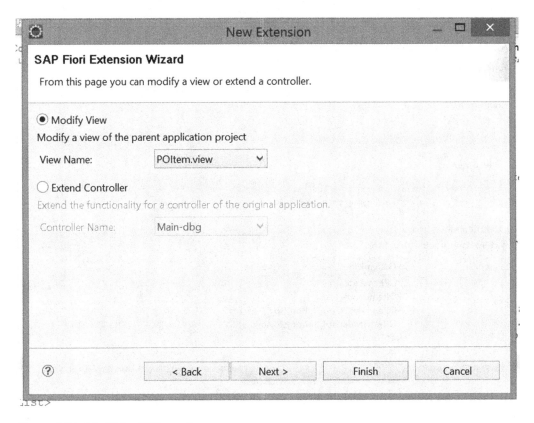

Figure 4-54.   Modifying POItem.view

6.   On the next page, select Hide Control, and choose delivery_form (see Figure 4-55).

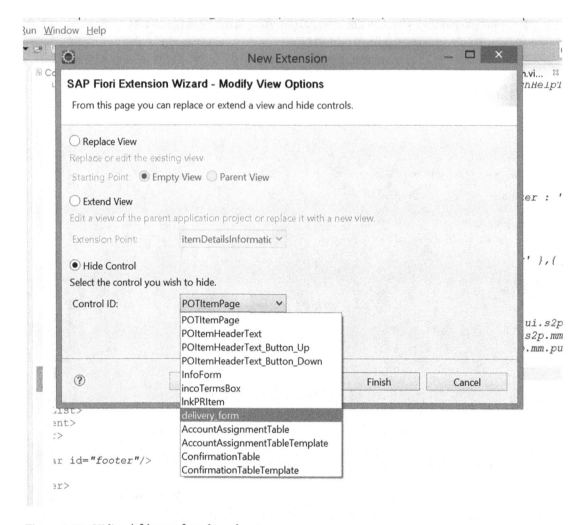

Figure 4-55. *Hiding delivery_form from the view*

You can see the changes being made in Component.js. If you modify a control, a separate file is not generated; instead, the property of the control to be modified is defined in Component.js. In this case, it is under sap.ui.ViewModifications, and the form's Visible property is made false (see Figure 4-56).

```
ui.s2p.mm.purord.tracking.Component.extend("ui.s2p.mm.purord.tracking.TrackPurchaseOrder_v2Extension.Component
    metadata: {
        version : "1.0",
        config : {
            "sap.ca.i18Nconfigs": {
                "bundleName":"ui.s2p.mm.purord.tracking.TrackPurchaseOrder_v2Extension.i18n.i18n"
            },
            "sap.ca.serviceConfigs":[{
                name:"ZTRCK_PO_EXT_SRV",
                serviceUrl:" /sap/opu/odata/sap/ZTRCK_PO_EXT_SRV",
                isDefault:true
            }]
        },

        customizing: {
            "sap.ui.viewModifications": {
                "ui.s2p.mm.purord.tracking.view.POItem": {
                    "delivery form": {
                        "visible": false
                    },
                },
            },

            "sap.ui.viewReplacements": {
                "ui.s2p.mm.purord.tracking.view.S2": {
                    viewName: "ui.s2p.mm.purord.tracking.TrackPurchaseOrder_v2Extension.view.S2Custom",
                    type: "XML",
                },
            },

        }
    }
});
```

Figure 4-56. *Component.js updated with the view-modification code*

7. To extend a view, select S3.view (see Figure 4-57).

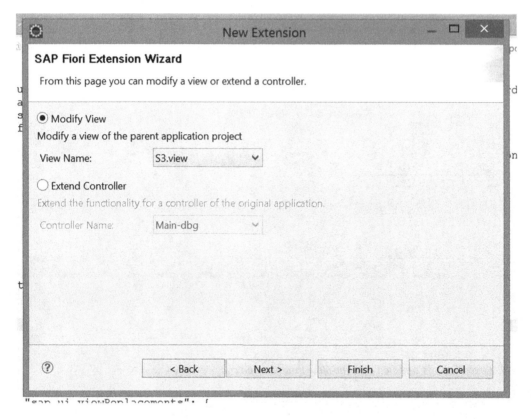

Figure 4-57. *Modifying the S3 view*

8. Extend detailsHeader (see Figure 4-58).

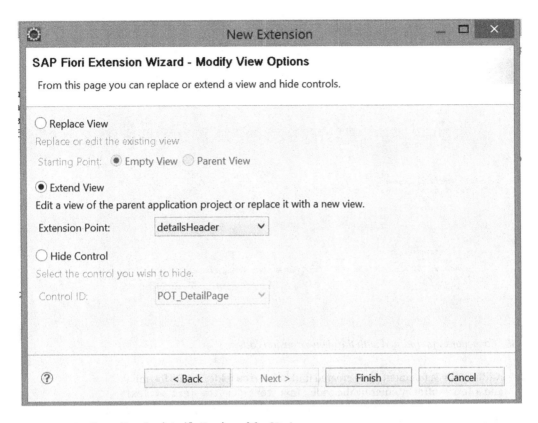

Figure 4-58. *Extending the* detailsHeader *of the S3 view*

For the extension, the Component.js file is modified (see Figure 4-59).

```
                    name:"ZTRCK_PO_EXT_SRV",
                    serviceUrl:" /sap/opu/odata/sap/ZTRCK_PO_EXT_SRV",
                    isDefault:true
                }]

        },

        customizing: {
        "sap.ui.viewExtensions": {
            "ui.s2p.mm.purord.tracking.view.S3": {
                "detailsHeader": {
                    className: "sap.ui.core.Fragment",
                    fragmentName: "ui.s2p.mm.purord.tracking.TrackPurchaseOrder_v2Extension.view.detailsHeaderCustom",
                    type: "XML",
                },
            },
        },

            "sap.ui.viewModifications": {
                "ui.s2p.mm.purord.tracking.view.POItem": {
                    "delivery_form": {
                        "visible": false
                    },
                },
            },

            "sap.ui.viewReplacements": {
                "ui.s2p.mm.purord.tracking.view.S2": {
                    viewName: "ui.s2p.mm.purord.tracking.TrackPurchaseOrder_v2Extension.view.S2Custom",
                    type: "XML",
                },
            },

        }
```

Figure 4-59. *Component.js updated with the view-extension code*

9. Additionally, a fragment file is created under the view folder. In the fragment,
    add a Text control by entering the code `<Text text="Custom Text"></Text>`
    between the `<Core:FragmentDefinition></code:FragmentDefinition>` tags, as
    shown in Figure 4-60.

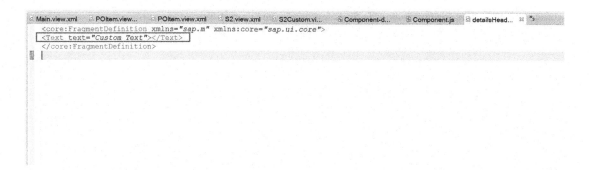

Figure 4-60. *detailsHeader fragment file*

Uploading the Extension Project to the Gateway Server

You have now made all the modifications. It's time to upload the file to the front-end server. Follow these steps:

1. Log on to the Gateway server, and execute the /UI5/UI5_REPOSITORY_LOAD program in SE38. In the input field, give a name for the BSP app you are uploading (see Figure 4-61).

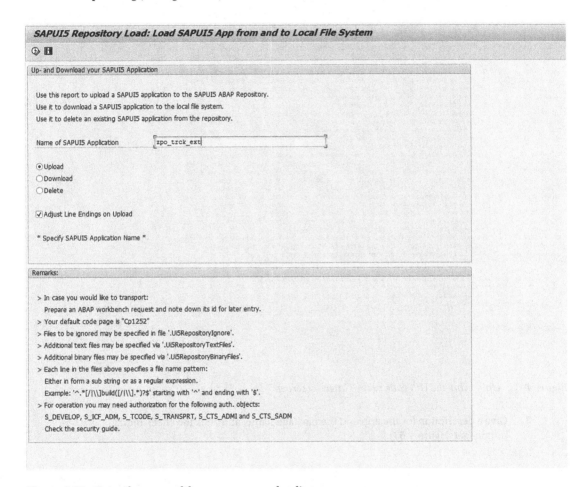

Figure 4-61. *Enter the name of the app you are uploading*

2. Click the Click Here To Upload button. The program uploads the files and registers the BSP app as a UI5 app (see Figure 4-62).

```
Load SAPUI5 Application from File System to the SAPUI5 ABAP Repository

This is going to happen when you confirm at the end of this list ...

* Create SAPUI5 Application    ZPO_TRCK_EXT *

Upload File     :   C:\Users\Bince\Desktop\Po Tracking Extended\WebContent\Component.js  ( Text )
Upload File     :   C:\Users\Bince\Desktop\Po Tracking Extended\WebContent\index.html   ( Text )
Create Folder   :   C:\Users\Bince\Desktop\Po Tracking Extended\WebContent\i18n
Upload File     :   C:\Users\Bince\Desktop\Po Tracking Extended\WebContent\i18n\i18n.properties  ( Text )
Upload File     :   C:\Users\Bince\Desktop\Po Tracking Extended\WebContent\i18n\i18n_ar.properties  ( Text )
Upload File     :   C:\Users\Bince\Desktop\Po Tracking Extended\WebContent\i18n\i18n_bg.properties  ( Text )
Upload File     :   C:\Users\Bince\Desktop\Po Tracking Extended\WebContent\i18n\i18n_cs.properties  ( Text )
Upload File     :   C:\Users\Bince\Desktop\Po Tracking Extended\WebContent\i18n\i18n_de.properties  ( Text )
Upload File     :   C:\Users\Bince\Desktop\Po Tracking Extended\WebContent\i18n\i18n_en.properties  ( Text )
Upload File     :   C:\Users\Bince\Desktop\Po Tracking Extended\WebContent\i18n\i18n_en_US_sappsd.properties  ( Text )
Upload File     :   C:\Users\Bince\Desktop\Po Tracking Extended\WebContent\i18n\i18n_en_US_saptrc.properties  ( Text )
Upload File     :   C:\Users\Bince\Desktop\Po Tracking Extended\WebContent\i18n\i18n_es.properties  ( Text )
Upload File     :   C:\Users\Bince\Desktop\Po Tracking Extended\WebContent\i18n\i18n_fr.properties  ( Text )
Upload File     :   C:\Users\Bince\Desktop\Po Tracking Extended\WebContent\i18n\i18n_hr.properties  ( Text )
Upload File     :   C:\Users\Bince\Desktop\Po Tracking Extended\WebContent\i18n\i18n_hu.properties  ( Text )
Upload File     :   C:\Users\Bince\Desktop\Po Tracking Extended\WebContent\i18n\i18n_it.properties  ( Text )
Upload File     :   C:\Users\Bince\Desktop\Po Tracking Extended\WebContent\i18n\i18n_iw.properties  ( Text )
Upload File     :   C:\Users\Bince\Desktop\Po Tracking Extended\WebContent\i18n\i18n_ja.properties  ( Text )
Upload File     :   C:\Users\Bince\Desktop\Po Tracking Extended\WebContent\i18n\i18n_no.properties  ( Text )
Upload File     :   C:\Users\Bince\Desktop\Po Tracking Extended\WebContent\i18n\i18n_pl.properties  ( Text )
Upload File     :   C:\Users\Bince\Desktop\Po Tracking Extended\WebContent\i18n\i18n_pt.properties  ( Text )
Upload File     :   C:\Users\Bince\Desktop\Po Tracking Extended\WebContent\i18n\i18n_ro.properties  ( Text )
Upload File     :   C:\Users\Bince\Desktop\Po Tracking Extended\WebContent\i18n\i18n_ru.properties  ( Text )
Upload File     :   C:\Users\Bince\Desktop\Po Tracking Extended\WebContent\i18n\i18n_sh.properties  ( Text )
Upload File     :   C:\Users\Bince\Desktop\Po Tracking Extended\WebContent\i18n\i18n_sk.properties  ( Text )
Upload File     :   C:\Users\Bince\Desktop\Po Tracking Extended\WebContent\i18n\i18n_sl.properties  ( Text )
Upload File     :   C:\Users\Bince\Desktop\Po Tracking Extended\WebContent\i18n\i18n_tr.properties  ( Text )
Upload File     :   C:\Users\Bince\Desktop\Po Tracking Extended\WebContent\i18n\i18n_zh_CN.properties  ( Text )
Create Folder   :   C:\Users\Bince\Desktop\Po Tracking Extended\WebContent\META-INF
Upload File     :   C:\Users\Bince\Desktop\Po Tracking Extended\WebContent\META-INF\MANIFEST.MF  ( Text )
Create Folder   :   C:\Users\Bince\Desktop\Po Tracking Extended\WebContent\view
Upload File     :   C:\Users\Bince\Desktop\Po Tracking Extended\WebContent\view\detailsHeaderCustom.fragment.xml  ( Text )
Upload File     :   C:\Users\Bince\Desktop\Po Tracking Extended\WebContent\view\S2Custom.view.xml  ( Text )
Create Folder   :   C:\Users\Bince\Desktop\Po Tracking Extended\WebContent\WEB-INF
Upload File     :   C:\Users\Bince\Desktop\Po Tracking Extended\WebContent\WEB-INF\web.xml  ( Text )

* Items to be ignored have been determined from the built-in standard settings.  *
* Text files have been identified from standard settings.  *
* Binary files have been identified from standard settings.  *
* The adjustment of line endings has been requested.  *

[  Click here to Upload  ]
```

Figure 4-62.   *Uploading the UI5 code to the Gateway server*

3.   Give a description for the app and the package name, and click the check mark button (see Figure 4-63).

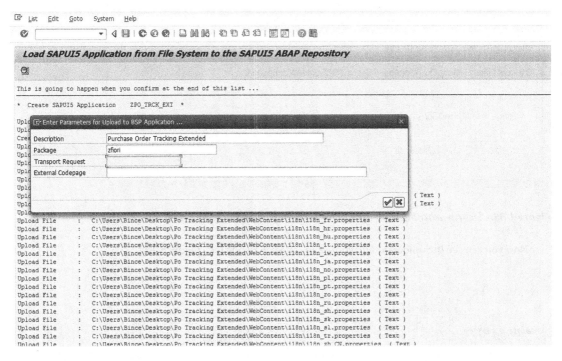

Figure 4-63. *Specify the package for the app*

4. Enter a workbench request, or create a new one if necessary (see Figure 4-64).

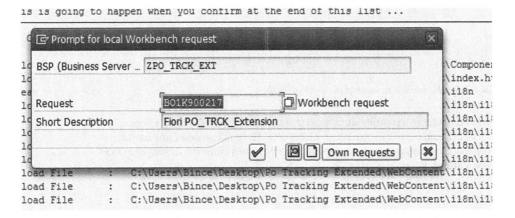

Figure 4-64. *Enter a workbench request for creating the BSP app*

5. Give the app permission to access your system files (see Figure 4-65). You can disable this pop-up by making changes in the SAP GUI configuration in the control panel.

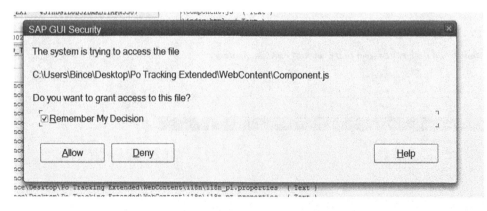

Figure 4-65. *Security warning from the system regarding accessing system files*

Now you can see the uploaded app service in the SICF t-code (see Figure 4-66).

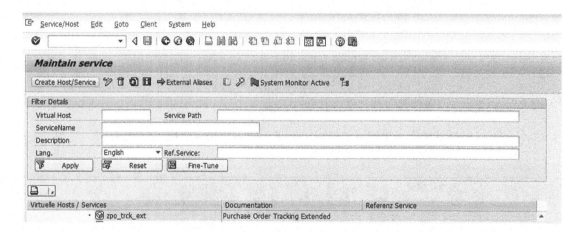

Figure 4-66. *SICF with the service activated for the BSP app*

6. You need to create a custom launchpad using the LPD_CUST t-code. Execute LPD_CUST, and enter the role name **ZLPD_PO_TR** (you can enter any name you want). For Instance, enter **TRANSACTIONAL**; and enter the description **PO Track Extended** (see Figure 4-67).

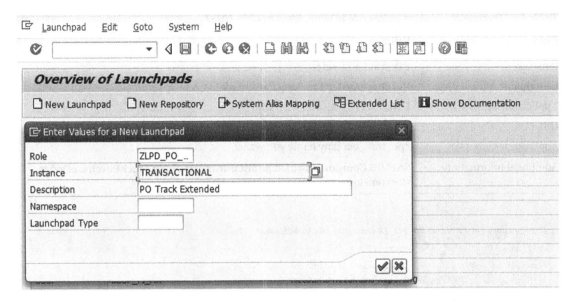

Figure 4-67. *Creating a new launchpad in LPD_CUST*

7. Click Yes in the pop-up screen (see Figure 4-68).

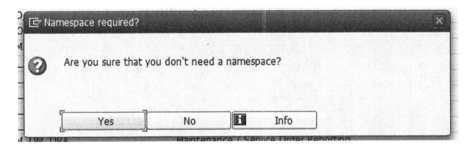

Figure 4-68. *Ignore the namespace warning*

8. Click the New Application button, and enter the parameter values from Table 4-1 in the fields. Click Show Advanced (Optional) Parameters to expand the fields (see Figure 4-69).

Table 4-1. *Parameter Values to Create a New Launchpad in LPD_CUST*

Field	Value
Link Text	**PO Track Extended**
Description	**Purchase Order Tracking Extended**
Application Type	**URL**
URL	**/sap/bc/ui5_ui5/sap/zpo_trck_ext**
Application Alias	**zpo_trck_ext** (any name you want)
Additional Information	**SAPUI5.Component=ui.s2p.mm.purord.tracking.TrackPurchaseOrder_v2Extension**

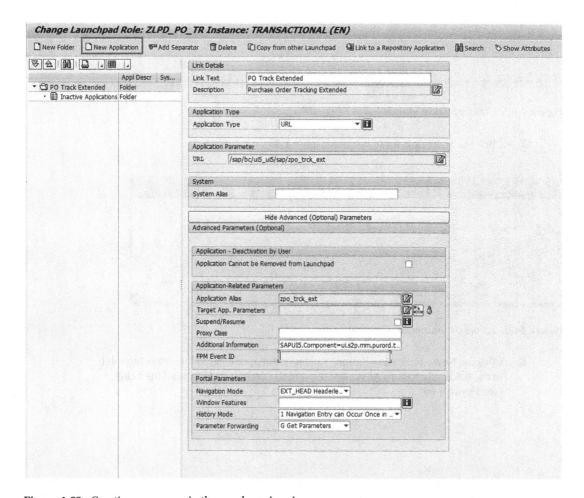

Figure 4-69. *Creating a new app in the new launchpad*

You can get the value for the Additional Information field from the app source code (see Figure 4-70).

```
🕮 Component.js ⋈   🗏 Main.view.xml      🗏 POItem.view...      🗏 POItem.view.xml      🗏 S2.view.xml      🗏 S2Custom.vi...      🕮 Component-d...      🕮 Component.js    ⁿ₈
    jQuery.sap.declare("ui.s2p.mm.purord.tracking.TrackPurchaseOrder_v2Extension.Component");

    // use the load function for getting the optimized preload file if present
    sap.ui.component.load({
        name: "ui.s2p.mm.purord.tracking",
        url: jQuery.sap.getModulePath("ui.s2p.mm.purord.tracking.TrackPurchaseOrder_v2Extension") + "/../mm_purord_tpo" //
        // we use a URL relative to our own component; might be different if
        // extension app is deployed with customer namespace
    });

    ui.s2p.mm.purord.tracking.Component.extend("ui.s2p.mm.purord.tracking.TrackPurchaseOrder_v2Extension.Component", {
        metadata: {
            version : "1.0",
            config : {
                "sap.ca.i18Nconfigs": {
                    "bundleName":"ui.s2p.mm.purord.tracking.TrackPurchaseOrder_v2Extension.i18n.i18n"
                },
                "sap.ca.serviceConfigs":[{
                    name:"ZTRCK_PO_EXT_SRV",
                    serviceUrl:" /sap/opu/odata/sap/ZTRCK_PO_EXT_SRV",
                    isDefault:true
                }]
            },
        },
```

Figure 4-70. *Value for the Additional Information field in the LPD_CUST app*

Creating a Custom Tile in the Fiori Launchpad

Log in to the Fiori launchpad designer (see Figure 4-71). To add a custom tile to the launchpad, you need to create a new catalog and add your custom app. Follow these steps:

Figure 4-71. *Creating a new catalog in the launchpad designer*

1. Click the Create Catalog icon at lower-left.

2. Give the catalog a name and ID in the pop-up (see Figure 4-72).

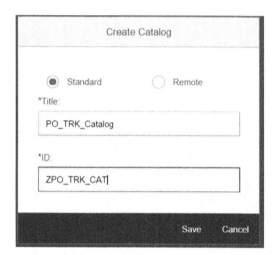

Figure 4-72. *Assign a unique ID for the catalog*

3. Click the + sign to create a new tile in your catalog (see Figure 4-73).

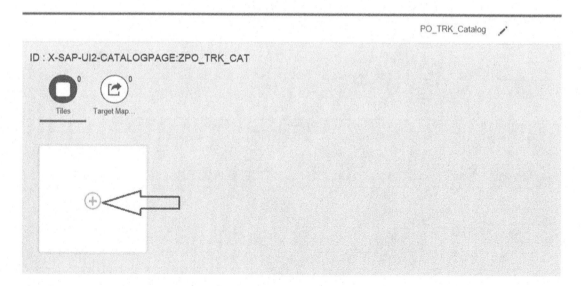

Figure 4-73. *Creating a tile for the new catalog*

4. Because your tile does not show data dynamically, select App Launcher – Static, as shown in Figure 4-74.

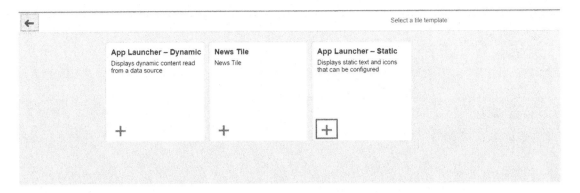

Figure 4-74. *Choose App Launcher – Static*

5. Give the General and Navigation details for your app (see Figure 4-75). In the
    Navigation area, enter the same semantic object and action as the standard app;
    because it's an extension of the standard app, you don't need to create a custom
    semantic object. Click Save.

Figure 4-75. *Static tile configuration for the extended Track Purchase Order app*

6. Click the target mapping icon at upper-left, and then click Create Target Mapping
    at lower-right (see Figure 4-76).

149

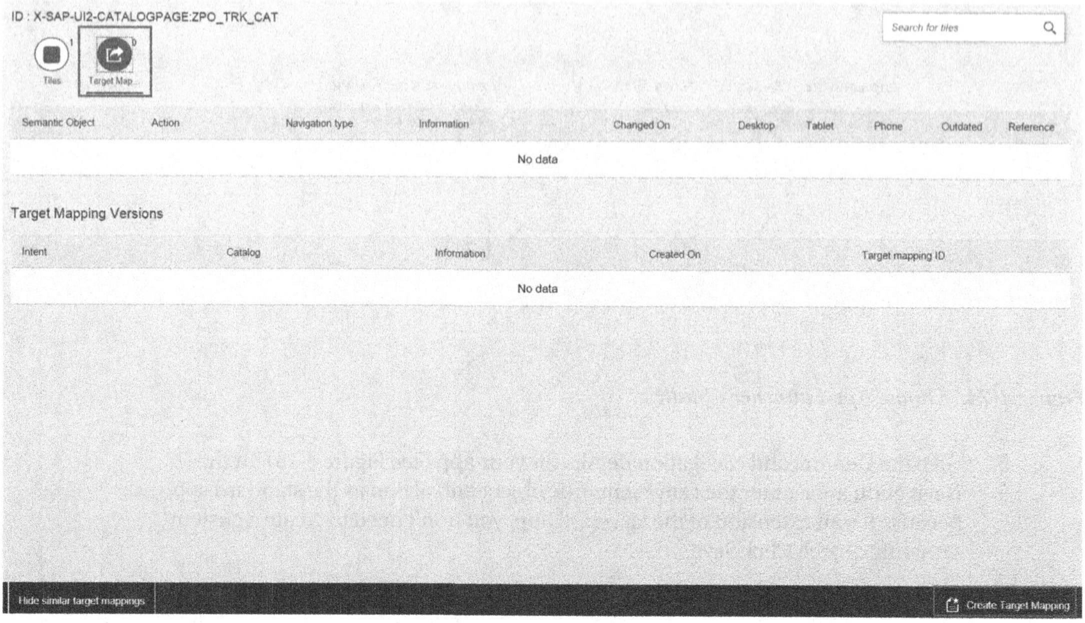

Figure 4-76. *Creating a target mapping*

7. In the Intent area, specify the same semantic object and action that you specified for the app launcher static tile, so that the visible static tile and the target-mapping tile are linked. In the Target area, enter the custom launchpad role you created earlier using LPD_CUST, the Launchpad Instance value **TRANSACTIONAL**, and the Application Alias **zpo_trck_ext** (see Figure 4-77).

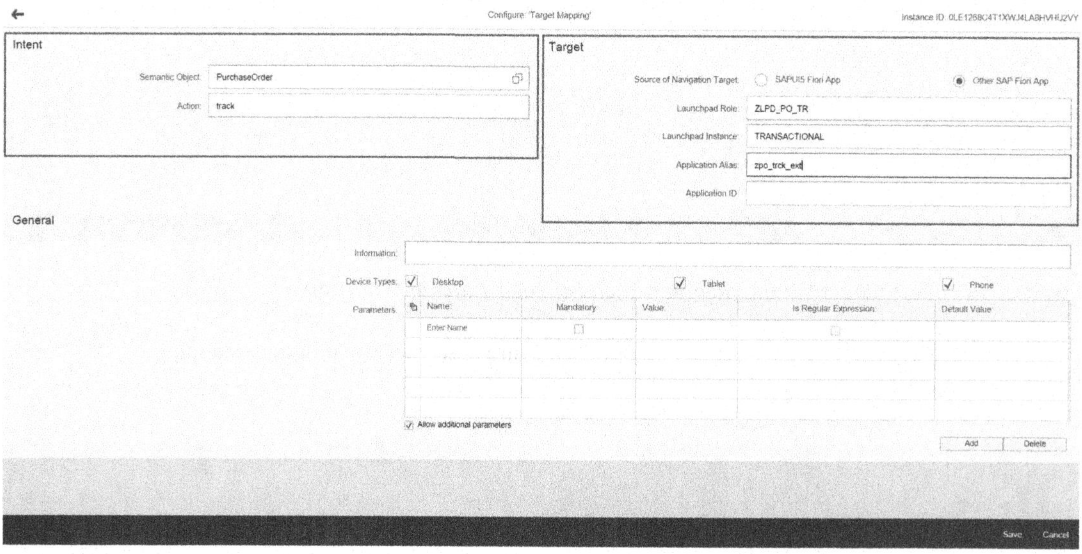

Figure 4-77. *Target-mapping configuration for the extended Track Purchase Order app*

Assigning Roles to End Users

The catalog setup is complete in the Fiori launchpad, but in order for end users to access these tiles, you must assign them the catalog ID that you specified when you created the catalog in the launchpad designer. To assign the catalog role to the user, follow these steps:

1. Log on to the Gateway server, and execute the PFCG transaction. Create a new role called zpo_TRCK_ROLE by clicking the Single Role button (see Figure 4-78).

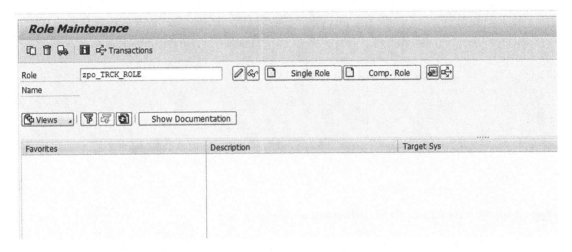

Figure 4-78. *Create a new role for the user, to assign the catalog*

2. On the Menu tab, click the Transaction button, and select SAP Fiori Tile Catalog (see Figure 4-79).

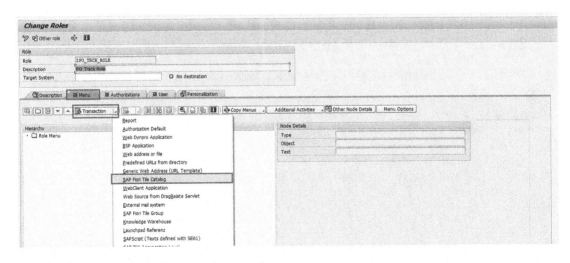

Figure 4-79. *Adding the catalog ID to the new role*

3. From the pop-up select the catalog ID ZZPO_TRK_CAT that you created in the Fiori launchpad designer (see Figure 4-80).

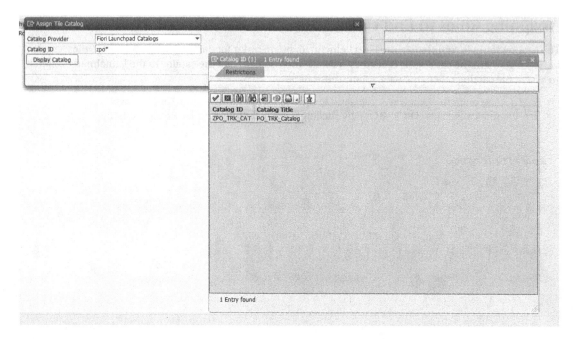

Figure 4-80. *Enter the Catalog ID created in the launchpad designer*

4. On the User tab, enter the user ID of the end user you want to give access to the catalog (see Figure 4-81).

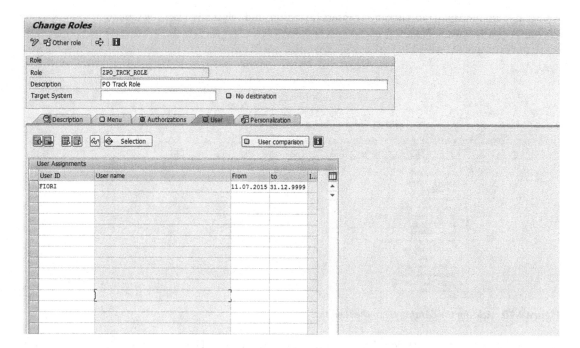

Figure 4-81. *Map the role to the end user*

Adding a Custom Tile to the Home Page

When the user logs in to the Fiori launchpad (see Figure 4-82), they need to be able to access the tile you added to the catalog assigned to the user. To add the tile to the home page, follow these steps:

Figure 4-82. Tile Catalog on the end user's home page

1. Click the icon at upper-left on the home page, and then click the Tile Catalog button at lower-left.

The new tile appears in the catalog you assigned to the user (see Figure 4-83).

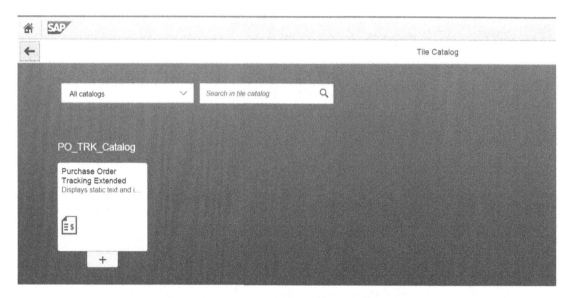

Figure 4-83. *Selecting the custom tile for the home page*

2. Click the + icon at the bottom of the tile and add it to an existing group on the home page, or add a new group specifically for this tile. To create a group, click the New Group button on the list (see Figure 4-84).

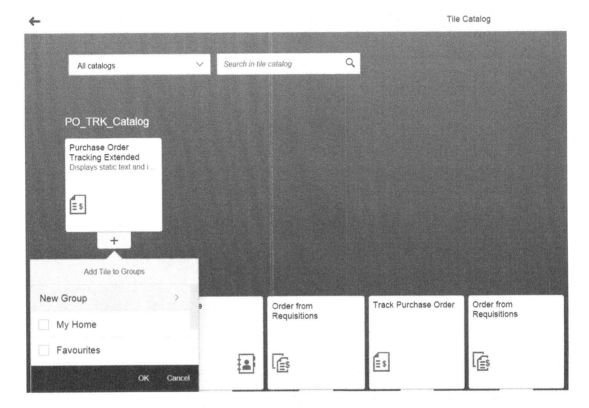

Figure 4-84. *Select the group to which you want to add the tile*

3.   Give the group a name, and click OK (see Figure 4-85).

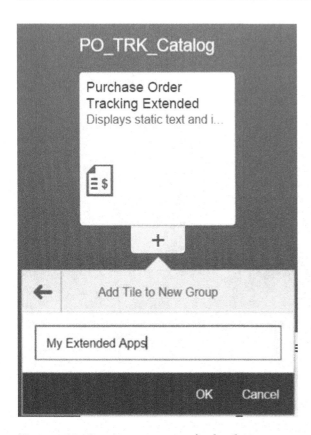

Figure 4-85. *Creating a new group for the tile*

4. On the home page, you can see your new tile (see Figure 4-86).

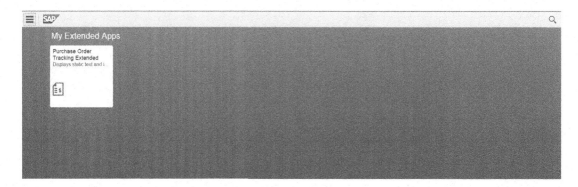

Figure 4-86. *Extended tile on the end user's home page*

5. Click the tile to launch the extended app. The custom data appears in the Track Purchase Order app (see Figure 4-87).

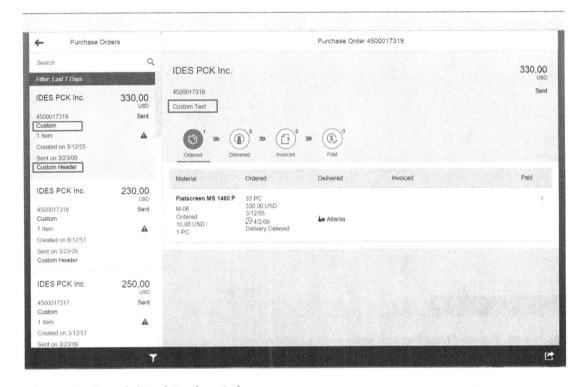

Figure 4-87. *Extended Track Purchase Order app*

The delivery form is hidden on the Item Details screen (see Figure 4-88).

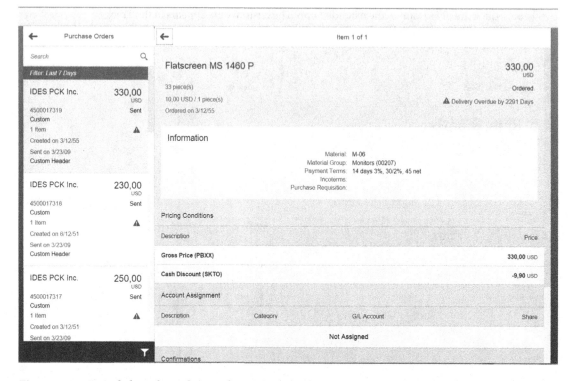

Figure 4-88. *Extended Track Purchase Order app's S3 view*

In Figure 4-89, the original screen is on the left, and the modified screen is on the right. The Delivery form is hidden on the modified app.

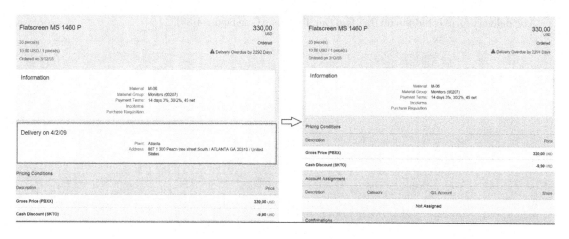

Figure 4-89. *S3 view with* delivery_form *hidden*

Extending a Fiori Standard Application in Web IDE

Now, let's look at how to extend the Track Purchase Order app using Web IDE. You can get a trial version of Web IDE by registering on the SAP Hana Cloud Platform at `https://account.hanatrial.ondemand.com/register`. Once you have registered and logged in to Hana Cloud Platform, you can access Web IDE at `/subscriptions/webide`. You can also install an on-premises version of Web IDE (Chapter 6 covers Web IDE in more detail).

Connecting Web IDE to Back-End Systems

Because you are using a Web IDE that is deployed on Hana Cloud Platform, you need to do two things to connect Web IDE to your SAP back-end systems:

- Install the HANA Cloud connector on your system (you can download the cloud connector installation file from `https://tools.hana.ondemand.com/#cloud`). Installation details for the cloud connector can be found at `https://help.hana.ondemand.com/help/frameset.htm?204aaad4270245f3baa0c57c8ab1dd60.html`.

- Create a new service in your Hana Cloud Platform cockpit.

Let's get on with creating a new service:

1. Log on to Hana Cloud Platform at `https://account.hanatrial.ondemand.com`.

2. Click Destinations. At right, click the New Destination link.

3. Enter the data from Table 4-2 in the input fields.

Table 4-2. *Hana Cloud Destination Parameter Values*

Field Name	Value
Name	**<ServerName>**
Type	**HTTP**
Description	**MyServer**
URL	Your local SAP system URL, which you configured while installing the cloud connector in step 1
ProysType	**OnPremise**
Cloud Connector Version	**2**
Authentication	**NoAuthentication**

4. Click the New Property button next to the input fields, and add the parameter values from Table 4-3.

Table 4-3. *Hana Cloud Destination Additional Parameter Values*

Field Name	Value
WebIDEEnabled	**True**
WebIDEUsage	**odata_abap,dev_abap,ui5_execute_abap**
WebIDESystem	**<ServerName>**

Creating a New Extension Project in Web IDE

One of the advantages of Web IDE is that you can download and upload standard UI5 apps directly from the Web IDE interface. You can download apps directly in Eclipse; but when you upload apps, the app folder structure is not exactly the same, because the Fiori architecture is designed to run standard apps. To create an extension project, open Web IDE in the browser and then follow these steps:

1. Click New Extension Project (see Figure 4-90).

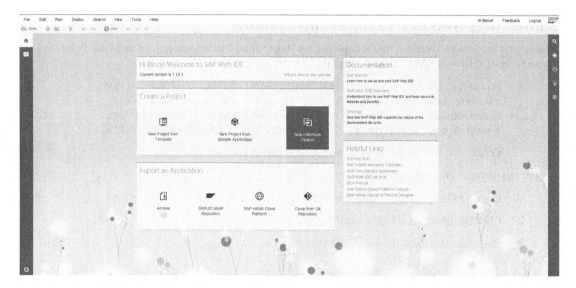

Figure 4-90. *Web IDE home page*

2. Click the Remote button, and select SAPUI5 ABAP Repository (see Figure 4-91).

Figure 4-91. *Creating an extension project using Web IDE*

3. Select the Gateway server from the list, enter the standard app's name, and click OK (see Figure 4-92).

***Figure 4-92.** Selecting the back-end system to choose a standard app for extension*

4. Select the check box to import the original app (see Figure 4-93).

***Figure 4-93.** Give the details for the extension project*

5. Click Finish to create the extension project (see Figure 4-94).

Figure 4-94. *Completing the creation of the extension project*

Adding Extensions to the Project

After the standard app is downloaded, just as in the Eclipse version, you can create extensions. Here are the steps:

1. Right-click the project, and create an extension on it (see Figure 4-95). The phrases *extension project* and *adding an extension* may be confusing: the extension project you created previously is just a blank project with the standard source code imported into it. After you import the code, you can tell Web IDE what type of extensions you want to add to this standard app.

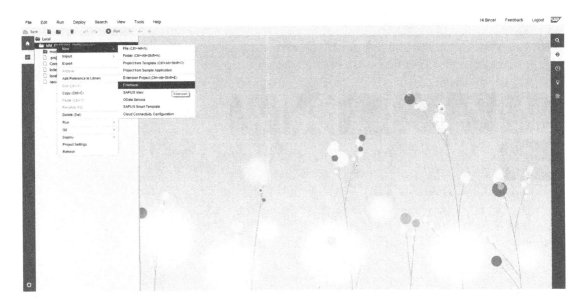

Figure 4-95. *Creating an extension for the custom app*

2. Give your extension project a name (see Figure 4-96).

Figure 4-96. *Give the extension project a name*

3. Define the type of extension you want to perform on the standard app. In this case, select Replace View (see Figure 4-97).

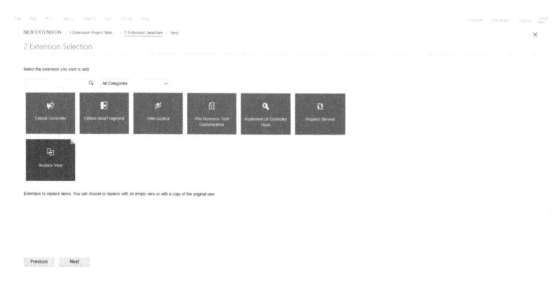

Figure 4-97. *Select the Replace View extension*

4. To replace the S2 view, copy the code of the original view into your replacement view; then you can modify it (see Figure 4-98).

Figure 4-98. *Creating an extension for the S2 view*

5. Click Finish to create the extension project (see Figure 4-99).

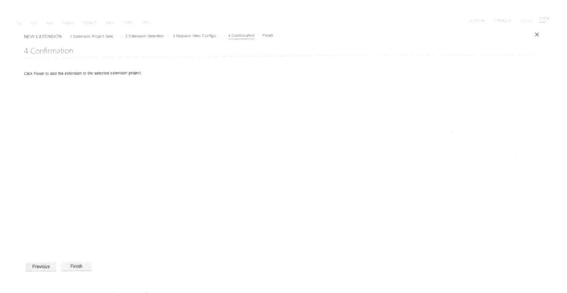

Figure 4-99. *Completing the extension*

6. Open the S2Custom view in the `view` folder, and add the custom fields as you did earlier in Eclipse (see Figure 4-100).

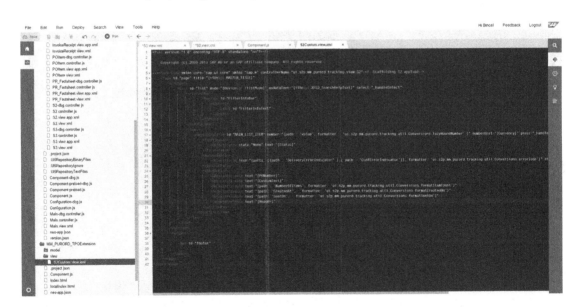

Figure 4-100. *Extension view for the S2 view*

7. In addition to manual coding, Web IDE has a drag-and-drop feature you can use to add controls to views. To add controls via drag-and-drop, right-click the view, select Open With, and select Layout Editor (see Figure 4-101).

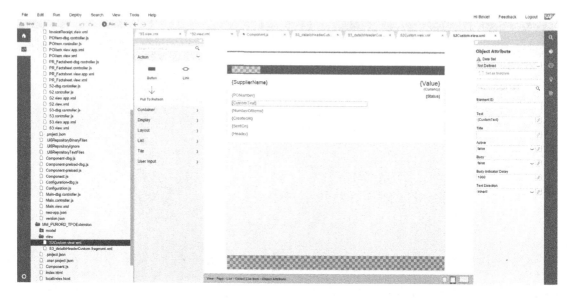

Figure 4-101. *Layout editor for the S2Custom view*

8. In the left pane, select the desired control; drag to the preview pane to add the control (see Figure 4-102).

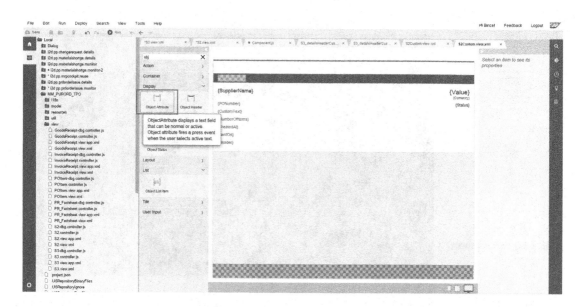

Figure 4-102. *Drag and drop controls in the layout editor*

9. Next you can extend an existing control. Just as you did for the S2 view, right-click the project, select New ➤ Extension, select Extend View/Fragment, and click Next (see Figure 4-103).

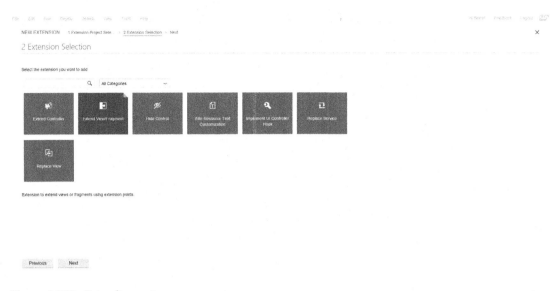

Figure 4-103. *Extending a view*

10. Select the S3 view, and choose detailsHeader as the extension point
    (see Figure 4-104).

Figure 4-104. *detailsHeader extension for the S3 view*

11. Click Finish to complete the extension (see Figure 4-105).

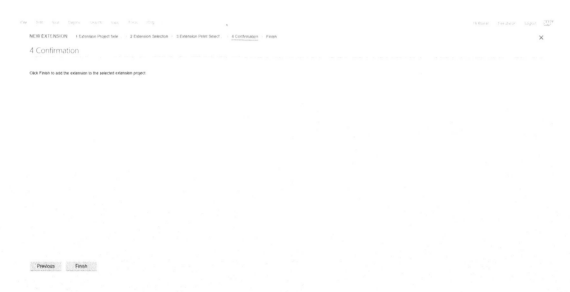

Figure 4-105. *Completing the extension for the S3 view*

12. The extension for the controller is created in the view folder as a fragment (see Figure 4-106).

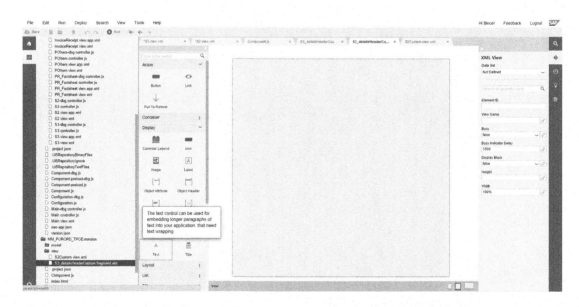

Figure 4-106. *Fragment file for the detailsHeader extension*

13. You can choose to manually code the page or open the fragment in the layout editor (see Figure 4-107).

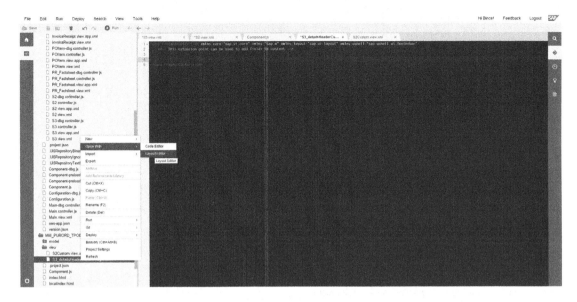

Figure 4-107. *Open the S3 extension view in the layout editor*

14. Drag and drop the custom controls you want to add to the fragment (see Figure 4-108).

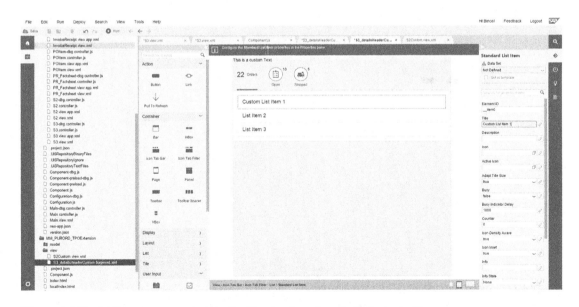

Figure 4-108. *Adding custom controls to the S3 extension view via the layout editor*

15. To replace the standard OData service of the extended project, click Replace Service from the extension view (see Figure 4-109).

Figure 4-109. *Creating a Replace Service extension*

16. On the next screen, select the desired back-end system. From the drop-down list, select your OData service (see Figure 4-110).

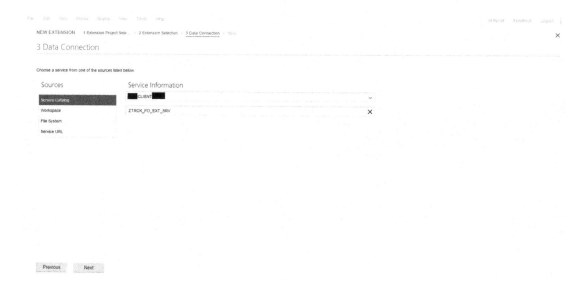

Figure 4-110. *Select the custom OData service from the back-end server*

17. The new OData service is added to the metadata: JSON body along with other extensions and modifications you chose earlier (see Figure 4-111).

Figure 4-111. Component.js *updated with the replaced OData service URL*

18. You can also hide an existing control as you did in the Eclipse project. Select Hide Control from the extension view (see Figure 4-112).

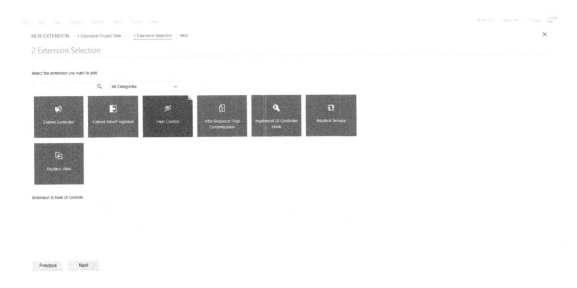

Figure 4-112. *Hiding a control in the view*

19. Select the control you want to hide. In this example, hide delivery_form (see Figure 4-113).

Figure 4-113. *Hiding* delivery_form

20. Click Finish to complete the extension (see Figure 4-114).

Figure 4-114. *Completing the extension*

21. All the enhancements, customizations, and modifications are now complete (see Figure 4-115).

Figure 4-115. Component.js updated with all the extensions in the metadata: JSON

22. To preview the app, select the project's main folder or Component.js, and click the green Run button on the toolbar (see Figure 4-116).

Figure 4-116. Previewing the app

23. You need to deploy this extended project back to the Gateway server as a BSP app and activate the service for the app. To deploy the app, right-click it, select Deploy, and click Deploy To SAPUI5 ABAP Repository (see Figure 4-117).

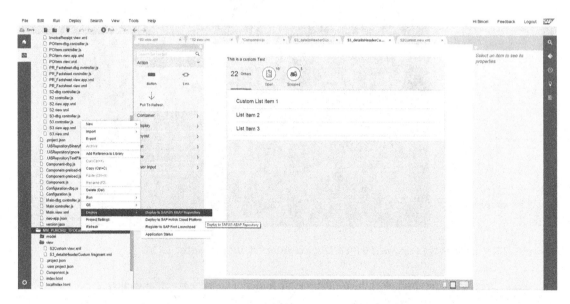

Figure 4-117. *Deploy the app to the ABAP repository*

24. Select the Gateway system from the drop-down list, and click Next (see Figure 4-118).

Figure 4-118. *Select the Gateway system to deploy the app*

25. Enter the app name, a description, and a package name to deploy the app to the Gateway server (see Figure 4-119).

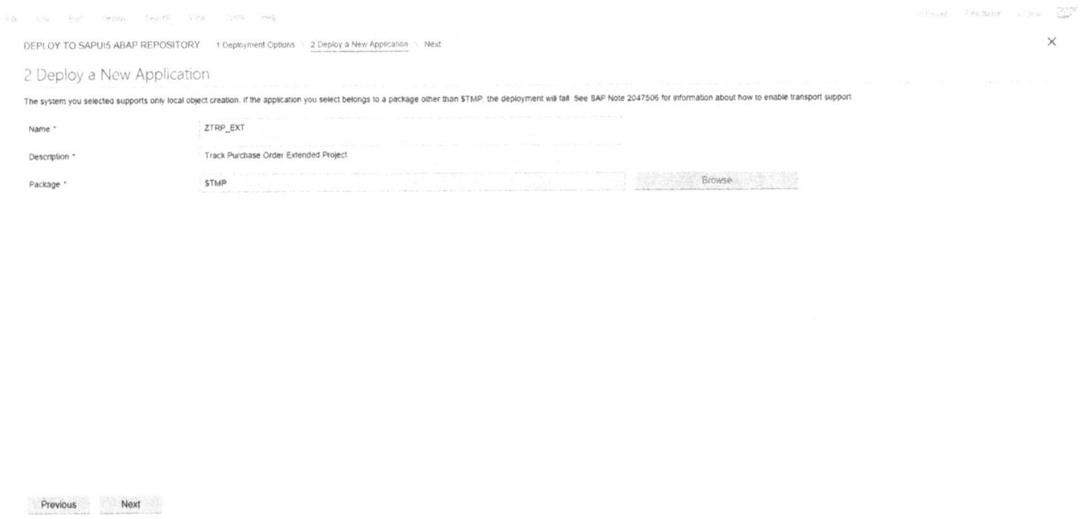

Figure 4-119. *Give the package and details for the app*

26. Click Finish to deploy the project (see Figure 4-120).

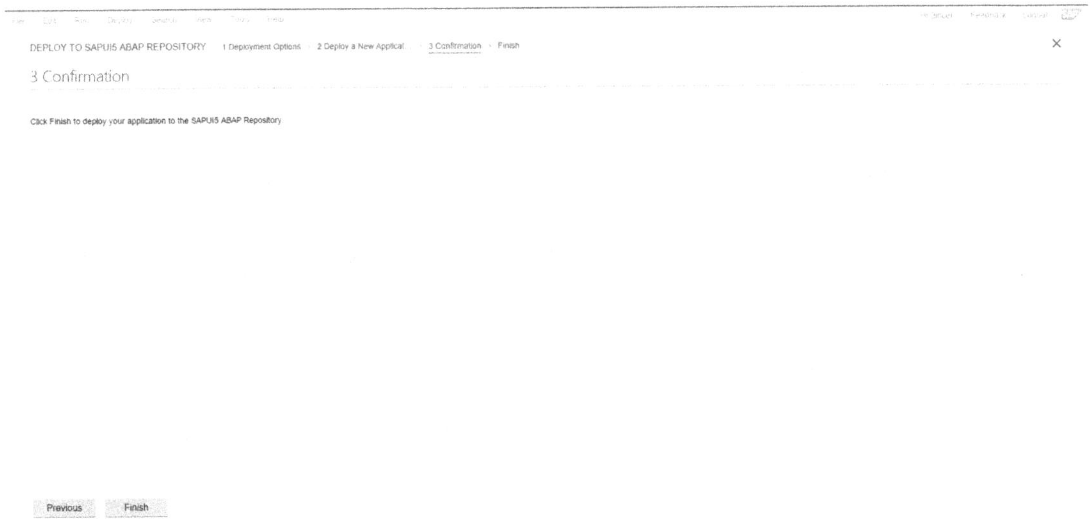

Figure 4-120. *Completing the deployment of the app*

The next chapter covers Fiori OData customizations and NetWeaver Gateway in detail.

CHAPTER 5

Fiori OData Customization and NetWeaver Gateway Overview

In addition to the Fiori UI, to make changes to the standard data from SAP ERP, you need to modify the standard OData service or develop a custom OData service for Fiori apps. In this chapter, you learn about the basics of OData, creating a custom OData service from scratch, and building a UI5 application to use that custom OData service.

OData Overview

OData (Open Data Protocol) is standard for generating and consuming RESTful APIs. SAP has the NetWeaver Gateway you can use to build an OData service so that it can be consumed by UI5 applications. RESTful APIs are easy to consume. These services enable UI5 apps to perform CRUD (create read update delete) operations on the SAP back end via the NetWeaver Gateway server.

The NetWeaver Gateway allows even developers who are new to SAP to consume or modify SAP data from SAP business applications. Basically, SAP NetWeaver Gateway (now called as just SAP Gateway) is a RESTful service provider based on OData technology that connects applications to the SAP business suite.

The OData service is not limited to UI5 apps. It is a generic standard used by many websites, cloud services, and even social media sites like Facebook and Twitter. The apps uses OData services to receive data from their respective back-end data sources and send data to the front-end UI. Similarly, SAP allows apps like enterprise software, social media apps, cloud-based services, and so on to access the SAP data source with NetWeaver Gateway as the service provider and authenticator of these services from SAP's side. From SAP 2.3, OData support has been introduced to the SDK; now, with SMP 3.0, offline OData support also has been added. Figure 5-1 shows how OData helps the SAP Gateway to communicate with different back-end and front-end services.

Electronic supplementary material The online version of this chapter (doi:10.1007/978-1-4842-1335-3_5) contains supplementary material, which is available to authorized users.

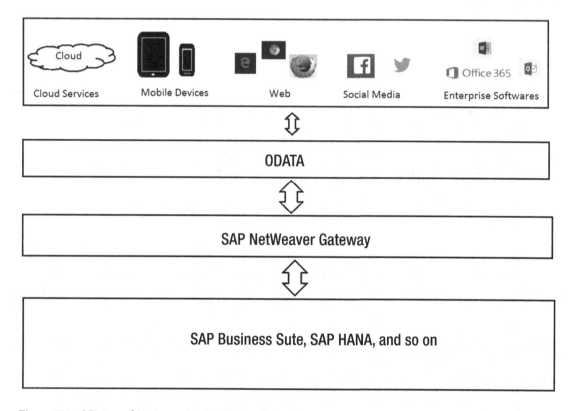

Figure 5-1. *OData architecture using NetWeaver Gateway*

OData Development Using NetWeaver Gateway

In this section, you learn how to implement a custom OData service to fetch business data from the SAP business suite. You create an OData service that supports CRUD operations; later, you build a simple UI5-based app as an interface for the new OData service.

Custom Table for the OData Service

Log in to the NetWeaver Gateway, and create a new OData service. For this scenario, you are fetching a few records from a custom table created in the back end (see Figure 5-2), You can download the details of the table elements and field names from the Apress website (this book doesn't cover ABAP basics about creating database tables in the SAP back end).

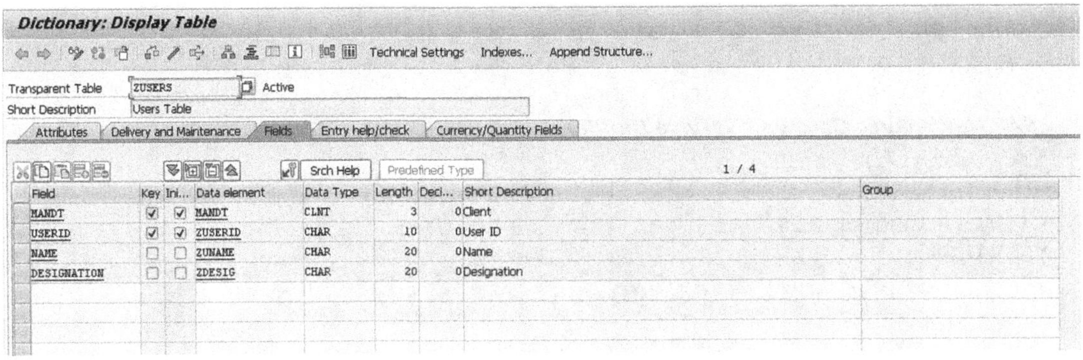

Figure 5-2. *ZUSERS table created for the custom OData service*

The table contains records you will fetch with the OData service via the `GetEntitySet` method (see Figure 5-3).

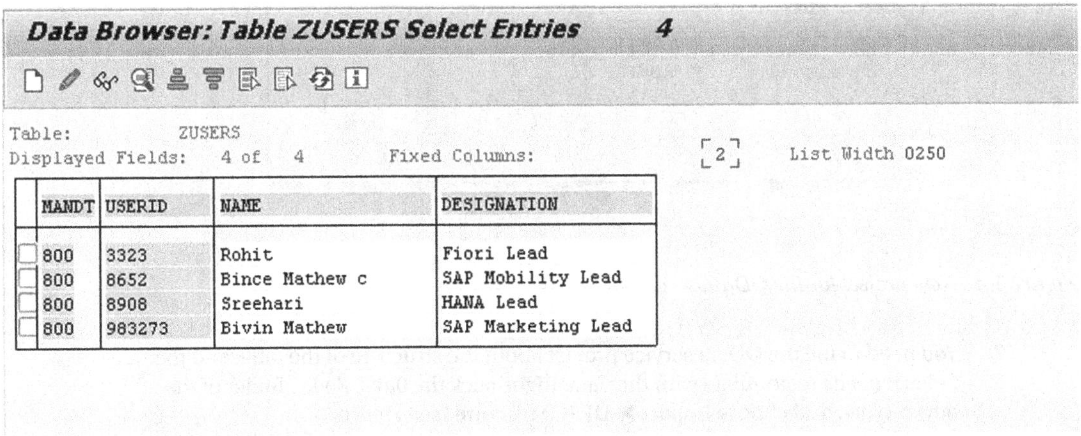

Figure 5-3. *The table is filled with records to fetch via OData*

After you create the table, it's time to create a new OData service to fetch the data from this table.

Creating an OData Service in Gateway

Go to the SEGW t-code, and create a new OData Project. Then, follow these steps:

1. Give the new OData project a name, as shown in Figure 5-4. Here the name is **ZEMP_RECORDS**.

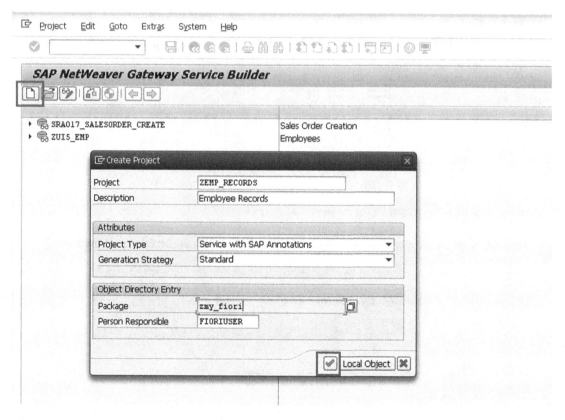

Figure 5-4. *New project for the OData service in SEGW*

2. You need to tell the OData service project about the structure of the table and the fields it needs to populate with the data. Right-click the Data Model folder of the new project, and choose Import ➤ DDIC Structure (see Figure 5-5).

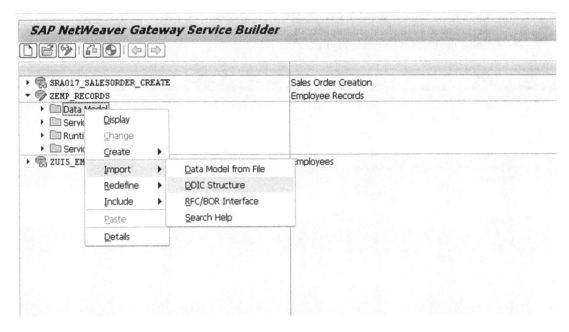

Figure 5-5. *Importing the DDIC structure to define OData entity fields*

3. Create a new entity, and select your custom table from the DDIC in order for the OData service to get the structure definitions it needs to create the new entity. Name the entity table **Users** and the ABAP structure **ZUSERS**, and click Next (see Figure 5-6).

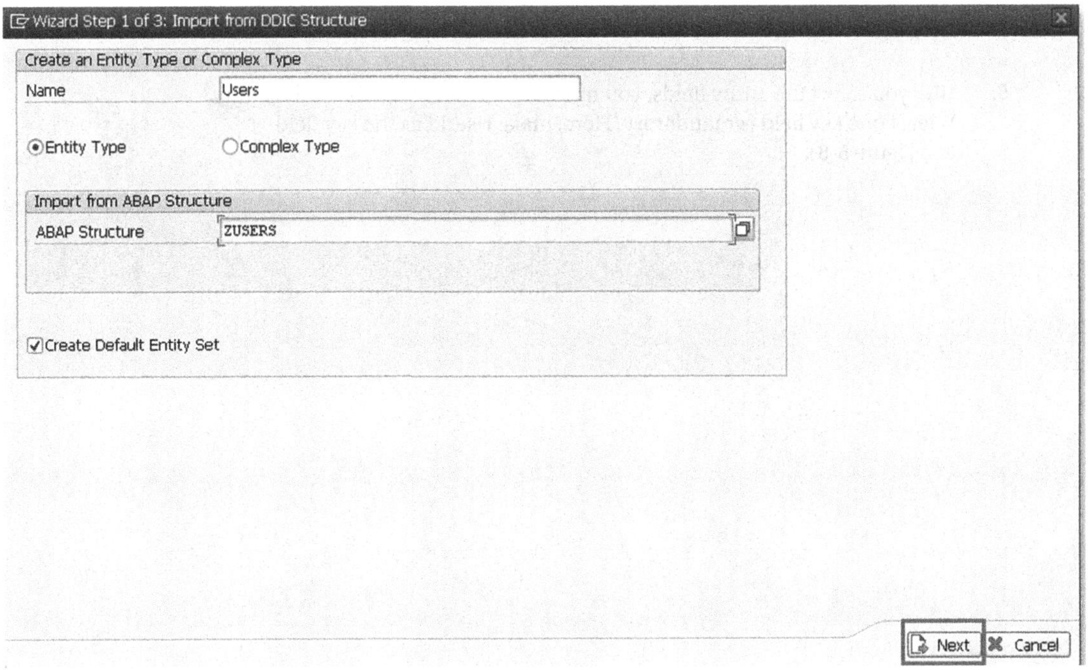

Figure 5-6. *Defining the entity name and DDIC structure*

4. Select the required fields for the entity. When creating entities, sometimes you may not need all the fields to implement your logic. For the OData service, choose the fields as shown in Figure 5-7.

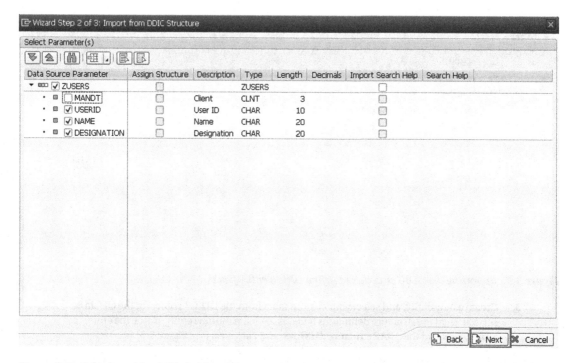

Figure 5-7. *Selecting entity fields for the service*

5. After you select the entity fields, you must define the key fields for the entity. At least one key field is mandatory. Here, make Userid as the key field (see Figure 5-8).

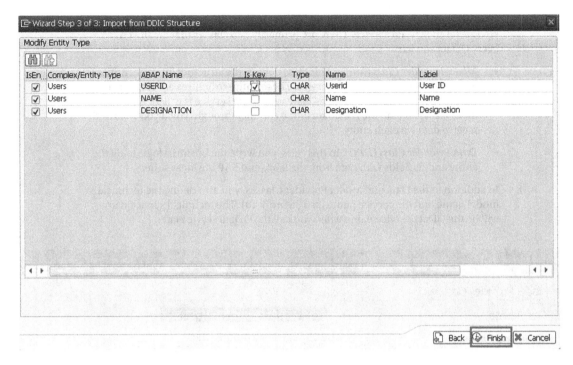

Figure 5-8. *Define the key field for your entity*

6. Activate the OData service by clicking the Generate button (see Figure 5-9).

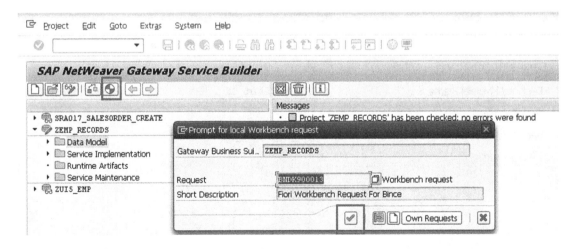

Figure 5-9. *Activate the OData definition*

7. When you activate the service, you see a pop-up with the class names that will be created for the OData service. There are primarily two classes that are linked to every OData service.

   • *Model Provider Class (MPC)*: This class defines the structure for your entities when you activate the OData service. These entity structures are created at runtime via the Model Provider Classes when the service is called. Basically, these classes create the metadata or the channel through which you send and receive data via each entity.

   • *Data Provider Class (DPC)*: In this class, you write the business logic to fill the entity and its fields with data from the back-end SAP business suite.

8. In addition to the Data and Model Provider Classes, you also define the technical model name and the service name (see Figure 5-10). The technical service name will be the OData service name when you call the OData service later.

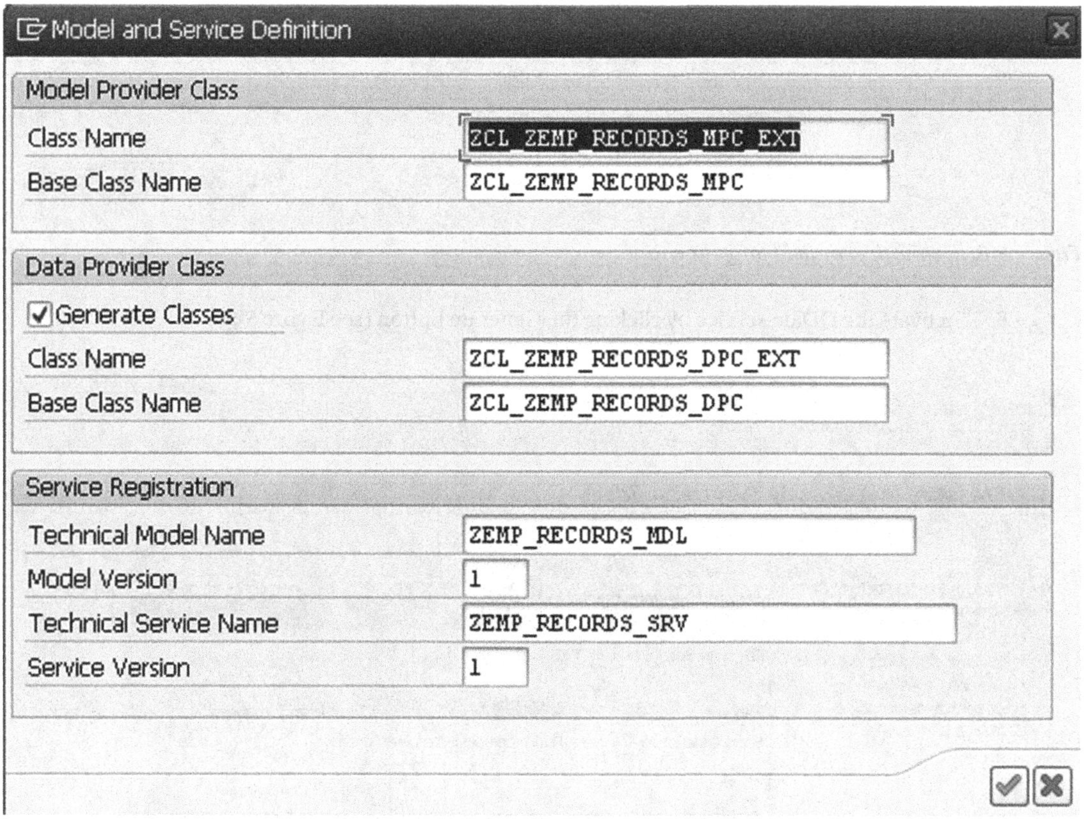

Figure 5-10. *Data Provider and Model Provider Class definitions*

9. When you activate the service, you see the list of classes associated with your OData service in the `Runtime Artifacts` folder of your OData project (see Figure 5-11). Double-click the `ZCL_ZEMP_RECORDS_DPC_EXT` class. Here you see a set of classes that will help you fetch the data required for your OData service. You can directly activate the OData service without editing these classes, but then your OData service will not return any valid data based on your business logic. In the next section, you see how to implement your custom logic in these classes to fetch the data from your custom table.

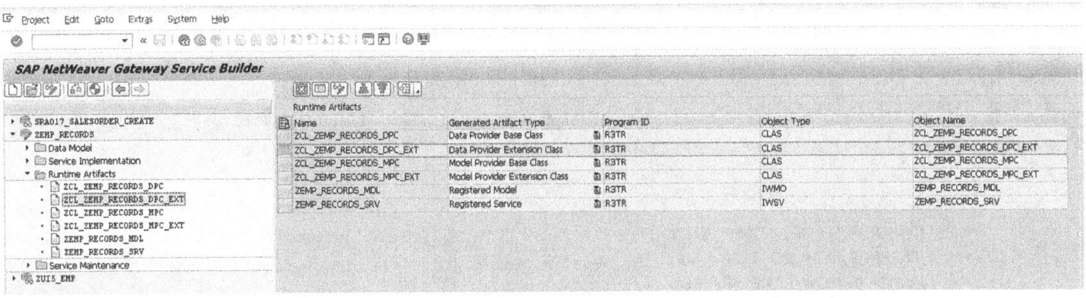

Figure 5-11. *Runtime Artifacts folder*

The standard methods of an OData DPC are mainly for CRUD functionalities. You can find these classes in the `Methods ➤ Inherited Methods` folder of your DPC. By default, these methods have standard code that raises an exception whenever they're called, saying that the method has not been defined. You need to redefine these classes and write custom code to fill the entity structure you defined earlier.

You can write custom code in the inherited methods without redefining them, but when you modify the OData project to edit any of the entity fields or create a new entity and then click Generate in the OData service, all the code you wrote in the inherited methods will be reinitialized. To avoid that, you must first redefine the methods and then write your business logic in those methods.

Implementing Business Logic in the OData Service

In this section, you redefine the `USERSET_GET_ENTITYSET` method. `GET_ENTITYSET` is equivalent to firing up a `select *` query to a database table. This method is usually implemented to fetch all the data from a table without any conditions. But, of course, you can control what data you receive at the consuming end by using filter conditions that ensure you aren't bombarded with thousands if not millions of records. To learn more about OData and the URI operations, visit `www.odata.org`, and see the PDF `http://docs.oasis-open.org/odata/odata/v4.0/odata-v4.0-part2-url-conventions.pdf`.

Now, follow these steps:

1. Right-click `USERSET_GET_ENTITYSET`, and redefine the method (see Figure 5-12).

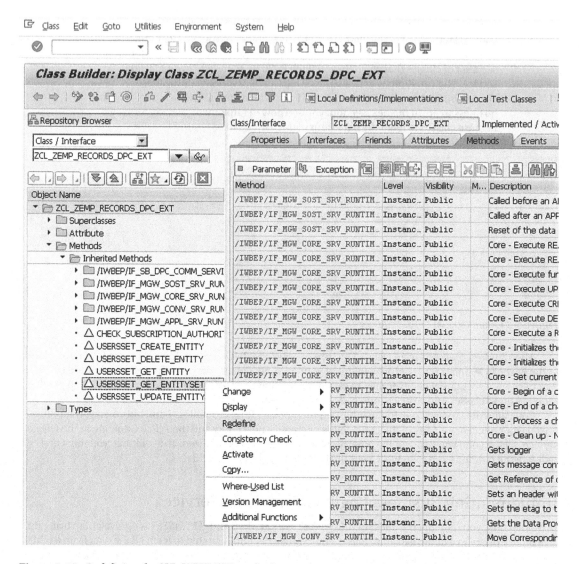

Figure 5-12. *Redefining the GET_ENTITYSET method*

2. Here you can implement the logic to fetch the data from the back end. In this example, you are fetching the records from the custom table. On the Signature tab, notice the ET_ENTITYSET of type ZCL_ZEMP_RECORDS_MPC=>TT_USERS (see Figure 5-13): this is a returning data that you give to the OData query as a response. The data type for the ET_ENTITYSET is a table type that is created in the MPC of your OData service, and it is the same type as your custom table.

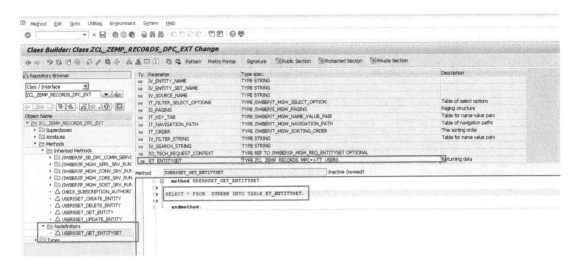

Figure 5-13. GET_ENTITYSET method for fetching all records

3. Similarly, you redefine the GET_ENTITY method. To get a new record, you need the key fields in order to carry out the fetch. All the key fields passed from the OData calls are stored in the IT_KEY_TAB parameter, which you can see on the Signature tab (see Figure 5-14). You need to loop the internal table and search for the key fields. Notice the data type of the returned data, ER_ENTITY: it's a table structure that was generated in the MPC. So, based on the key fields you get from IT_KEY_TAB, you populate the ER_ENTITY parameter and send it back as the response.

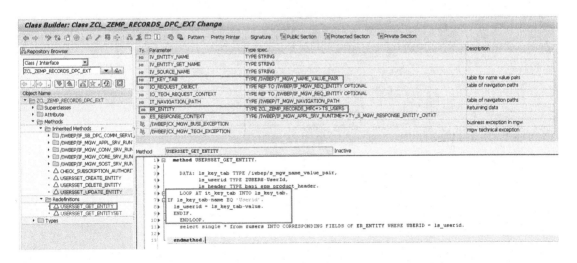

Figure 5-14. GET_ENTITY method for fetching a single record based on a condition

4. To create a new record, you need all the required fields, including the key fields. In the case of CREATE_ENTITY, you can retrieve the fields sent via the OData service call from the IO_DATA_PROVIDER in the Signature field. Based on the records from IO_DATA_PROVIDER, you can create a new record in your table, as shown in Figure 5-15.

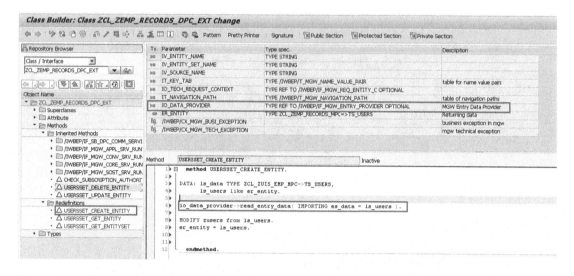

Figure 5-15. Creating a new entry in the custom table

5. Updating a record is similar to creating a new record. You get the full record value, including the changes to the fields that need to be updated, from IO_DATA_PROVIDER (see Figure 5-16).

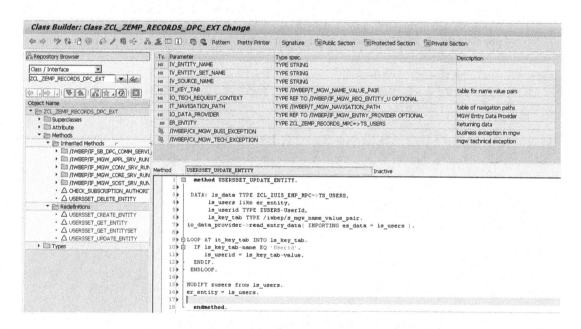

Figure 5-16. Updating an existing record in the custom table

6. To delete a record, you need a key field value. You can get the key field from IT_KEY_TAB, similar to the GET_ENTITY method (see Figure 5-17).

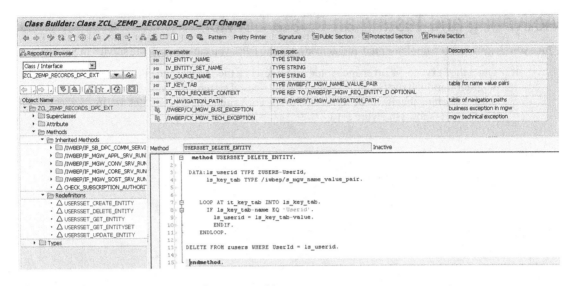

Figure 5-17. *Deleting a record from the custom table*

In addition to redefining the methods just discussed, you can also use functionalities including expand, deep inserts, function imports, media resources, and others:

- Expand is used to access or view results from multiple entities/entity sets using a single service call. This is especially useful when you have multiple service calls at the same time. To invoke an expansion, you use $expand after the primary entity name followed by the entity you want to expand. For example, the sample OData service is /sap/opu/odata/sap/ZEMP_RECORDS_SRV/Users(ID='1822')?$expand= UserDetails. This calls the Get_Entity/Get_EntitySet method of the appropriate entity and gives you a nested structure as a result.

- A deep insert is the opposite of $expand. Instead of giving you a nested structure as a result, it creates (POST) a nested record at the back end. An example is creating multiple purchase orders and posting the header and multiple items to the back end in a single service call.

- You can use function imports when you cannot use the CRUD methods. For example, if you want to start a workflow based on a custom flag, you can use a function import to pass data to the back end and trigger the workflow. To learn more about function imports, see http://scn.sap.com/docs/DOC-55336.

- Media resources are used mainly to post or retrieve media files such as images and videos; you can also use them to access binary data files (PDF, Word files, and so on). You can use any normal entity as a media resource: set a flag in the OData service builder by selecting the M check box on the entity type page, or change the code in the MPC of your OData service by using set_is_media() method.

Activating and Testing an OData Service

Once your logic has been implemented and activated in the DPC, you can activate the service in SEGW:

1. Open the Service Maintenance folder, double-click the service, and click the Register button. If the Gateway system is a hub-based system, the wizard will show a warning that it will be redirected to the corresponding server. Click Yes to continue, as shown in Figure 5-18.

Figure 5-18. *Registering the OData service*

2. A pop-up appears with the OData service name and version details. Click the check mark to activate your service as, shown in Figure 5-19.

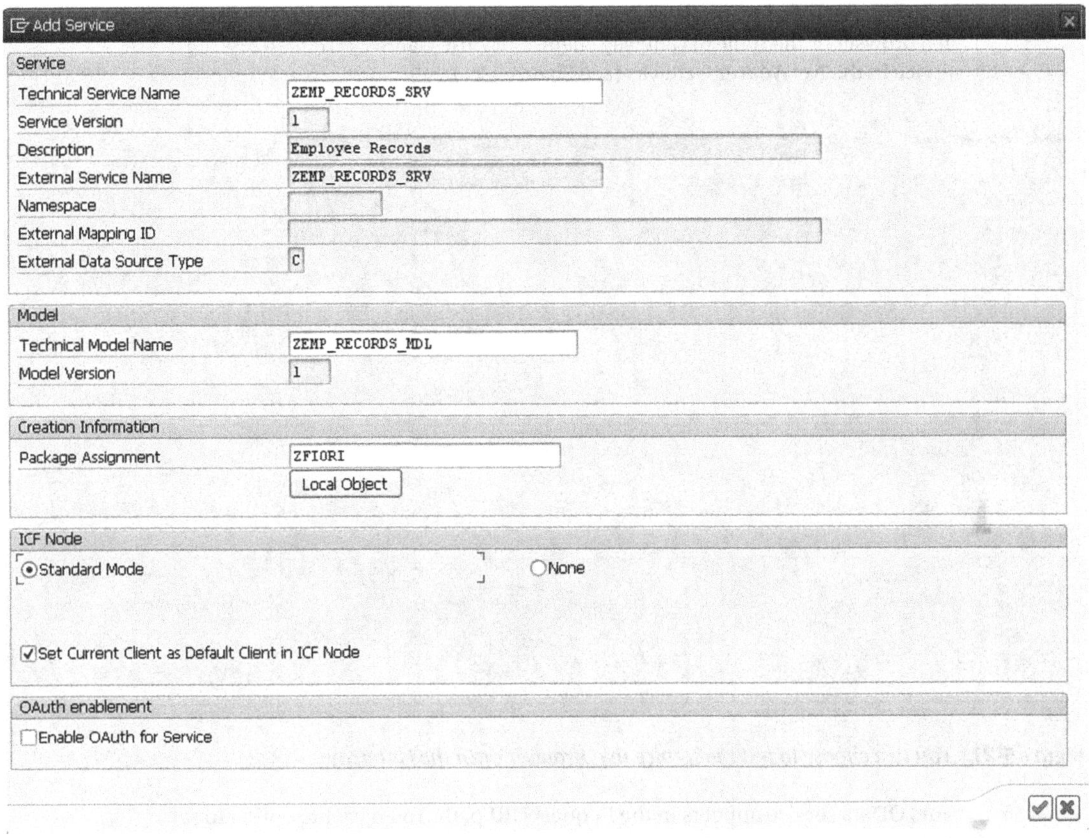

Figure 5-19. *Activating the OData service*

3. Go to the maintenance view to test your OData service. Click the Maintain button, as shown in Figure 5-20.

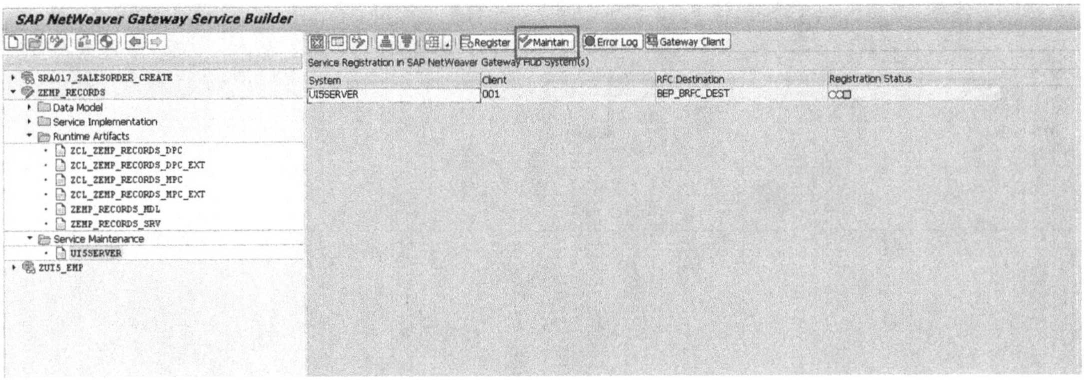

Figure 5-20. *Maintaining the registered service*

4. On the Activate and Maintain Services screen, you can choose to test the service on a browser or the built-in Gateway client. Click the Gateway client to test the service in the NetWeaver Gateway (see Figure 5-21).

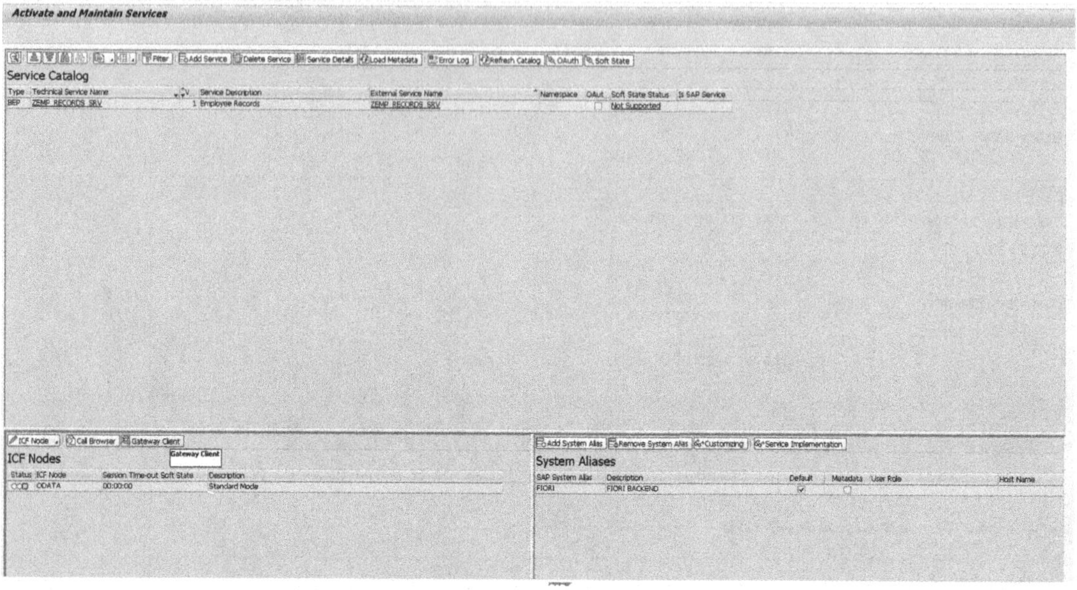

Figure 5-21. *You can choose to test the service in a browser or in the Gateway*

5. Yours OData service appears in the Request URI path. You have the option to set the OData call method as GET, POST, PUT, PATCH, MERGE, or DELETE. These options are your CRUD methods, so when you click the Get radio button and execute the OData service along with your required entity-set name, the GET_ENTITYSET method is invoked in the DPC of your OData service. Similarly, if you click the Post radio button, it invokes the CREATE_ENTITY method in the DPC (see Figure 5-22).

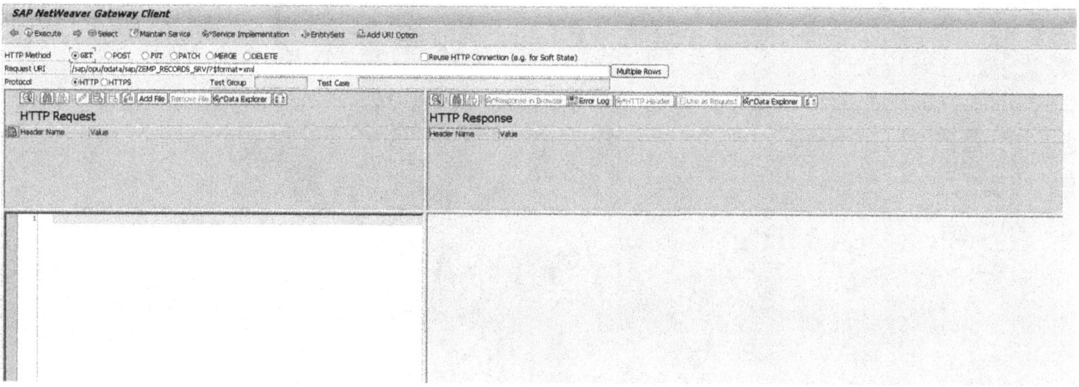

Figure 5-22. *NetWeaver Gateway client*

6. To test your entity, click the EntitySets button; you get the list of entities available in your OData service. In this case, you have created only one entity, so you see UsersSet in the pop-up (see Figure 5-23).

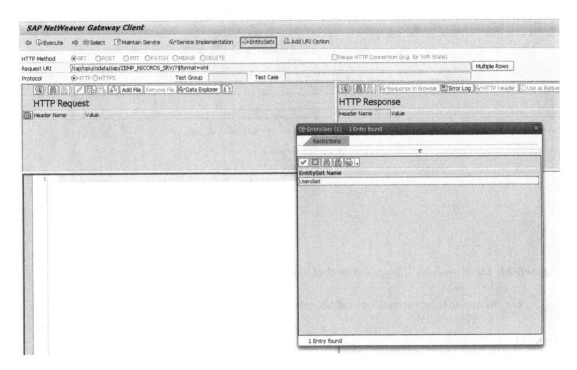

Figure 5-23. *List of available entity sets in the OData service*

7. You can also see the list of available standard OData URIs by clicking the Add URI Option button (see Figure 5-24).

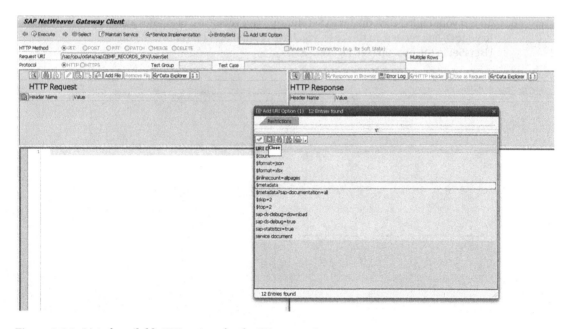

Figure 5-24. *List of available URI options for the OData service*

    8.   To see the OData service's metadata, select the URI option `$metadata` (see Figure 5-25).

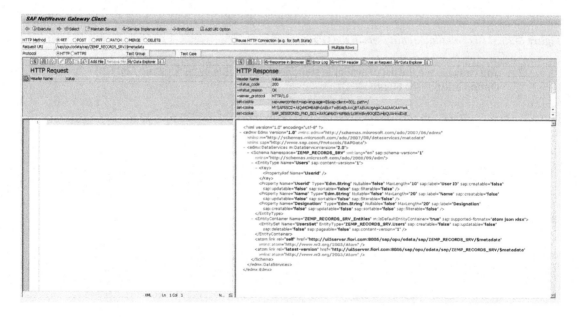

Figure 5-25. *List of available entity sets in the OData service*

9. Click the Execute button. Your entity invokes the `GET_ENTITYSET` method in the back end, and you get all the records from your custom table in response (see Figure 5-26).

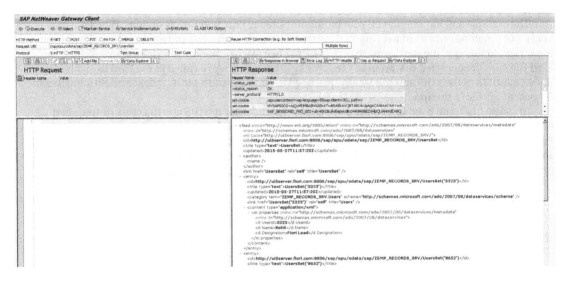

Figure 5-26. `GET_ENTITYSET` method being invoked

10. If you pass the key field value along with the entity set name, in this case the URI is /UserSet('3323'); it in turn invokes the `GET_ENTITY` method, which listens to the incoming key fields according to your logic and fetches the records based on the key field (see Figure 5-27).

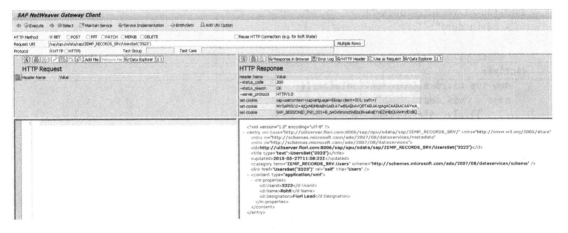

Figure 5-27. `GET_ENTITY` method being invoked

Building a UI5 App to Consume the OData Service

After testing the app on the Gateway client, you can build a simple UI5 app to consume the OData service and use the CRUD features. In this section, you create a UI5 app in Eclipse. You can find the steps to create a UI5 app in Chapter 4.

The example app has one screen with buttons for Create, Edit, and Delete options. When the page loads, a GET method is invoked to bring all the data from the custom table and load it into a UI5 table on the screen. In this app, the starting page is index.html because you are running it locally on Eclipse. But Fiori UI5 apps are designed to start from Component.js because they're called in the Fiori launchpad in the scenario. To make a UI5 app run locally, you need to write reroute logic in index.html so it invokes the Component.js file in the app.

In index.html, you need to bootstrap a few things in order for the UI5 app to access the required libraries (see Listing 5-1). You enter those in src and data-sap-ui-libs in the script tag, as shown in Figure 5-28. Next you need to make a call to the ComponentContainer() method of the standard UI5 library so it will in turn call the Component.js file. After calling ComponentContainer(), you place the response in a div in index.html so that at runtime, the entire app will be loaded under that div.

Listing 5-1. index.html

```
<!DOCTYPE HTML>
<html>
    <head>
        <meta http-equiv="X-UA-Compatible" content="IE=edge">
        <meta http-equiv='Content-Type' content='text/html;charset=UTF-8'/>
<link type="text/ccss" rel="stylesheet" href="css/style.css" />
<script type="text/javascript" src="./Js/jquery-1.11.2.min.js"></script>

<script src="resources/sap-ui-core.js"
        id="sap-ui-bootstrap"
 data-sap-ui-libs="sap.ui.commons,sap.m, sap.ui.table,sap.ui.ux3,sap.ui.layout,sap.viz"
        data-sap-ui-theme="sap_bluecrystal"
        data-sap-ui-resourceroots='{
        "ui5.odata.demo": "./"
                }' >
        </script>
    <script>
        new sap.ui.core.ComponentContainer({
        name : "ui5.odata.demo"
                }).placeAt("content");
        </script>
    </head>
    <body class="sapUiBody" role="application">
        <div id="content"></div>
    </body>
</html>
```

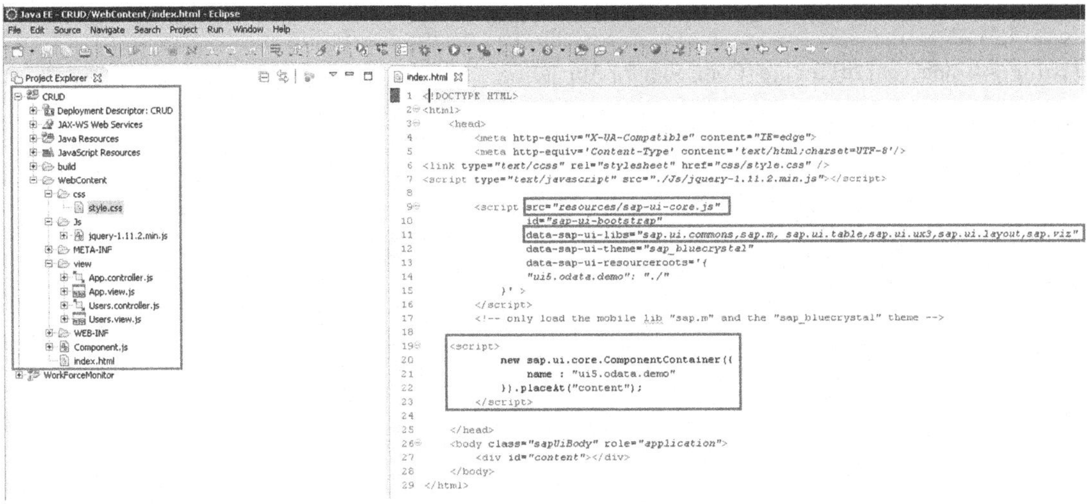

Figure 5-28. *`index.html` start page for the custom app*

In the `Component.js` file, you have to bind the OData service to the model, because UI5 apps use model-view-controller (MVC) architecture. (Chapter 6 gets into more detail about MVC architecture.) Here you define the OData service URL and set it to the model of your root view (see Listing 5-2).

Listing 5-2. `Component.js` (Binding the OData Service to the Root View)

```
var url = "http://ui5server.fiori.com:8006/sap/opu/odata/sap/ZEMP_RECORDS_SRV/";
    if(!oModel)
        {
oModel = new sap.ui.model.odata.ODataModel(url, true, "username", "password");
        }
// Set the model
```

oView.setModel(oModel);

In `app.view.js`, you define what type of app you are going to use as a view (see Listing 5-3). The two main app types are `SplitApp` and the normal `App`. Because you only need one screen for this app, you use `App`. You also need to specify the path of the view/screen for this app.

Listing 5-3. `App.view.js` (Defining the Type of App)

```
//create app
 this.app = new sap.m.App();
//load the master page
var master = sap.ui.jsview("users","ui5.odata.demo.view.Users");
master.getController().nav = this.getController();
this.app.addPage(master);
```

Listing 5-4 shows the code for the controller file of App.js, which handles context binding and navigation.

Listing 5-4. App.controller.js (Controller for App.js)

```
var master = ("Master" === pageId);
        if (app.getPage(pageId, master) === null) {
            var page = sap.ui.view({
                id : pageId,
                viewName : "ui5.odata.demo.view." + pageId,
                type : "JS"
            });
            page.getController().nav = this;
            app.addPage(page, master);
        }

        // show the page
        app.to(pageId);

        // set data context on the page
        if (context) {
            var page = app.getPage(pageId);
            page.setBindingContext(context);
        }
    },
```

In the Users view, you add the controls required for the app view (see Listing 5-5). First you declare a Layout container to hold all the buttons, and then you add the buttons for the CRUD functions.

Listing 5-5. Users.view.js (Users View Page Code Containing the App UI Design)

```
sap.ui.jsview("ui5.odata.demo.view.Users", {

    getControllerName : function() {
       return "ui5.odata.demo.view.Users";
    },

    createContent : function(oController) {

        var oLayout1 = new sap.ui.commons.layout.MatrixLayout({
            id:"matrix1",
            layoutFixed: true,
            width : "50%",
            widths : [ "10%","10%", "80%" ]

        });

        var oLayout2 = new sap.ui.commons.layout.MatrixLayout({
            id:"matrix2",
            layoutFixed: true,
            width : "80%",
            widths : [ "80%","20%" ]

        });
```

```
var oButton1 = new sap.ui.commons.Button({
    id:"Create",
    style:"Accept",
    text: "Create",
    press: oController.Create
});
var oButton2 = new sap.ui.commons.Button({
    id:"Edit",
    text: "Edit",
    style:"Emph",
    press: oController.Edit
});
var oButton3 = new sap.ui.commons.Button({
    id:"Delete",
    style:"Reject",
    text: "Delete",
    press: oController.Delete
});
```

Now you create a Form control for creating a new record in the Users view (see Listing 5-6). This form contains all the fields from your custom table as input fields so users can enter new records. Then you add a Save button to the form: when clicked, it invokes the CREATE_ENTITY method. You also add a Close button with some JQuery animations for sliding, because this form will be invisible when the screen is loaded. Only when the user clicks Create or Edit on the screen will this form be made visible.

Listing 5-6. Users.view.js (Creating an Input Form)

```
//Create a Simple Form

var oForm = new sap.ui.layout.form.SimpleForm("form1",{
    content:[
            new sap.ui.commons.Label({text:"Userid"}),
            new sap.ui.commons.TextField("Userid",{width:'200px',editable:true}),

            new sap.ui.commons.Label({text:"Name"}),
            new sap.ui.commons.TextField("Name",{width:'200px',editable:true}),

            new sap.ui.commons.Label({text:"Designation"}),
            new sap.ui.commons.TextField("Designation",{width:'200px',editable:true}),

            new sap.ui.commons.Label({text:""}),
            new sap.ui.commons.Button({
              text:"Save",
              style:"Emph",
              press: oController.Save,
              width:'200px'
            }),
            new sap.ui.commons.Button({
              id:"btn_close",
              text:"Close",
              style:"Reject",
```

```
                    press: function(){
                            $('#form1').slideUp('1000');
                    },
                    width:'200px'
                })
    ]
});
```

On the same Users page, add a new UI5 table similar to your custom back-end table to show the contents of the table when the app loads (see Listing 5-7). This table is added to a new Layout container. Now you have a Layout container holding the CRUD buttons, a Form container with fields for creating new records, and another Layout holding the Table control. You put these three controls in a single main VerticalLayout control so they're grouped properly in the UI.

Listing 5-7. Users.view.js (Groups All Controls in a Single VerticalLayout Control)

```
//Create an instance of the table control
    var oTable = new sap.ui.table.Table("Table1",{
        title: "User List",
        editable:true,
        visibleRowCount: 15,
        firstVisibleRow: 10,
        selectionMode: sap.ui.table.SelectionMode.Single
    });
     //Define the columns and the control templates to be used
    oTable.addColumn(new sap.ui.table.Column({
        label: new sap.ui.commons.Label({text: "UserID"}),
        template: new sap.ui.commons.TextView().bindProperty("text", "Userid"),
        sortProperty: "Userid",
        filterProperty: "Userid",
        width: "75px",
        hAlign: "Center"
    }));
    oTable.addColumn(new sap.ui.table.Column({
        label: new sap.ui.commons.Label({text: "Name"}),
        template: new sap.ui.commons.TextField().bindProperty("value", "Name"),
        sortProperty: "Name",
        filterProperty: "Name",
        width: "75px",
        hAlign: "Center"
    }));
    oTable.addColumn(new sap.ui.table.Column({
        label: new sap.ui.commons.Label({text: "Designation"}),
        template: new sap.ui.commons.TextField().bindProperty("value", "Designation"),
        sortProperty: "Designation",
        filterProperty: "Designation",
        width: "75px",
        hAlign: "Center"
    }));
```

```
        oTable.bindRows("/UsersSet");
        oTable.attachRowSelectionChange(oController.selectedRow);
          oLayout1.createRow(oButton1,oButton2,oButton3);
          oLayout2.createRow(oTable);

        var oVerticalLayout = new sap.ui.layout.VerticalLayout("Layout1", {
            content: [oLayout1,oForm, oLayout2]
        });
                       return oVerticalLayout;
      }
    });
```

Next you create the controller page for your Users view, to handle events like button clicks, page loads, and so on (see Listing 5-8). The selectedRow function gets the details of any row the user clicks in the table. Similarly, you use JQuery functions to read values directly from fields and toggle the visibility of the form that contains the input fields for creating and editing records based on button clicks.

Listing 5-8. Users.controller.js (Controller Page to Handle the Events of the View)

```
selectedRow: function(oEvent){
        currentRowContext = oEvent.getParameter("rowContext").sPath;
        var start = currentRowContext.lastIndexOf('/') + 1;
        value = currentRowContext.substring(start, currentRowContext.length);

        var oTable = sap.ui.getCore().byId('Table1');
        index = oTable.getSelectedIndex();
        var data= oTable.getModel().oData[value];
        mode = "Update";
        $('#Userid').val(data.Userid);
        $('#Name').val(data.Name);
        $('#Designation').val(data.Designation);
         var userId = sap.ui.getCore().byId('Userid');
         userId.setEditable(false);
    },
    Create: function(){
        $('#form1').slideDown();
        mode = "Create";
        $('#Userid').val("");
        $('#Name').val("");
        $('#Designation').val("");
        var userId = sap.ui.getCore().byId('Userid');
         userId.setEditable(true);
    },
    Edit: function(){
        $('#form1').slideDown('1000');
        mode = "Update";
        var oTable = sap.ui.getCore().byId('Table1');
        index = oTable.getSelectedIndex();
        var data= oTable.getModel().oData[value];
        $('#Userid').val(data.Userid);
```

```
        $('#Userid').editable = false;
        $('#Name').val(data.Name);
        $('#Designation').val(data.Designation);
    },
```

Based on the action required (Create, Delete, or Update), you call the OData service along with the parameters that need to be sent to the Gateway server. The OData service is invoked by oModel.create() for Create (oModel is the name of the variable created in Component.js that holds ODataModel). For Delete, the method is oModel.remove(); and for Update, it is oModel.update()(see Listing 5-9). When you have finished coding, right-click index.html and choose Run As ➤ Web App Preview to run the UI5 app.

Listing 5-9. Users.controller.js (Invoking OData Operations)

```
Save: function(){
     var oParameters = {
             "Userid" : $('#Userid').val(),
             "Name" : $('#Name').val(),
             "Designation" : $('#Designation').val(),
         };

if(mode=="Update"){
  var sServiceUrl = currentRowContext;
  oModel.update(sServiceUrl, oParameters,null,function(odata,response){
      console.log("success");
  },function(err){
     console.log(err);
  });
    }
else if(mode=="Create"){
    var sServiceUrl = "/UsersSet";
    oModel.create(sServiceUrl, oParameters,null,function(odata,response){
          console.log("success");
      },function(err){
         console.log(err);
      });
}
},
Delete: function(){
    mode="Delete";
    var sServiceUrl = currentRowContext;
    oModel.remove(sServiceUrl, null,null,function(odata,response){
        mode = "";
         console.log("success");
      },function(err){
        mode = "";
        console.log(err);
    });

},
```

When you test the app on a Chrome browser, you may sometimes face issues with an Allow-Access-Origin security issue when the app is run locally. To bypass this security check, edit the Target properties in Chrome and add the `--disable-web-security` line shown in Figure 5-29 to the end of the target path.

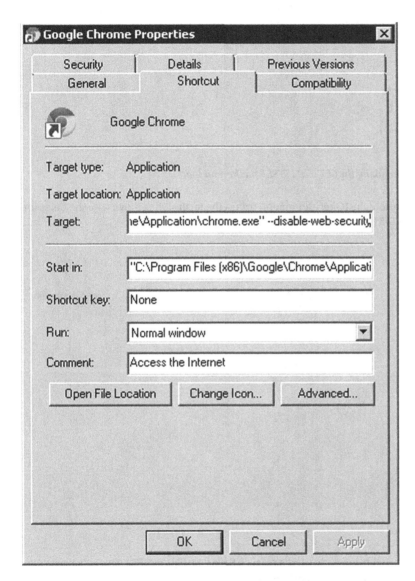

Figure 5-29. *Disabling Chrome web security checks for local testing*

Previewing and Testing the UI5 App

When you run the application, the initial GET_ENTITYSET method brings all the records from the back end to the Table control you created for the UI (see Figure 5-30).

Figure 5-30. *CRUD application invoking the* `GET_ENTITYSET` *method on load*

When you click the Create button, the JQuery animation brings the form sliding down with the fields for creating a new record (see Figure 5-31).

Figure 5-31. *Creating a new record*

The new record appears in the table instantly when you click Save (see Figure 5-32). This is because the table is bound to the model, which you update with the button click.

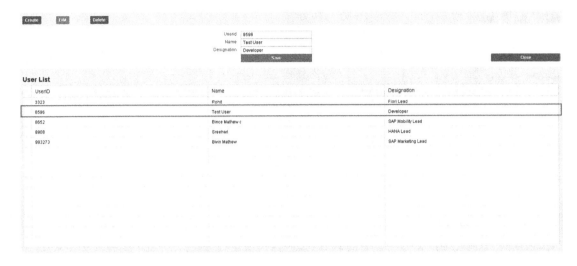

Figure 5-32. *New record updated instantly in the table*

The back-end table is updated with a new row via the OData CREATE_ENTITY method (see Figure 5-33).

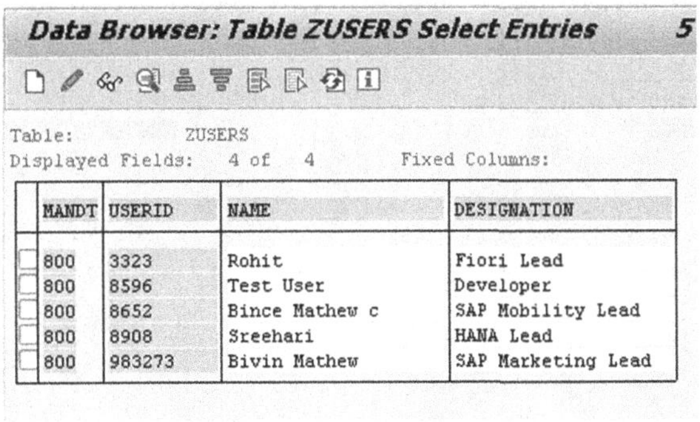

Figure 5-33. *The back-end custom table gets a new row*

When you click the Edit button and select a row in the table (see Figure 5-34), you can update values in that row. The UserID field is non-editable so the key field is not changed accidently.

Figure 5-34. *Updating an existing record*

Your modifications are also reflected instantly in the table rows (see Figure 5-35).

Figure 5-35. *Table row updated successfully*

When you click the Delete button (see Figure 5-36), the DELETE_ENTITY method is invoked, and the data is removed from the model as well as from the back-end table.

Figure 5-36. *Deleting a record*

The deletion of the records is also instantly reflected in the table (see Figure 5-37).

Figure 5-37. *Successful record deletion*

Error Log Monitoring and Troubleshooting Techniques

Some times you set up your OData service and everything is working fine, but suddenly, out of nowhere, you don't get a response, or you're getting errors in the app or in the browser (see Figure 5-38). It can be really frustrating to pinpoint the error if you don't use proper debugging methods.

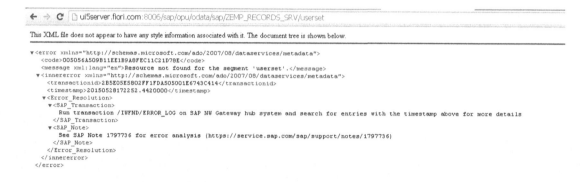

Figure 5-38. *Failed OData request*

There are two primary approaches to debugging OData services to find errors. One is to use the browser's Debug mode. In Chrome, you can press F12 or right-click the page and click Inspect Element (see Figure 5-39).

Figure 5-39. *Switching to Debug mode in the browser*

In Debug mode, on the Network tab, you can see the OData request that was fired from the browser to the back end (see Figure 5-40). In this case, that request is red because it failed.

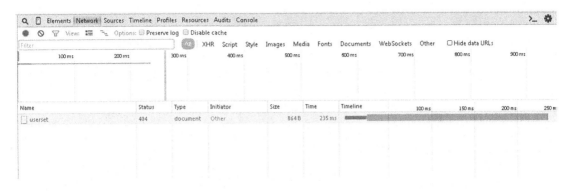

Figure 5-40. *Network tab in the Chrome browser's Developer tools*

If you double-click the request, you see a detailed description of what went wrong (see Figure 5-41). In this case, the requested entity was not found, and the type of request fired was a GET method.

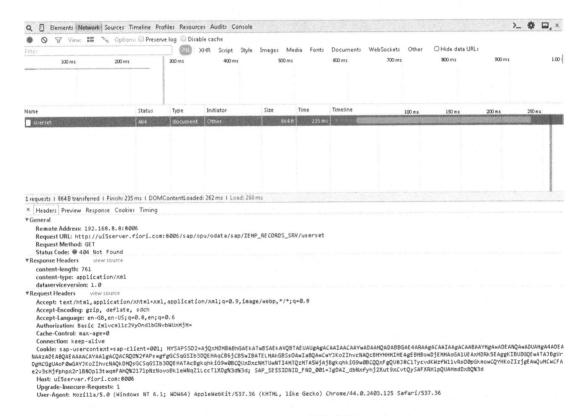

Figure 5-41. *Detailed error description in response to the failed OData request*

If you want more details about what went wrong, the second option is to log in to the Gateway server and check the error logs using the t-code /n/IWFND/ERROR_LOG, as shown in Figure 5-42.

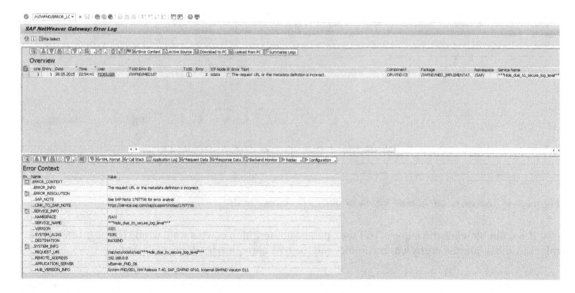

Figure 5-42. *Error Log console in the Gateway server*

If you click the Response Data button, you see the details of the request from the browser to the Gateway in XML format (see Figure 5-43).

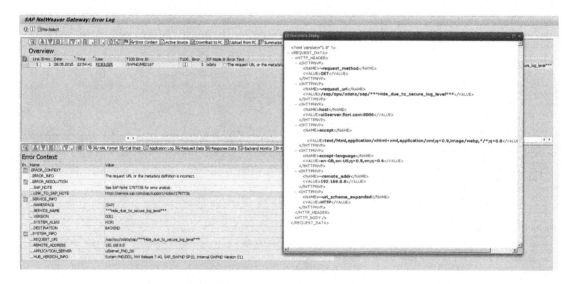

Figure 5-43. *Inbound browser OData request in an XML view*

You can also see a detailed technical error description by clicking the Application Log button in the Error Log console (see Figure 5-44).

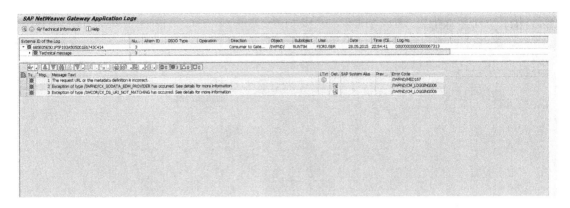

Figure 5-44. *Application log*

Some other useful tools are available to explore the OData service and its features. You can use the online tools offered by www.odata.org (see Figure 5-45); they come in handy especially when you are a front-end developer and you don't have proper authorizations to check the OData properties in SEGW in the back-end SAP system.

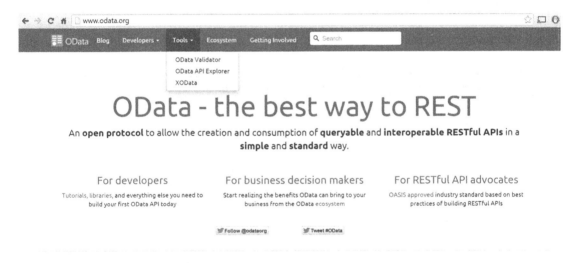

Figure 5-45. *Tools for exploring OData services*

OData API Explorer is one such tool. It lets you traverse all the entity sets and execute queries that you want to test (see Figure 5-46).

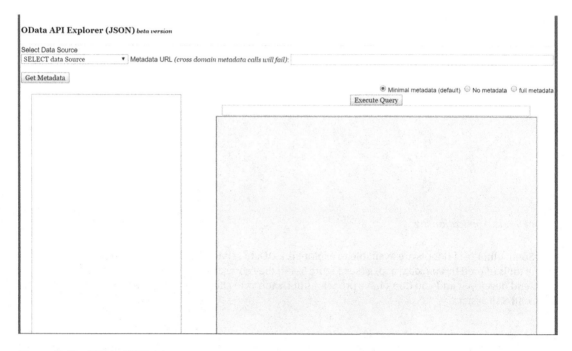

Figure 5-46. *OData API Explorer*

In Figure 5-47, you see the list of all entities for the Northwind OData service. This is a free OData service offered by odata.org for developers to test apps or explore the features of OData services.

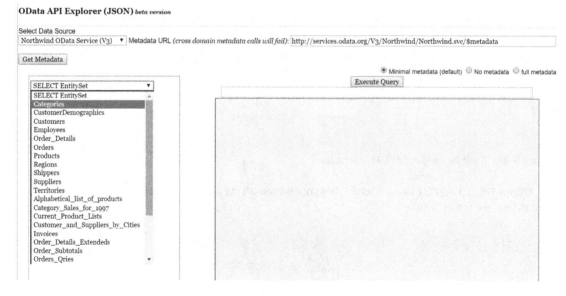

Figure 5-47. *Entity list of the OData service in OData API Explorer*

You can even type custom queries in the input field on the Execute Query tab (see Figure 5-48).

Figure 5-48. Query result for the Categories entity of the Northwind OData service

Another useful tool is XOData (see Figure 5-49). It presents a visual, chart-like overview of all entities and their relations with other entities, such as associations. This tool helps front-end developers design their app navigation effectively by giving them an overall picture of how one entity is linked to another.

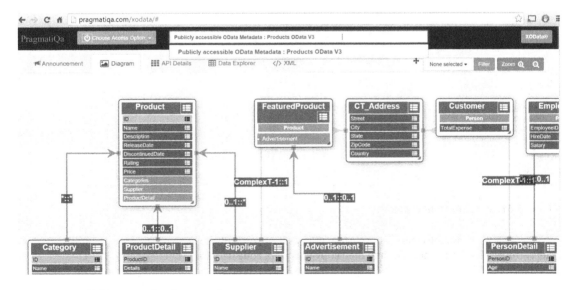

Figure 5-49. XOData service diagram view

The API Details tab gives you a better understanding of each entity's properties and fields (see Figure 5-50). You can easily check the field type: whether it's a DateTime field or String, and so on.

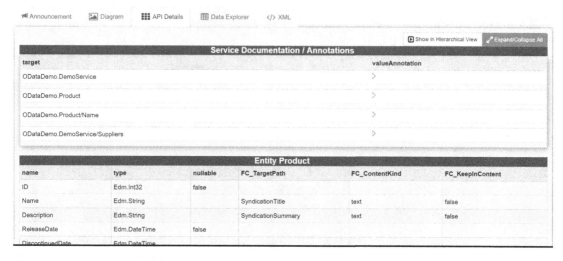

Figure 5-50. *XOData API Details view*

The Data Explorer helps you build queries with conditions and expand associated entities with the click of a few buttons, without knowing the URI conventions of the OData queries (see Figure 5-51).

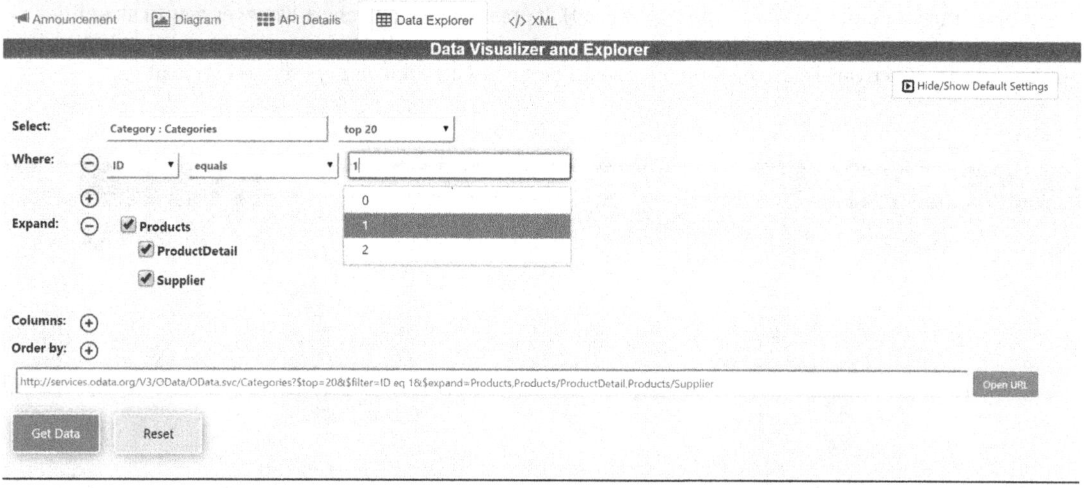

Figure 5-51. *XOData Data Explorer*

Figure 5-52 shows the result of the custom query string you built. You can use this tool to build complex query strings with filter conditions and then copy the query code back into your app.

214

Figure 5-52. *Custom OData query result*

Using REST Clients

A REST client is a browser plug-in that is a dedicated tool you can use instead of a website to test OData services. There are many REST clients in the Chrome plug-ins list. The one I use most often is the Postman client (see Figure 5-53). The choice of REST clients depends on how comfortable you are with the UI.

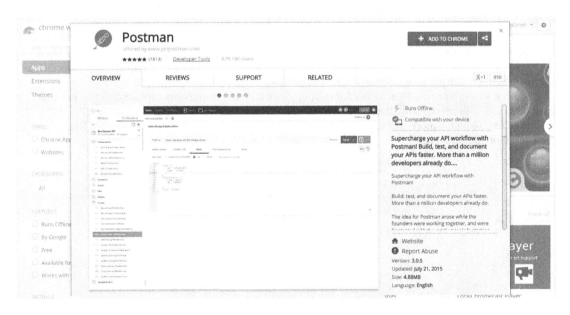

Figure 5-53. *The Postman REST client*

Using the Postman client, you can choose the method (POST, PUT, PATCH, and so on) of the request you are sending to the back end (see Figure 5-54). You can also attach payloads such as PDF files or image files to test OData services that accept attachments.

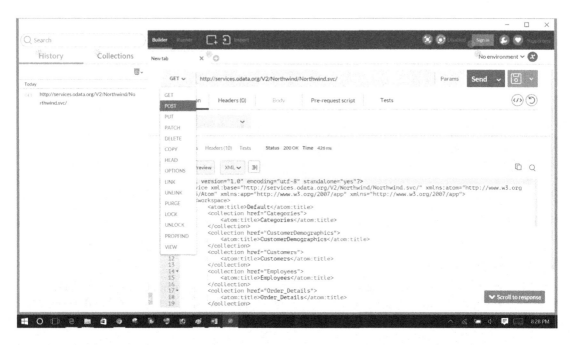

Figure 5-54. *Using Postman*

Another useful Chrome plug-in is JSONView, which lets you see the OData response in JSON format that your UI app understands. This helps developers create mock JSON files to test without an actual OData service, when it is difficult to access the live OData service.

You can also explore the Fiori Stars Chrome plug-in, which lets developers explore the UI5 controls used in an app without checking the source code.

The next chapter explores IDEs used for UI5 app development. You develop a full-fledged UI5 app with the latest Fiori architecture.

CHAPTER 6

Fiori Custom Application Development and Tools

Before you can start developing custom Fiori UI5 applications, you must first install and configure an IDE and a few required tools.

Eclipse

One of the main IDEs used for developing Fiori apps is Eclipse. The recommended version of Eclipse is Luna. You can download Eclipse Luna (32-bit and 64-bit) from `https://eclipse.org/downloads/packages/release/luna/sr2`. The download page is shown in Figure 6-1.

Electronic supplementary material The online version of this chapter (doi:10.1007/978-1-4842-1335-3_6) contains supplementary material, which is available to authorized users.

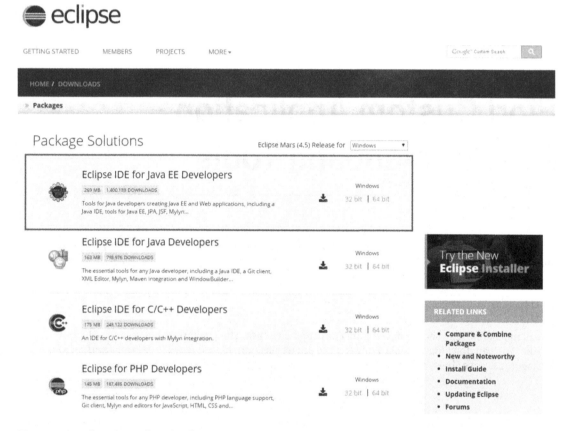

Figure 6-1. *Eclipse Luna download page*

Open the `Eclipse.exe` file from the extracted folder. In Eclipse, go to Help ➤ Install New Software. Enter the URL `https://tools.hana.ondemand.com/luna/` in the input field, and click Add (see Figure 6-2). You see a list of files to be installed. For UI5 development, you only need to select the UI Development Toolkit for HTML5; the rest are optional. Click Next, and accept the terms and conditions. Eclipse will download and install the files and then restart.

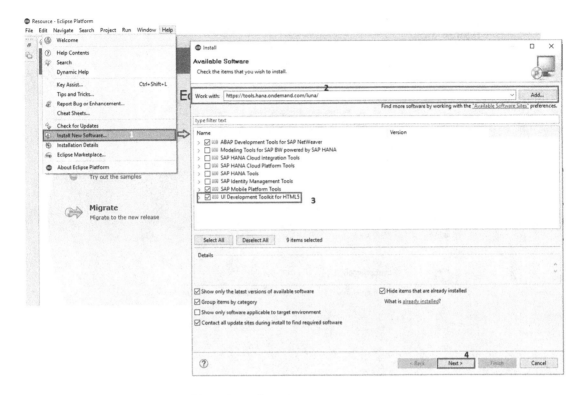

Figure 6-2. *Installing SAP UI5 add-ons into Eclipse*

Eclipse is ready for you to begin building new UI5 apps. But before you jump into development, let's look at a few other old and new IDEs and tools that are available for UI5 development.

AppBuilder

Early Fiori developers probably encountered the AppBuilder tool. This tool is no longer being supported or updated. It was SAP's initial approach to building a more user-friendly IDE that allowed users to quickly develop and design UI5 screens without much coding (at least, minimalistic apps that generated reports or fetched data via OData services).

You can find a detailed document on how to install AppBuilder at `https://tools.hana.ondemand.com/#sapui5`. Basically, you need to follow these steps:

1. Install Node.js on your system (you can find the steps at the link just mentioned).

2. Download AppBuilder from `https://tools.hana.ondemand.com/additional/appbuilder-1.0.1252.zip`.

3. Extract the files from the zip.

4. Start AppBuilder by double-clicking the `run.bat` file in the extracted folder. (Complete steps are at `http://infocenter.sybase.com/help/index.jsp?topic=/com.sybase.infocenter.appbuilder.1.0/doc/html/title.html`.)

5. Open AppBuilder in the browser using `http://127.0.0.1:9009/ide/ares/index.html` (see Figure 6-3).

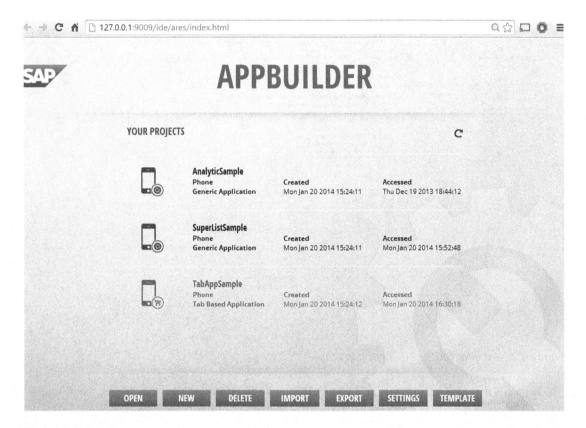

Figure 6-3. *AppBuilder home page*

Web IDE

This is the latest IDE solution from SAP (see Figure 6-4). This book doesn't say much about AppBuilder because Web IDE is now available. Web IDE has inherited and integrated the features of Eclipse, the UI development toolkit for UI5, AppBuilder, the Gateway Productivity Accelerator, the Fiori toolkit, and AppDesigner. It is an all-in-one tool for everything and anything related to Fiori development and extensions.

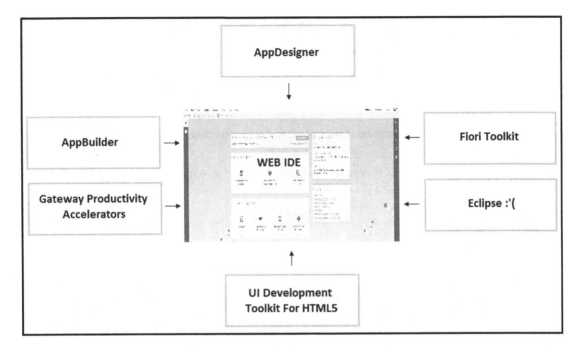

***Figure 6-4.** Web IDE, the new superhero in town*

At the time of writing, I am not a big fan of Web IDE. The main reason I don't feel at home with it is that it does not have the flexibility of a native desktop app (the feeling of using a web-based whatsapp compared to your native whatsapp). You cannot even drag-and-drop files from your desktop to the project folder or realign the order of open view tabs. Web IDE also lacks support for other third-party development plug-ins, which you can easily install in Eclipse. (Yes, this IDE is specific to SAP Fiori, but then why should I use Web IDE when I already have a platform that acts as an IDE for almost all programming languages under the Sun?) Another bottleneck I face with Web IDE is the inability to use SAP's HANA SDK for developing persistent Java apps to use the Internet of Things platform offered by HANA Cloud. I could easily install the same SDK in Eclipse.

Because Web IDE is in its beta stage, it has many bugs. One annoying issue in the cloud-based Web IDE is the session timeout (something I don't have to bother about while using the native desktop-based Eclipse). Another issue with Web IDE that I have noticed is that it doesn't allow you to check or navigate through the project source code while in Debug mode. I find this a little frustrating, especially because it is possible in Eclipse.

Web IDE has its positive points, too. Creating a Fiori app extension is a breeze with this tool compared to Eclipse, and it also has native git support (maybe not as powerful as in Eclipse, but it's getting there). Going forward, this will most likely be the single IDE that SAP will support; we will all have to move to Web IDE eventually (when the Fiori 2.0 architecture is released, Web IDE will be a more powerful option due to its native support for the new architecture).

This chapter covers how to port to Web IDE a custom app developed in Eclipse. Based on the current Web IDE bugs and limitations, I am still inclined toward Eclipse rather than Web IDE; but I am sure my view will change once the tool becomes more mature.

To use Web IDE, you have two options:

- On-premises installation

- Cloud-based Web IDE trial or full version

The easiest way to access Web IDE is to use the cloud-based solution. But to connect the Web IDE cloud to your on-premises or local network-based SAP back end, you need to configure the cloud connector.

To install Web IDE locally, follow these steps:

1. Download Web IDE from the SAP store (see Figure 6-5) at `https://store.sap.com/sap/cp/ui/resources/store/html/SolutionDetails.html?pid=0000013489&catID=&pcntry=US&sap-language=EN&_cp_id=id-1413816705087-0`.

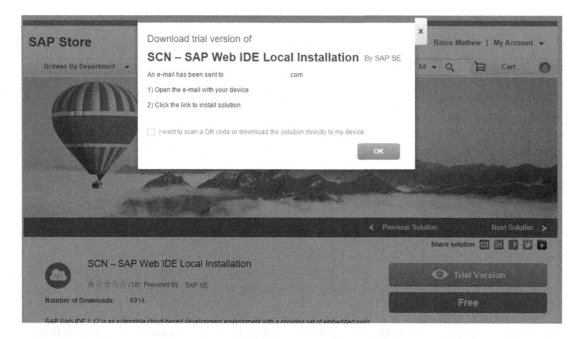

Figure 6-5. *Download Web IDE from the SAP Store*

2. Download the Developer Guide, which provides detailed information about Web IDE solution: `https://scn.sap.com/docs/DOC-58848`.

3. Make sure you have Java Runtime 7 (at least version 1.7) or higher.

4. Create a new folder named `SAPWebIDE`.

5. Download Orion from `http://www.eclipse.org/downloads/download.php?file=/orion/drops/R-10.0-201510301610/eclipse-orion-10.0-win32.win32.x86.zip`.

6. Unzip the contents into the `SAPWebIDE` folder.

7. Download Director from `http://www.eclipse.org/downloads/download.php?file=/tools/buckminster/products/director_latest.zip`.

8. Unzip the contents into the `SAPWebIDE` folder.

9.   Unzip the Web IDE file downloaded in step 1 into a folder. You find two more zip files: one for Web IDE (updates.zip) and one for Hybrid App Toolkit (see Figure 6-6).

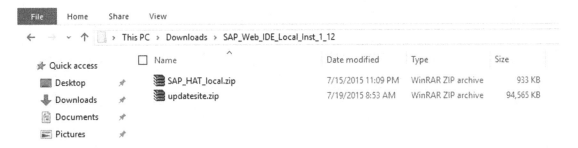

Figure 6-6. *Extract Web IDE files*

10.   Open the command line (press the Windows button + R, type **CMD**, and then press Enter). Navigate to the directory folder in the SAPWebIDE folder via cd: for example, cd C:\SAPWebIDE\director.

11.   Execute

director -repository jar:file:/<*Full path of the SAP Web IDE file you unzipped in step 9*>!/ -installIU

and

com.sap.webide.orionplugin.feature.feature.group -destination c:\SAPWebIDE\eclipse

12.   Go to C:\SAPWebIDE\eclipse and start orion.exe.

13.   To start Web IDE after installation, execute the following URL in your browser (see Figure 6-7): http://localhost:8080/webide/index.htm. You are asked to create a new account in Orion; create the account, and log in.

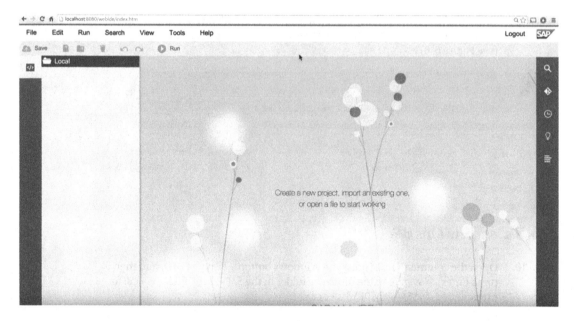

Figure 6-7. *Web IDE main page*

Theme Designer

The theme designer is a very useful tool that lets you change the look and feel of the launchpad and Fiori apps. You can add a custom background, change the default logo, and so on. Let's start with a scenario in which you modify the home page background image and the login page image and add custom CSS to standard tiles.

Launching the Theme Designer

You can launch the theme designer from the Gateway SAP system by executing the t-code /UI5/THEME_ DESIGNER. When you do, the theme designer opens in a web browser automatically. From the list of standard themes, select the SAP Blue Crystal theme, and click Open (see Figure 6-8).

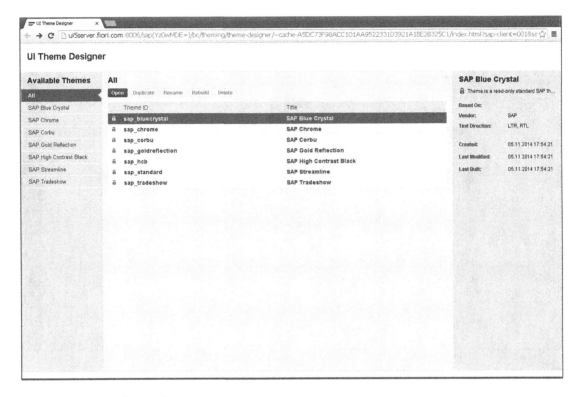

Figure 6-8. *Theme designer home page*

When you open the theme, the name of the project changes to Custom Blue Crystal. This is a copy of the standard Blue Crystal theme. For Link to Application, enter **/sap/bc/ui5/ui2/ushell/shells/abap/FioriLaunchpad.html**; and for Name of Application, enter **Home**. Click Add (see Figure 6-9).

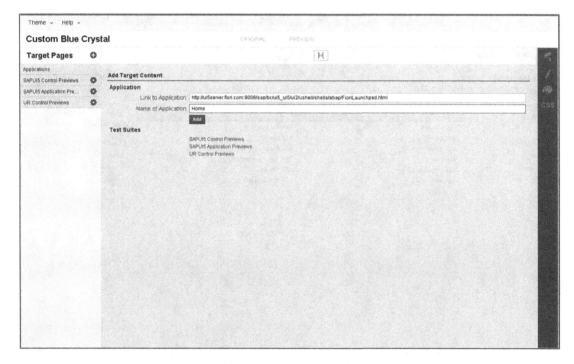

Figure 6-9. *Creating a custom theme for the launchpad*

Customizing the Home Screen Background Image

Now you can begin customizing the Fiori launchpad. To add a custom background image, click the image field; you see a pop up screen in which to upload your custom image (see Figure 6-10).

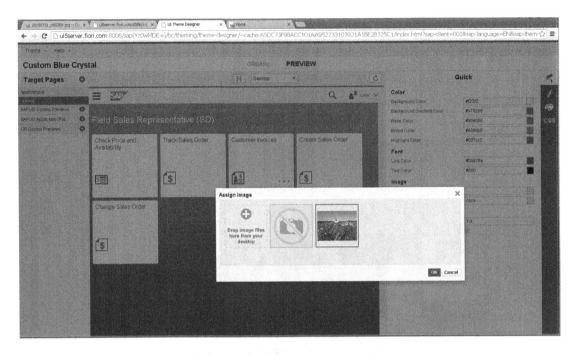

Figure 6-10. Uploading a custom background image

When you upload the custom image, the background image of the Fiori home page changes immediately, as shown in Figure 6-11.

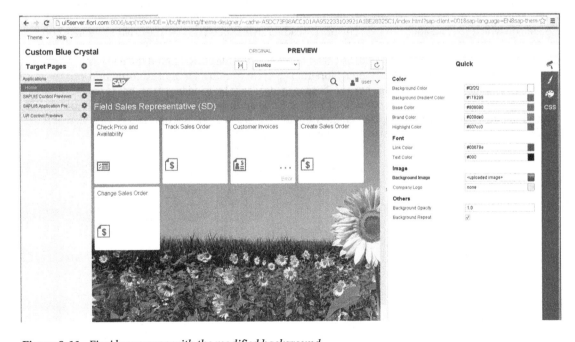

Figure 6-11. Fiori home page with the modified background

Customizing Standard Tiles

You can also edit the colors of any of the elements on the home page, including text (see Figure 6-12).

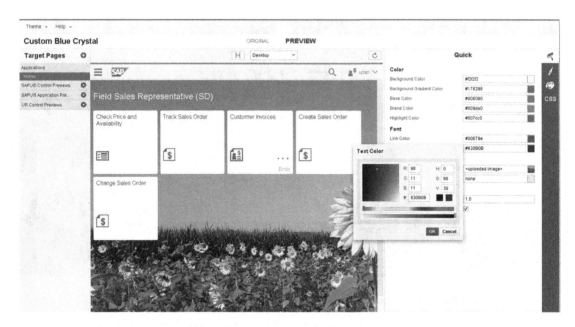

Figure 6-12. *Changing color parameters for the home page elements*

But sometimes just changing the color won't be enough: you may need to change an element's size, add transparency effects, change the shape of objects, and so on. For this purpose, the theme designer also has a CSS tab on which you can add your own custom cascading style sheets (CSS) to the existing elements on the home page. In Figure 6-13, I changed the shape of the tiles to be more round at the edges, using the border-top-radius and border-radius CSS properties of the tile class. I found the relevant classes by inspecting the tiles of the original Fiori home page in Chrome. For more information about the standard theme classes, see http://help.sap.de/saphelp_uiaddon10/helpdata/en/91/ a4946b0dcf4356aaaedc4e502864f4/content.htm. (Note that adding custom CSS to standard controls is not a recommended method because it can lead to compatibility issues when you upgrade the UI5 elements in the future. So, be careful when you use this technique.)

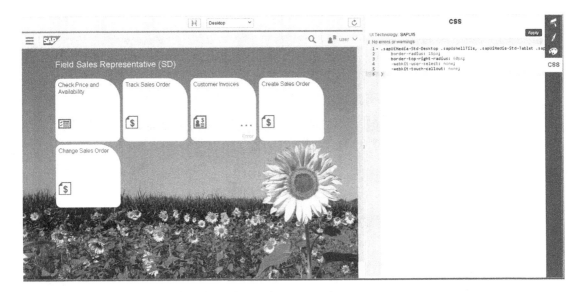

Figure 6-13. *Apply custom CSS to alter the home page elements*

After you make customizations, continue with these steps to add them to the launchpad:

1. Save the changes, and go to Theme ➤ Save & Build to build the theme, as shown in Figure 6-14.

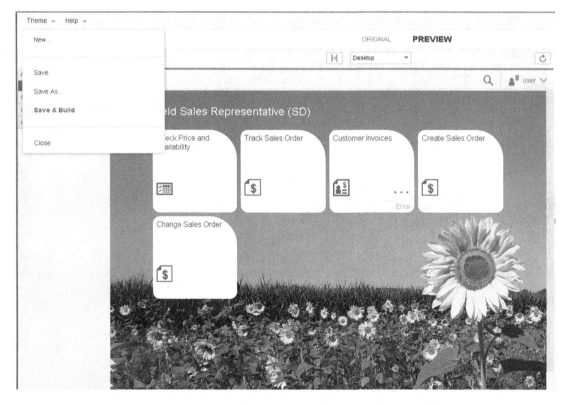

Figure 6-14. *Save and build the custom theme*

2. Once the build is complete, test the new theme for your home page (see Figure 6-15).

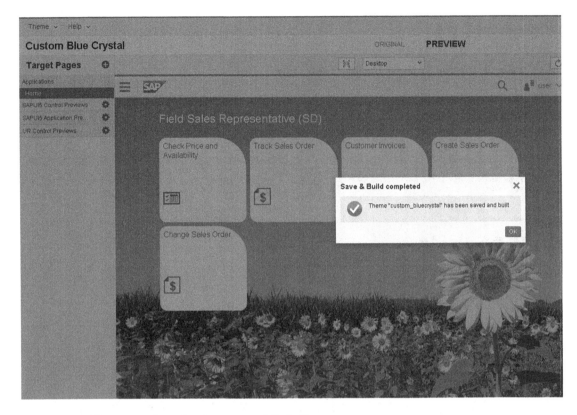

Figure 6-15. *The custom theme has been successfully built*

3. To get the theme URL parameters for your custom theme, log in to the Gateway system and execute the transaction /UI5/THEME_TOOL. Click the Info button next to the theme's name (see Figure 6-16).

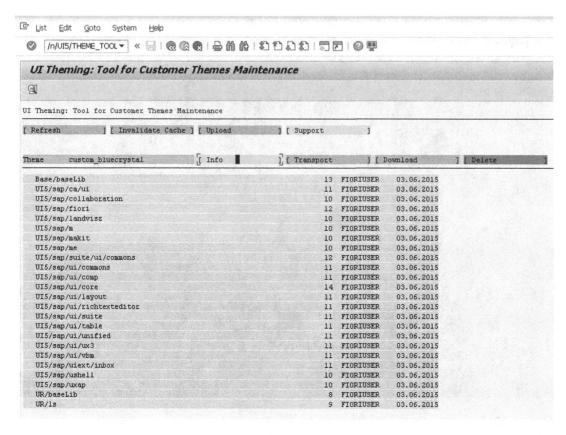

Figure 6-16. *UI5 theme tool*

4. Copy the `sap-theme-custom-bluecrystal@XXXXXXX` URL parameters (see Figure 6-17).

Figure 6-17. *URL parameters for the custom theme*

5. Add `?sap-theme-custom-bluecrystal@XXXXXXX` to the end of your standard Fiori launchpad URL to see the custom theme. You can also change the standard Fiori launchpad URL to show the custom theme by executing the transaction `/UI2/NWBC_CFG_CUST` in the Gateway system. On the NetWeaver Business Client (NWBC) configuration screen, add the following values (see Figure 6-18):

Field Name	Value
Filter	**SAP_FLP**
Parameter Name	**THEME**
Value	**Custom_blue_crystal** (the name of your custom theme)

Figure 6-18. *Fiori launchpad with the custom theme*

Be aware that these changes make the default standard Fiori launchpad always launch with your custom theme.

Customizing the Login Screen Background Image

Your home page displays the new theme, but the Fiori login screen remains the standard one. To change the background wallpaper of your Fiori login screen, follow these steps:

1. Go to transaction SE80, click MIME Repository, and then navigate to SAP ➤ PUBLIC ➤ BC ➤ UI2 ➤ Logon ➤ img. Here you can see the Fiori login screen default background image for different screen sizes. Make a backup of the standard image. Then right-click the login_background.jpg image and select Upload/Download ➤ Download (see Figure 6-19).

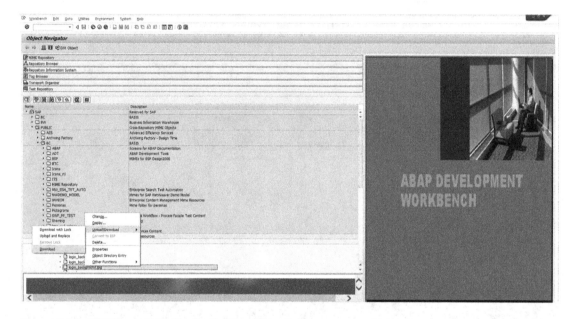

Figure 6-19. *MIME repository files for the Fiori login page*

2. Enter a path on your system, and save the image as shown in in Figure 6-20.

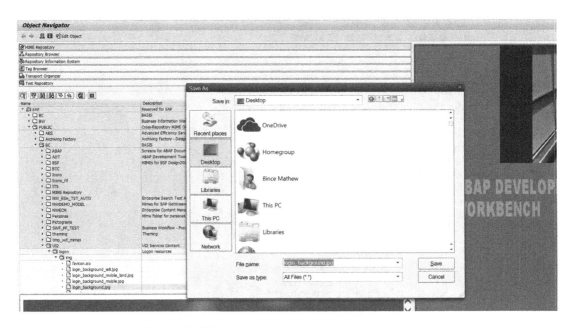

Figure 6-20. *Backing up the standard login screen image*

3. Replace the standard image with your custom wallpaper (see Figure 6-21).

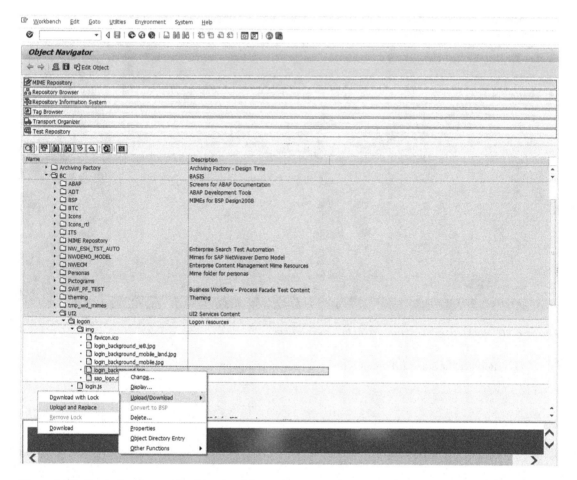

Figure 6-21. *Replacing the standard image with a custom image*

4. Once the upload is complete, you can preview the changed image in the MIME repository (see Figure 6-22).

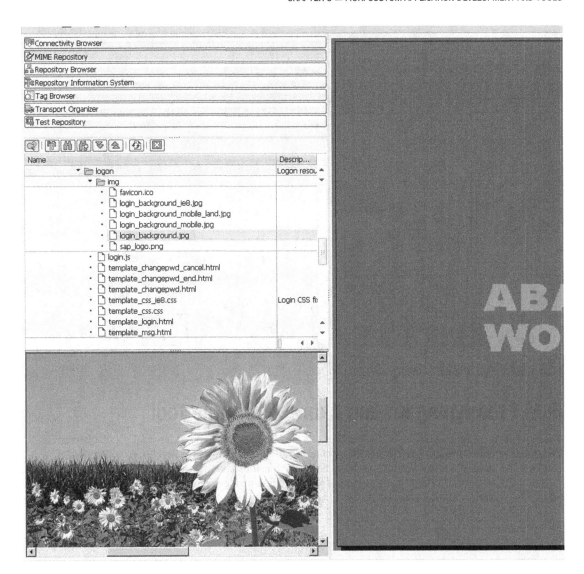

Figure 6-22. Custom image uploaded

5. Go to your standard login screen to see the new background image (see Figure 6-23). You may have to clear your browser cache to see the new image if the login page was already loaded with the old image.

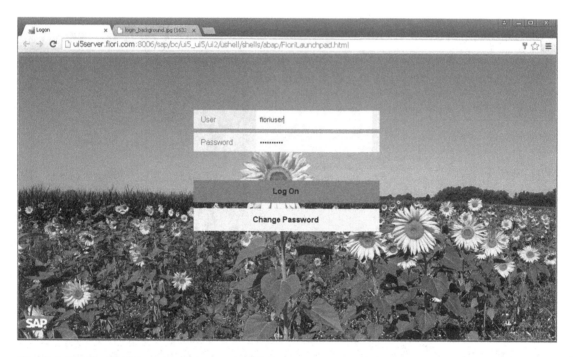

Figure 6-23. *Fiori login screen with custom wallpaper*

Fiori Prototyping Kit and Axure Wireframe Tool

The Fiori prototyping kit was one of the first files released by SAP to help designers make a mockup screen without any coding. It was a PowerPoint file containing all the UI5 controls as images, so you could combine the images to make a mockup screen. Now SAP has replaced the prototyping kit with a new solution: a third-party wireframing/prototyping tool called Axure (see Figure 6-24). You can download an Axure trial version at http://www.axure.com/download.

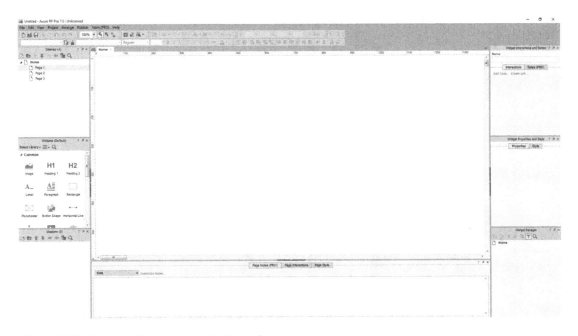

Figure 6-24. *Axure tool for creating wireframe designs*

SAP provides a set of stencil files and icon fonts that you can import into Axure so the Axure wireframe library is updated with SAP Fiori UI5 controls and icons (see Figure 6-25). You can download the stencils from `https://experience.sap.com/fiori-design/resources/downloads/`.

Figure 6-25. *Importing Fiori stencils into the Axure library*

Once you import the libraries, you can re-create every Fiori UI5 control and even the Fiori login screen (see Figure 6-26).

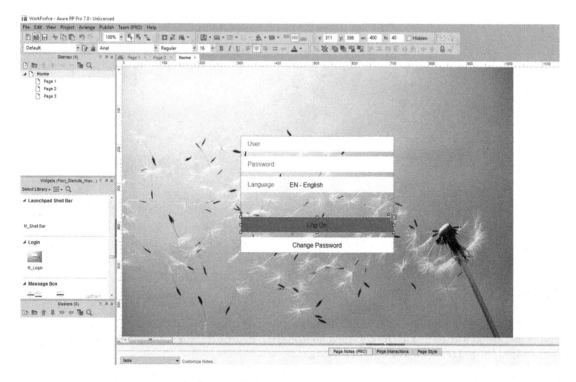

Figure 6-26. *Fiori login screen wireframe added from the Axure library*

You can create multiple pages in a single project. Tiles with custom icons can also be added from the SAP icons pack, which is added to the Axure library as shown in Figure 6-27.

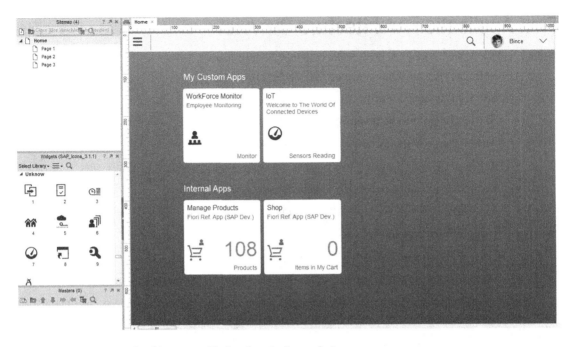

Figure 6-27. *SAP standard icon set added to the wireframe design*

There is even an action builder wizard that lets you create a website-like navigation from one screen to the next. This is helpful for making interactive presentations of the mockup screen (see Figure 6-28).

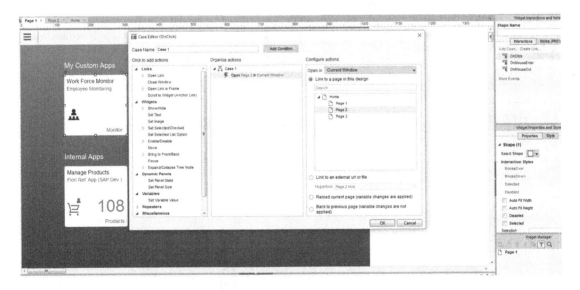

Figure 6-28. *Action builder wizard for adding interactions to wireframes*

Fiori Application Architecture Overview

When it comes to developing Fiori apps, there are ten golden rules:

- SAP Fiori apps must have an approved UX design.

- SAP Fiori UIs are built with SAP UI5.

- SAP Fiori apps must be based on OData services.

- An SAP Fiori app should have only one OData service.

- SAP Fiori UIs and OData services must be defined in different software components.

- Every SAP Fiori app is defined by a set of metadata.

- No custom CSS is allowed for SAP Fiori apps.

- Every SAP Fiori app must run as a web app.

- Every SAP Fiori app must run in the SAP Fiori launchpad.

- Every SAP Fiori app must run on mobile devices along with the native app paradigm.

When you're doing custom app development, in some scenarios you may choose to use custom CSS (especially when you need to meet a customer's specific design requirements). But using of lot of custom CSS may prevent the app from qualifying as a Fiori app—especially if the CSS customization crosses the line of being a simple UI with flat design.

Fiori apps are based on the model-view-controller (MVC) architecture. Before explaining MVC, let's first consider how a normal web page works (see Figure 6-29). Let's say you are accessing a website. The browser requests the HTML page and renders it on screen. When you interact with the page, it may require a back-end call to fetch the data from a database. This single web page has all the code to render the view, listen to user interactions, navigate, and handle database requests. After processing user input, the web page returns the result to the browser, and the browser renders the UI logic received from the web page. This is fine, but a single page cluttered with all the presentation logic, user event-handling, and business data logic is difficult to debug or modify.

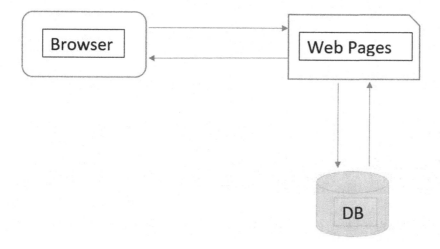

Figure 6-29. *Browser loading a regular web page*

What if you split this code into different files, each of which has a specific role in making the web page work? For example, you can have a model that encapsulates the data from the database or holds the business data logic, a view file that holds the presentation layer logic or UI code to render the GUI, a file controller that handles all the user interactions and page navigations, and so on. This makes the code more readable and modularized, giving developers a better understanding of and control over the app's source code. This approach is called MVC (see Figure 6-30).

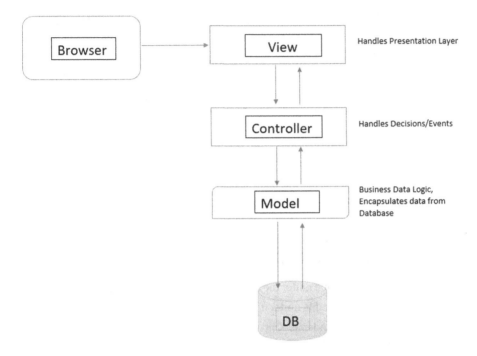

Figure 6-30. *Web page with MVC architecture*

Now let's see how this MVC architecture is embedded into a typical Fiori app. A Fiori app, when run locally from an Eclipse IDE, starts from index.html like any normal website. But when the app is loaded in the Fiori launchpad, the app starts from Component.js. This is mainly due to the way the Fiori launchpad is designed (see Figure 6-31 for the architecture and Table 6-1 for a file-name reference).

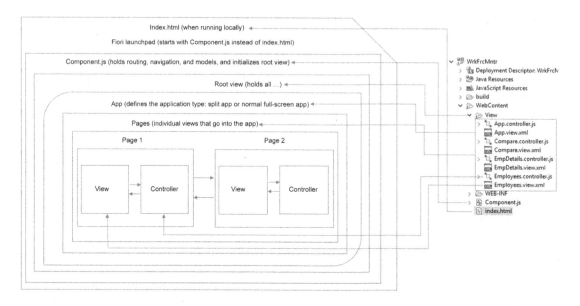

Figure 6-31. *Fiori app architecture*

Table 6-1. *Fiori Application Folder Structure Details*

Layer	Name	Example File Name in Project
1	Index.html	index.html file under the WebContent folder
2	Component.js	Component.js file under the WebContent folder
3	Root view	View folder under WebContent
4	App	App.controller.js file under WebContent\View
5	Pages	Pages including Compare.view.xml, EmpDetails.view.xml, and Employess.view.xml under WebContent\View
6	Views and controller	All the *.controller.js and *.view.xml files under WebContent\View

The second layer, Component.js, is the file that creates the model for your app. In addition to the model, Component.js contains the *routing*: a map or set of routes that specify how one page navigates to the next. Component.js also initializes a root view.

The third layer is the root view, which holds all the views for your app. The fourth layer is the app file, which defines what type of app this is: for example, a split app or a full-screen app. The fifth layer consists of the pages: a collection of view and controllers that are added to the app as pages.

The innermost layer shows the individual pages, each of which has a controller and a view. This layer implements the view controller architecture. You will understand the architecture better once you reach the app development section of the chapter.

Now it's time to begin developing a custom app. This section walks through how I made an app for workforce monitoring; that's a fancy name for an app that lets managers monitor employee attendance and working hours and analyze productivity.

The basic steps used to design the app are similar to the Personas approach used for SAP design; it's a thinking approach for building a Fiori app. These steps are as follows:

1. Visualize what the app is and whom it is for, and design a rough sketch on paper.

2. Design a wireframe/mockup design to give you a clearer idea of what UI controls you need to choose to build the app.

3. Build the final app.

Visualizing the App

As part of visualizing this example app, I thought about what a manager is interested in if they want to analyze an employee's productivity, check whether an employee is billable or non-billable, or analyze working hours to find a pattern for how best to utilize employees. I came up with a rough design that I drew on a piece of paper (see Figure 6-32), just to have an idea of how the app might work.

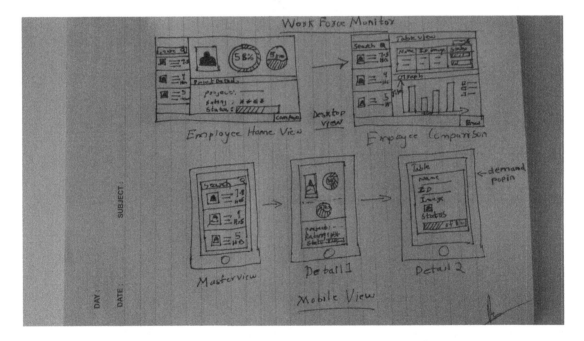

Figure 6-32. *I need more practice with my drawing skills* ☺

Designing a Wireframe/Mockup

Now that I had a rough sketch, I needed to finalize the exact UI5 elements required for this app. For this purpose, I used the Axure wireframe tool discussed earlier. I designed the first screen of the app (see Figure 6-33), which showed how the app would look with UI5 controls.

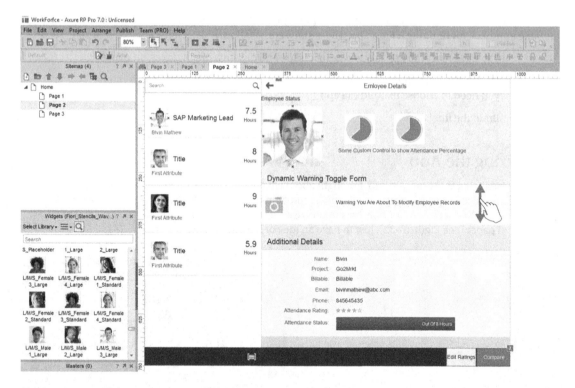

Figure 6-33. *Workforce monitor app home screen*

Then I designed the second screen, referring to my sketches. I added the table and chart controls to display employee comparison data, as shown in Figure 6-34.

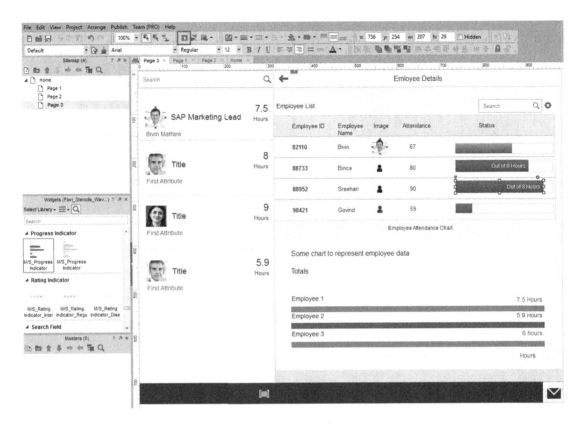

Figure 6-34. *Employee Details screen*

Finally, I added a Fiori login screen and home page with a tile pointing to my app. I also added some screen interactions by using the wizard to make the mockup navigate from the login screen to the app mockup screens (see Figure 6-35).

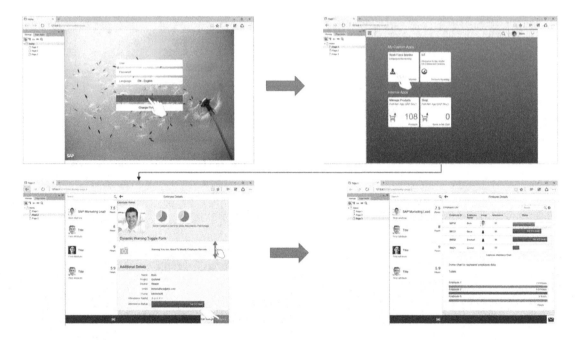

Figure 6-35. Interactive prototype design for the workforce monitor

Building the Final App

Now that I had a final render, it was time to build the app. See https://experience.sap.com/fiori-design/ for more detailed guidelines on how to build a custom Fiori app and what factors you need to consider. For example, Figure 6-36 shows you some UI design consideration when you're using a grid layout.

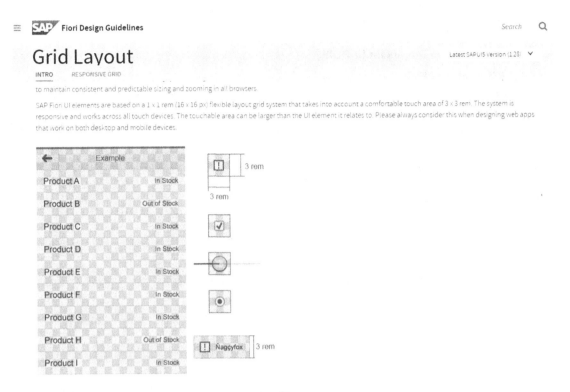

Figure 6-36. *Fiori design guidelines for creating a grid layout*

Developing a Custom Fiori Application

Now you have all the information required to begin development. Let's start building the example app!

Creating a New UI5 Project

Open Eclipse Luna, and create a new blank project as shown in Figure 6-37.

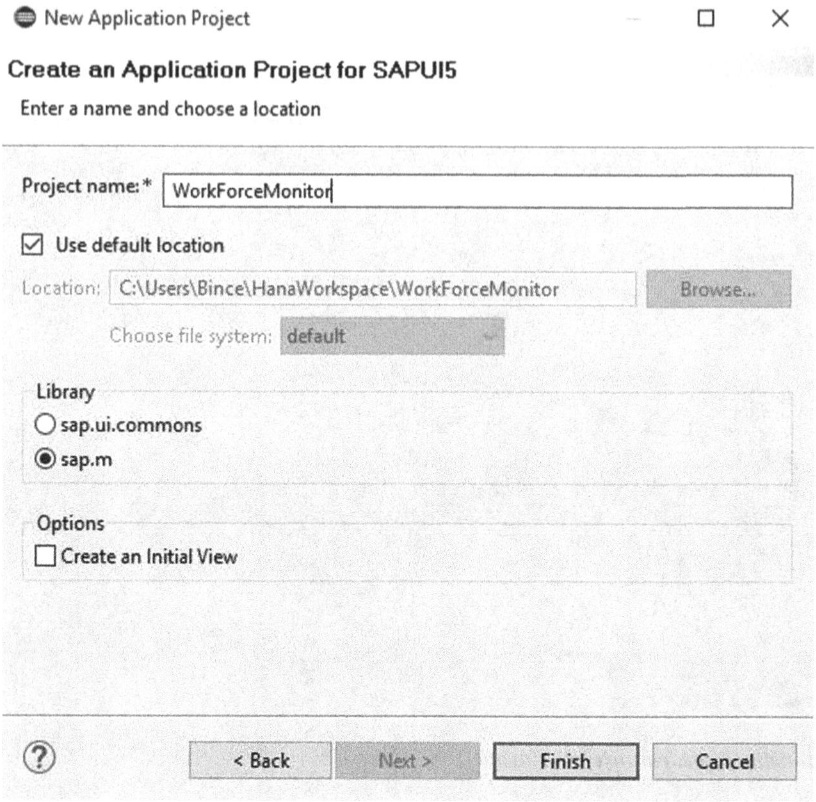

Figure 6-37. *Creating a new project for the WorkForceMonitor app*

Modify index.html as shown in Figure 6-38 (you can download the source code from the Apress website). As explained earlier, in Figure 6-31, index.html is used to run the app locally in Eclipse. In Figure 6-38, the first highlighted block bootstraps the SAP UI5 libraries in the src parameter. Similarly, you specify the theme, the library files used for this app, the complex binding syntax type (this helps bind multiple OData entity fields in one control, such as a text control), and the resource root name. Here, the resource root name is given as com.wfm, which is an alias for the actual root of the folder ./. This enters a unique name for the app's root folder.

📄 index.html ✕

```html
<!DOCTYPE HTML>
<html>
    <head>
        <meta http-equiv="X-UA-Compatible" content="IE=edge">
        <meta http-equiv='Content-Type' content='text/html;charset=UTF-8'/>
<!--    <link type="text/css" rel="stylesheet" href="styles/style.css"> -->

        <script
            id="sap-ui-bootstrap"
            src="https://sapui5.netweaver.ondemand.com/sdk/resources/sap-ui-core.js"
            data-sap-ui-theme="sap_bluecrystal"
            data-sap-ui-libs="sap.m"
            data-sap-ui-bindingSyntax="complex"                      1
            data-sap-ui-compatVersion="edge"
            data-sap-ui-preload="async"
            data-sap-ui-resourceroots='{
                "com.wfm": "./"
            }' >
        </script>
        <!-- only load the mobile lib "sap.m" and the "sap_bluecrystal" theme -->

        <script>
            sap.ui.getCore().attachInit(function () {
                new sap.m.Shell({
                    app : new sap.ui.core.ComponentContainer({
                        name : "com.wfm",                            2
                        height : "100%"
                    })
                }).placeAt("content");
            });
        </script>
    </head>
    <body class="sapUiBody" role="application">
        <div id="content"></div>                                    3
    </body>
</html>
```

Figure 6-38. *Index.html modified to run the app locally*

The second highlighted section in Figure 6-38 is where you make index.html call the Component.js file, which you will create in the app folder. This rerouting is required because the app starts from Component.js in the Fiori launchpad. Fiori launchpad apps run in a shell, so you declare a new shell sap.m.shell. Within the shell, you call the contents of Component.js, so you declare a component container (sap.ui.core.ComponentContainer). The controls you declare are placed on a div in index.html, so you place the response in a div named content using the PlaceAt() method. The third highlighted area is the content div that shows the contents you place in Component.js.

Now, create a new file named Component.js in the root folder. Component.js holds the Fiori app's references to include files, routing configurations, the root view containing app type details, resource bundles (i18n), model resources, and so on.

Figure 6-39 shows the jQuery.sap.declare (com.wfm.Component) declaration. It identifies the Component.js file's name and path. com.wfm is the name of the root folder declared under resourceroots in the index.html file.

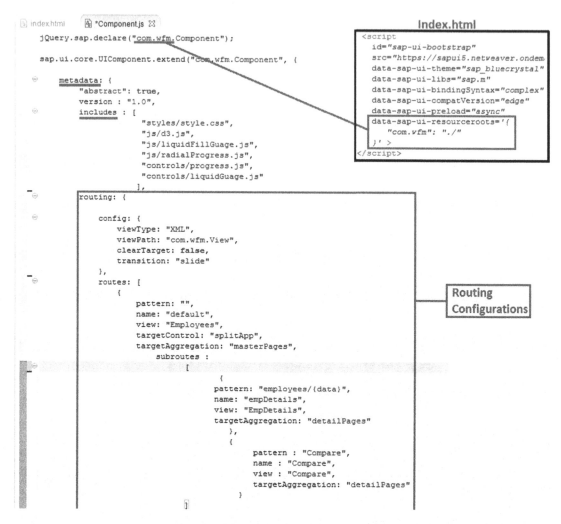

Figure 6-39. Component.js *with metadata definitions*

The component.js file contains the metadata; it is a faceless component that tells component.js about various resources and configurations required to run this app. (In the Fiori V2 architecture, this metadata will be a separate JSON file.) Some of the commonly used metadata parameters are as follows:

- abstract: Whether your component class is abstract or not

- version: Version of your component

- include: Custom CSS classes or third-party JS files

- dependencies: External dependencies

- library: Library the component belongs to

- config: Can be used to store static value pairs if you need to access them in the component level (kind of like declaring a global variable)

- `customizing`: Specific to Fiori extensions; not required for your custom app

- `routes`: Routes used to navigate to and between pages

In Figure 6-39, you can see the metadata JSON structure with the `includes` parameter, which holds the path to all the custom CSS and the third-party JS files used for this app.

The `routing` parameter holds the root view path under the `config` parameter. You can also see `targetControl`, with the value `SplitApp`; this is the name of the SplitApp control defined on the `App.view.xml` page (you see this page later in this chapter).

The `targetAggregation` for one of the routes is `masterPages` and for the remaining routes is `detailsPages`. This tells the router which view should be placed in the master view of the SplitApp control and which views are detail views.

The `pattern` parameter of `routes` is the path for each view, if the `pattern` value is `""`, then the page is the default view. If `pattern` has the value `employees/{data}`, it means the page name for the `EmpDetails` view can be accessed via the path `employees/{data}`. The `{data}` part is a dynamic variable that you need to pass at runtime; you could give the `pattern` value as `employees`, but you need to send an employee ID from the master page to the detail page as part of the logic to show the subsequent data in the `Employees` page.

`Component.js` uses two methods to control initial Instantiation (see Figure 6-40):

- `init`: Overwrites the standard `init` method. You can use it to call the `createContent` method and initialize your router.

- `createContent`: Inserts all the code to fill the component with your content. For example, you can use this method to replace the default view with your starting view (in this case, the app view), set the model for your view (JSON/OData), set the i18n resource bundle (`DefaultBindingMode`), and so on.

```
init: function() {
//      jQuery.sap.require("com.wfm.js.d3");          // you can call js library files like this also, but now we can do the same in the Metadata structure
//      jQuery.sap.require("com.wfm.js.liquidFillGuage");
//      jQuery.sap.require("com.wfm.js.radialProgress");
//      jQuery.sap.require("com.wfm.controls.progress");
//      jQuery.sap.require("com.wfm.controls.liquidGuage")

        jQuery.sap.require("sap.m.routing.RouteMatchedHandler");
        jQuery.sap.require("sap.ui.core.routing.HashChanger");

        //call createContent
        sap.ui.core.UIComponent.prototype.init.apply(this, arguments);

        this._router = this.getRouter();

        //initialize the router
        this._routeHandler = new sap.m.routing.RouteMatchedHandler(this._router);
        this._router.initialize();

    },

createContent: function() {

        var oView = sap.ui.view({
            id: "splitApp",
            viewName: "com.wfm.View.App",          Setting the path for the App view
            type: "XML",
            viewData: {
                component: this
            }
        });

        var oModel = new sap.ui.model.json.JSONModel('model/Employees.json');      Setting the model for the views; it can be a JSON/OData model
        oView.setModel(oModel);

        // set i18n model
        var i18nModel = new sap.ui.model.resource.ResourceModel({
            bundleUrl: "i18n/i18n.properties"                  Setting the i18n model
        });
        oView.setModel(i18nModel, "i18n");

        var deviceModel = new sap.ui.model.json.JSONModel({
            isPhone: sap.ui.Device.system.phone,
            listMode: (sap.ui.Device.system.phone) ? "None" : "SingleSelectMaster",
            listItemType: (sap.ui.Device.system.phone) ? "Active" : "Inactive"
        });
        deviceModel.setDefaultBindingMode("OneWay");
        oView.setModel(deviceModel, "device");
        return oView;

    }
```

Figure 6-40. *Setting the model for the views*

Adding Views to the App

Next, create a folder named View. Right-click the folder, and choose New ➤ Other. Under SAPUI5 Application Development, select View, and click Next (see Figure 6-41).

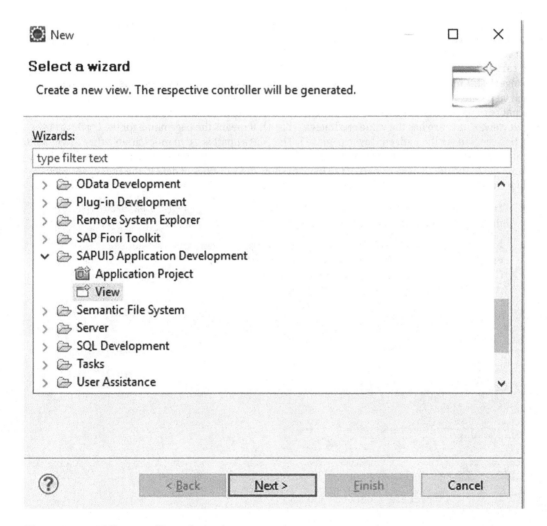

Figure 6-41. *Adding new files to the project*

For the view name, enter **App.** Select the XML radio button, and click Finish (see Figure 6-42).

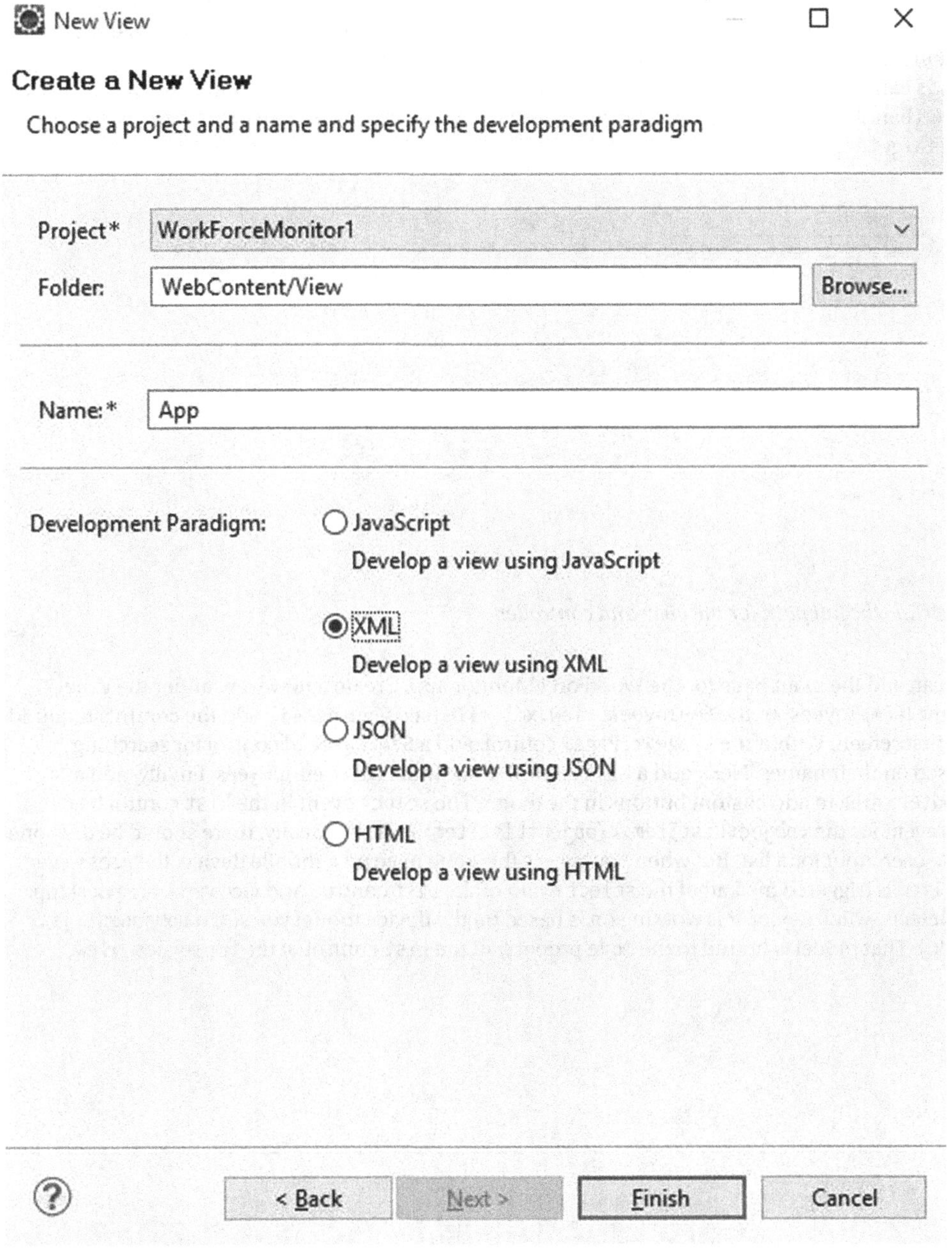

Figure 6-42. *Create a new XML view*

Open the default generated code in the view App.view.xml file and its corresponding controller file App.controller.js. The ControllerName for the view is View.App by default, but you need to change the path reference to com.wfm.View.App. This is important because com.wfm is the path of your root folder; in order for Component.js to find App.view, you must enter the full path from the root view to the View folder. Similarly, you need to modify the sap.ui.controller(View.App) of App.controller.js to sap.ui.controller (com.wfm.View.App). This change is mandatory for every new file you add to your project.

In addition to changing the controller name, in App.view you need to add an additional controller <SplitApp> </SplitApp> (see Figure 6-43). This makes your App view return a SplitApp controller to Component.js. In Figure 6-39, you can see a targetControl parameter in the metadata JSON in Component.js, so Component.js can find the application type in that target control. This is how you add the app type and the master view (handled by the parameter targetAggregation:masterPages) and detail view(handled by the parameter targetAggregation:detailPages) to the app via the routes in Component.js.

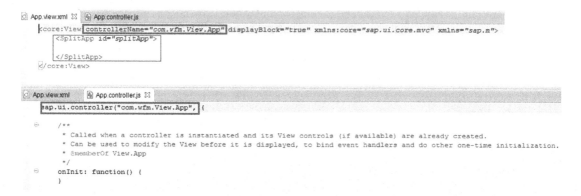

Figure 6-43. *Define the full path for the view and controller*

Now you can add the main page for the WorkForceMonitor app. Create a new view under the View folder, and name it Employees. In the Employees.view.xml file (see Figure 6-44), add the controls required to create your first screen. Within the <Page></Page> control, add a SearchField control for searching employees based on their names. Next, add a List control to show the list of employees. Finally, add a <Footer></Footer> area to add custom buttons in the footer. The select event in the List control has another press event for the <objectListItem></objectListItem> control. Ideally, there should be only one event to handle user input for a list. But when you access the same page on a mobile device, the press event of objectListItem is triggered instead of the select event of the List control, and vice versa on a desktop. How the app detects which device it is working on is based on the device model you set in Component.js (see Figure 6-40). That model is bound to the mode property of the List control of the Employees view.

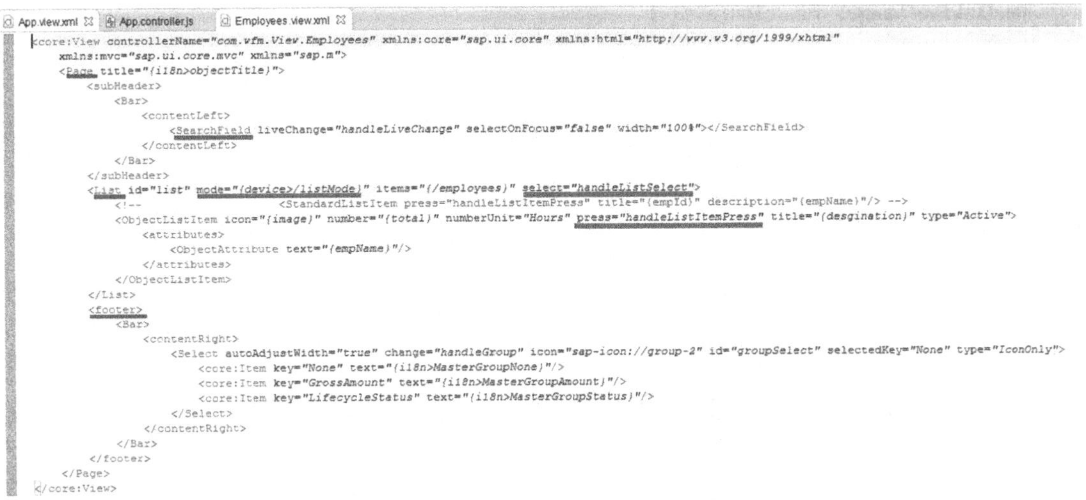


```xml
<core:View controllerName="com.vfm.View.Employees" xmlns:core="sap.ui.core" xmlns:html="http://vvv.v3.org/1999/xhtml"
    xmlns:mvc="sap.ui.core.mvc" xmlns="sap.m">
    <Page title="{i18n>objectTitle}">
        <subHeader>
            <Bar>
                <contentLeft>
                    <SearchField liveChange="handleLiveChange" selectOnFocus="false" width="100%"></SearchField>
                </contentLeft>
            </Bar>
        </subHeader>
        <List id="list" mode="{device>/listMode}" items="{/employees}" select="handleListSelect">
            <!--                <StandardListItem press="handleListItemPress" title="{empId}" description="{empName}"/> -->
            <ObjectListItem icon="{image}" number="{total}" numberUnit="Hours" press="handleListItemPress" title="{desgination}" type="Active">
                <attributes>
                    <ObjectAttribute text="{empName}"/>
                </attributes>
            </ObjectListItem>
        </List>
        <footer>
            <Bar>
                <contentRight>
                    <Select autoAdjustWidth="true" change="handleGroup" icon="sap-icon://group-2" id="groupSelect" selectedKey="None" type="IconOnly">
                        <core:Item key="None" text="{i18n>MasterGroupNone}"/>
                        <core:Item key="GrossAmount" text="{i18n>MasterGroupAmount}"/>
                        <core:Item key="LifecycleStatus" text="{i18n>MasterGroupStatus}"/>
                    </Select>
                </contentRight>
            </Bar>
        </footer>
    </Page>
</core:View>
```

Figure 6-44. *Employees XML view code*

In the controller file of the `Employees` view (see Listing 6-1), in the `onInit` hook method, you get the reference for your router using `sap.ui.core.UIComponent.getRouterFor(this)`. This reference is required in order to carry out page navigation.

The `handleListSelect` and `handleListItemPress` methods trigger based on the device. In those methods, the router method `navTo` is called. In the `navTo` method, you pass the pattern for the `EmployeeDetails` view defined in the `component.js` file. The `handleLiveChange` method is used to handle search queries based on the employee names in the search field in the view.

Listing 6-1. `Employees.controller.js` (Handles the Logic for the Employee List on the Master Page)

```javascript
jQuery.sap.require("com.wfm.util.Formatter");
sap.ui.controller("com.wfm.View.Employees", {

    onInit: function() {
        this.router = sap.ui.core.UIComponent.getRouterFor(this);
    },

    handleListSelect: function(evt) {
        var context = evt.getParameter("listItem").getBindingContext().sPath;
        sViewId = context.substring(context.lastIndexOf("/") + 1);
        this.router.navTo("empDetails", {
            data: sViewId
        });
    },
    handleListItemPress: function(evt) {
        var context = evt.getSource().getBindingContext().sPath;
        sViewId = context.substring(context.lastIndexOf("/") + 1);
        this.router.navTo("empDetails", {data: sViewId});
    },
```

```
handleLiveChange: function(evt) {

    // create model filter
    var filters = [];
    var sQuery = evt.getParameters().newValue;
    if (sQuery && sQuery.length > 0) {
        var filter = new sap.ui.model.Filter("empName", sap.ui.model.FilterOperator
        .Contains, sQuery);
        filters.push(filter);
    }

    // update list binding
    var list = this.getView().byId("list");
    var binding = list.getBinding("items");
    binding.filter(filters);
    },
});
```

Similarly, create the remaining views for the app, as shown in Figure 6-45. You can download the complete source code for all the examples in this book from the Apress website.

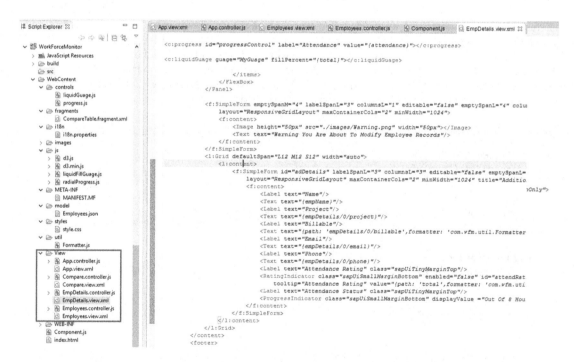

Figure 6-45. *Create all the views required for the app*

The compare.view.xml source code includes <core:Fragment> </core:Fragment> and
<viz:VizFrame></viz:VizFrame> controls (see Listing 6-2). The Fragment control loads another file that
contains the code for the Table control dynamically at runtime. To learn more about fragments, see
http://scn.sap.com/docs/DOC-55801. In short, a fragment is a method to modularize a page's code into
multiple files so that if a group of people are working on the same view and developing multiple controls,
they can work on the individual parts of the same page simultaneously. The viz control is required to show
the graphs on the page.

Listing 6-2. Compare.view.xml (Shows the Comparison Chart and Calls the Fragment Containing the
Employee Details Table)

```
<core:View controllerName="com.wfm.View.Compare" xmlns:viz="sap.viz.ui5.controls"
xmlns:core="sap.ui.core" xmlns:html="http://www.w3.org/1999/xhtml"
xmlns:mvc="sap.ui.core.mvc"
    xmlns="sap.m" xmlns:l="sap.ui.layout">
    <Page navButtonPress="backToEmpDetails" showNavButton="true"
    title="{i18n>CompareTitle}"<content>
<core:Fragment fragmentName="com.wfm.fragments.CompareTable" type="XML" />
    <Panel><ScrollContainer height="100%" width="100%" horizontal="false" vertical="true"
    focusable="true">
        <viz:Popover id="idPopOver"></viz:Popover>
        <viz:VizFrame id="idVizFrameColumn" uiConfig="{applicationSet:'fiori'}"
        vizType="column" width="100%" height="700px">
        </viz:VizFrame
    </ScrollContainer>
</Panel>
        </content>
    <footer>
            <Bar>
                <contentRight>
<Button icon="sap-icon://email" press="onEditBtn" text="Send Email"
type="Transparent"></Button>
    </contentRight>
    </Bar>
    </footer>
</Page>
</core:View>
```

Creating Custom Controls

This example also uses two third-party JS files from http://d3js.org/ (see Figure 6-46). I created custom
controls based on these third-party JS files to show the percentage and total hours worked by employees. For
more information about creating custom controls from scratch, see https://sapui5.netweaver.ondemand.
com/#docs/guide/d12d2ee6a5454d799358d425f9e7c4db.html.

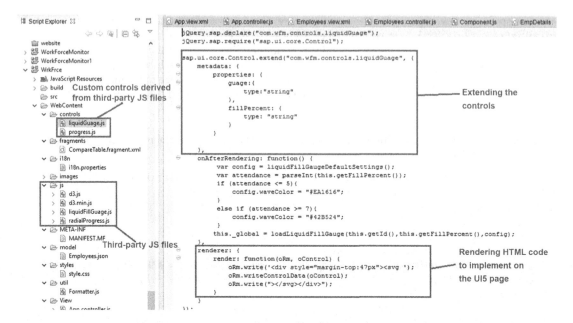

Figure 6-46. *Creating custom controls for the app*

You can see the custom controls rendered on the EmployeeDetails output page (see Figure 6-47).

Figure 6-47. *Custom controls preview on the view page*

When you click an employee name on the list and check the address bar, you can see the router pattern passing to the next page (see Figure 6-48).

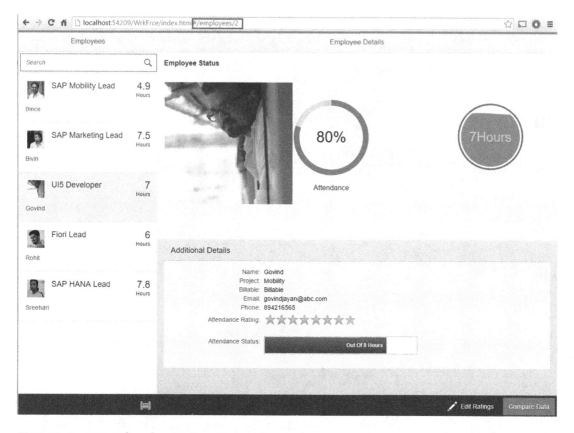

Figure 6-48. *Pattern-based navigation using routing*

Because this is a split app, when the screen size is reduced, the master view is hidden automatically (see Figure 6-49).

Figure 6-49. *The master view switches to Hide mode on smaller screens*

Deploying the Custom Application to HANA Cloud

Once you are done with your development, you can preview the app locally as a web app. But in this case, you want to port the app to Web IDE and deploy it in HANA Cloud.

This example uses the cloud Web IDE with a HANA trial account. You can register for a free HANA trial account at `https://account.hanatrial.ondemand.com/`.

Once you register the for the HANA trial, go to the HANA cockpit and click Subscriptions. At right, you can see sapwebide under Subscribed HTML5 Applications. Click the Web IDE link (see Figure 6-50).

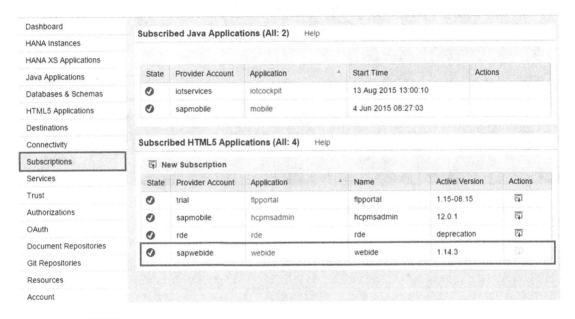

Figure 6-50. *HANA trial account*

You see a cloud Web IDE URL, as shown in Figure 6-51.

Figure 6-51. *HANA Cloud Web IDE*

Importing a UI5 App into Web IDE

Before you import your code into Web IDE, you have to first create a blank HTML5 app in HANA Cloud:

1. Click the HTML5 Applications link at left in the HANA Cloud portal, click New Application, enter the name of your new app, and click Save (see Figure 6-52).

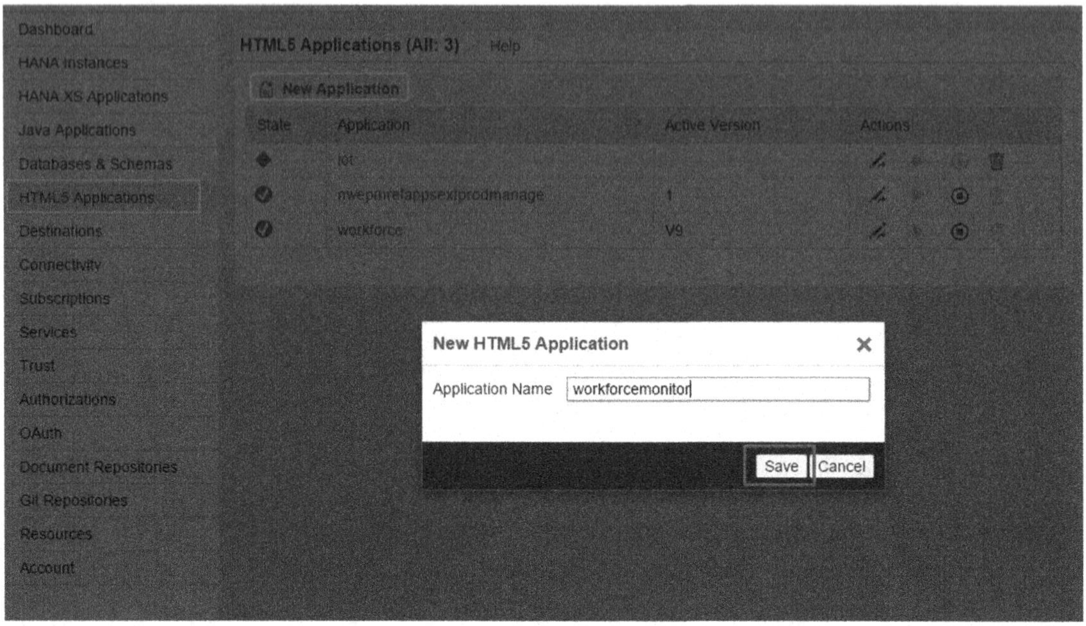

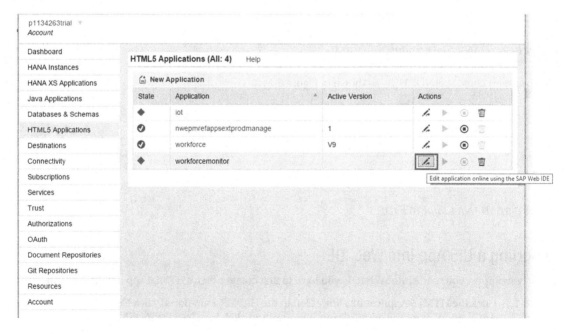

Figure 6-52. *Creating a new HTML5 app in HANA Cloud*

2. Click the Edit icon in the Actions column to open your new app in Web IDE (see Figure 6-53).

Figure 6-53. *Open your app in Web IDE*

3.   You are asked for your HANA trial credentials. This is required for Web IDE to connect to your HANA trial account and link the HTML5 app to its workspace (see Figure 6-54).

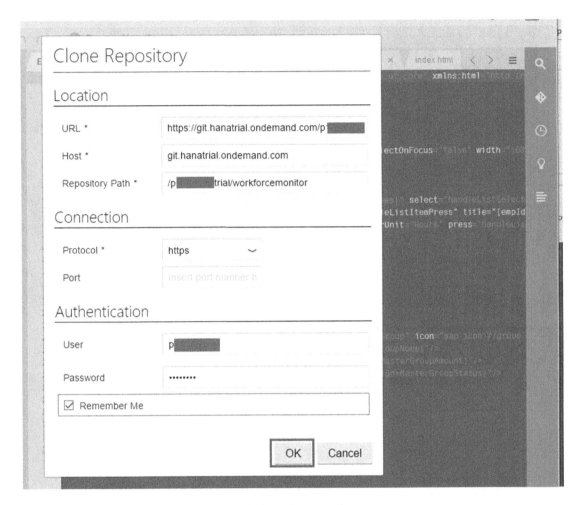

Figure 6-54. *Connecting the HTML5 app with the Web IDE workspace*

4.   Now that you have an app in Web IDE, it's time to upload your local app to Web IDE. To do this, make a zip file of the webapp folder of your local app. Right-click your Web IDE project, click Import, and select the project zip file, as shown in Figure 6-55.

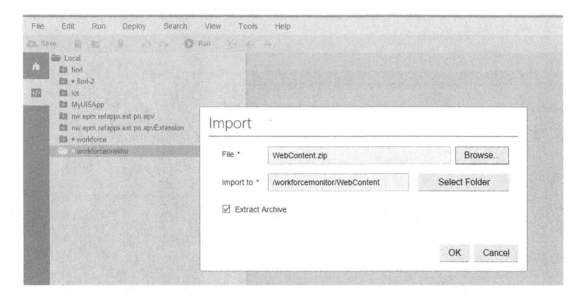

Figure 6-55.   *Importing the local UI5 app to Web IDE*

5.   Click the Git repository icon at right on the page, and click Commit and Push. This saves the files into the HANA Cloud (see Figure 6-56).

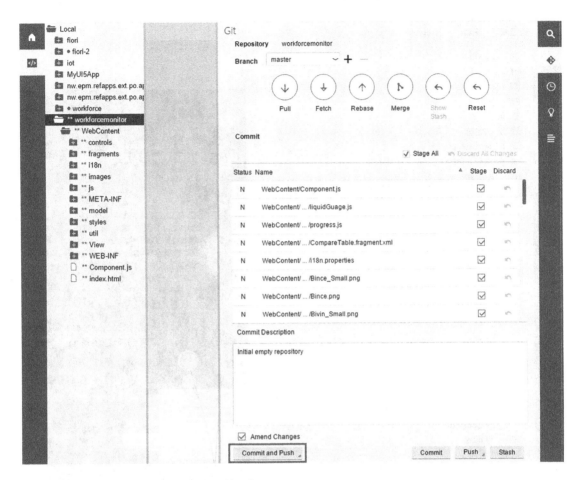

Figure 6-56. *Committing files to HANA Cloud*

6. Your files are saved to HANA Cloud as an HTML5 app. To access the app, you still need to activate it. To do so, right-click the project and choose Deploy ➤ Deploy to SAP HANA Cloud Platform, as shown in Figure 6-57.

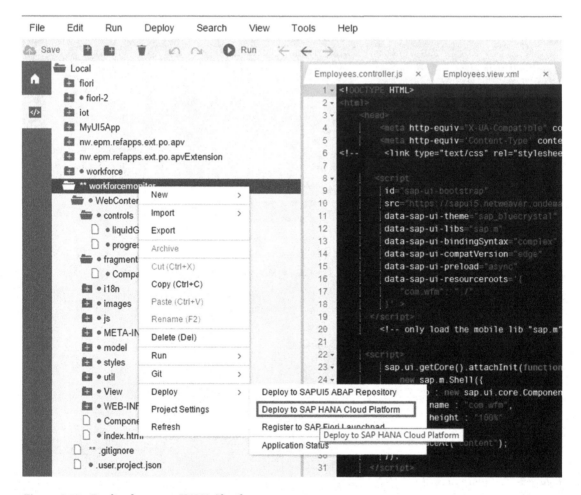

Figure 6-57. *Deploy the app to HANA Cloud*

7. A wizard pops up with details about the app to be activated. Click Deploy (see Figure 6-58).

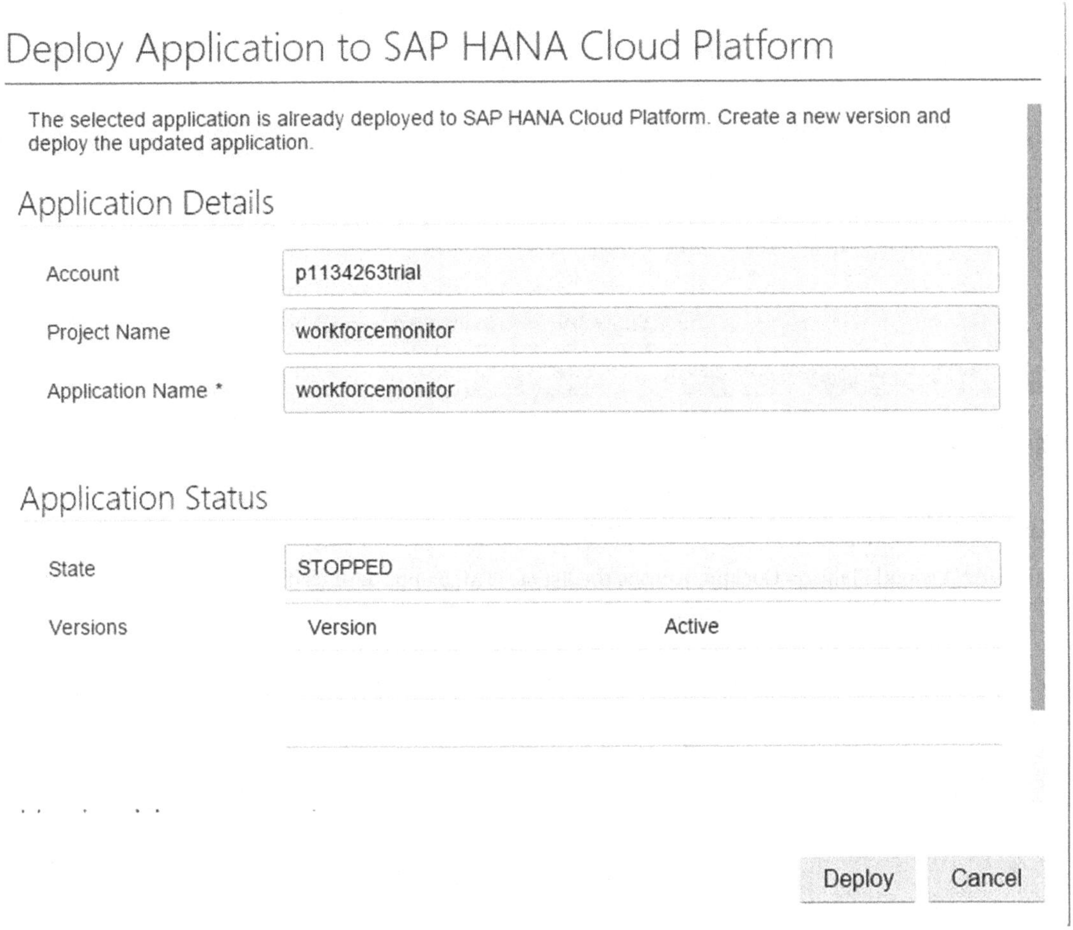

Deploy Application to SAP HANA Cloud Platform

The selected application is already deployed to SAP HANA Cloud Platform. Create a new version and deploy the updated application.

Application Details

Account

p1134263trial

Project Name

workforcemonitor

Application Name *

workforcemonitor

Application Status

State

STOPPED

Versions

Version   Active

Deploy   Cancel

Figure 6-58. Details of the app to be deployed to HANA Cloud

8.   Once the app is deployed, you get a confirmation message. Click Open The App's Page In The SAP HANA Cloud Platform Cockpit, as shown in Figure 6-59.

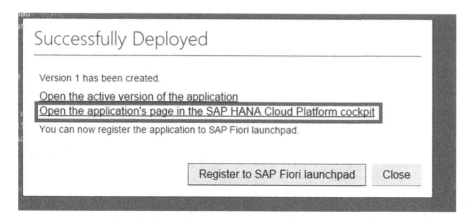

Figure 6-59. *The WorkForceMonitor app successfully deployed on HANA Cloud*

Running the App from HANA Cloud

In the HANA Cloud Platform Cockpit, you see the list of HTML5 apps deployed in HANA Cloud. Click the workforcemonitor app (see Figure 6-60).

Figure 6-60. *Activated HTML5 apps in HANA Cloud*

From here, you get the URL link of your deployed app (see Figure 6-61).

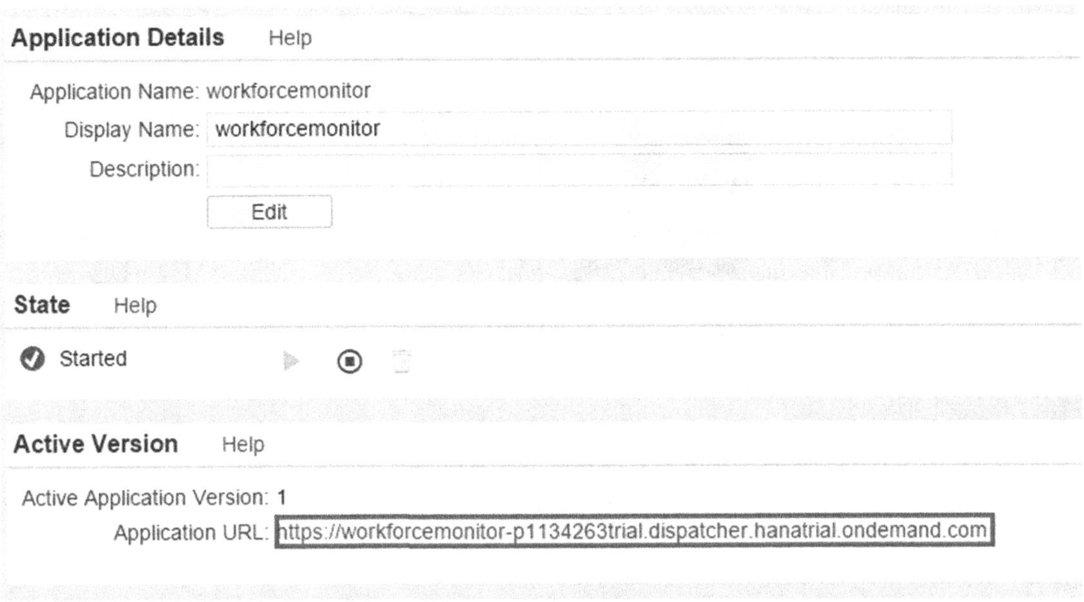

Application Details   Help

Application Name: workforcemonitor

Display Name: workforcemonitor

Description:

[Edit]

State   Help

✓ Started   ▷   ◉   ⬚

Active Version   Help

Active Application Version: **1**

Application URL: https://workforcemonitor-p1134263trial.dispatcher.hanatrial.ondemand.com

Figure 6-61. *URL link of your activated app*

If you directly open this URL, you get an error page. This is because HANA Cloud recognizes the app as an HTML5 app, unlike the Fiori launchpad, which opens the Component.js file in the app. You have to manually add the index.html path to the end of this URL (see Figure 6-62). For example, the URL for the WorkForceMonitor app is something like https://workforcemonitor-yourhanatrialusername. dispatcher.hanatrial.ondemand.com/WebContent/index.html.

Figure 6-62. *WorkForceMonitor app opened in HANA Cloud*

Now you can see your app via the cloud and access it from anywhere (see Figure 6-63).

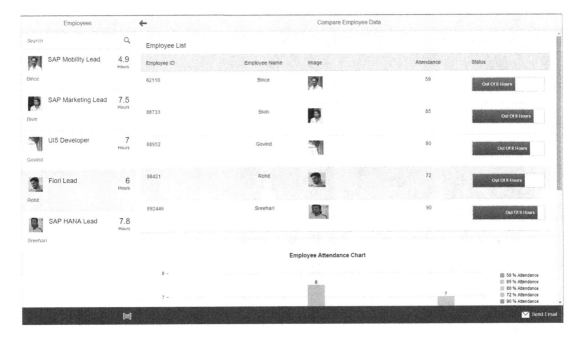

Figure 6-63. *Now your app is completely deployed in the cloud*

Web IDE Basics

If you want to develop UI5 apps using Web IDE, you have multiple options:

- Create a project from a template
- Create a project based on a sample app
- Use the Quick Start option with the Layout Editor
- Create an extension project

You saw how to create an extension project using Web IDE in Chapter 4. This section looks at the remaining options. You can access a trial version of Web IDE from the Hana Cloud Cockpit under Subscriptions ➤ Web IDE. By default, the URL for your cloud-based Web IDE is https://webide-<yourHANATrialId>.dispatcher.hanatrial.ondemand.com.

Creating a New Project from a Template

Creating a project from a template saves you the time of setting up a skeleton UI5 app. Follow these steps:

1. To create a new project, go to File ➤ New ➤ Project From Template. On the wizard page, you can choose from various preset templates to start your app (see Figure 6-64). In this case, select the SAPUI5 Application Project, which creates a blank project with one sample view.

273

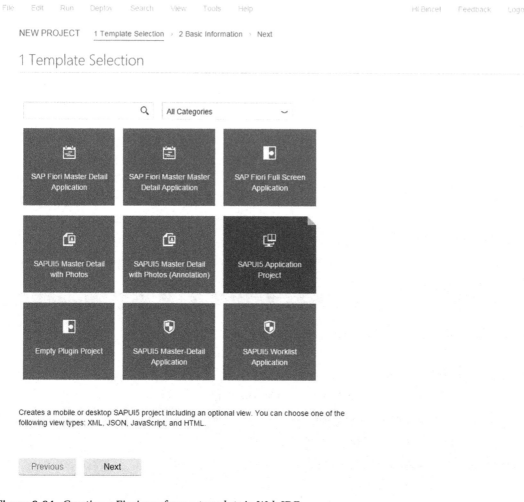

Figure 6-64. Creating a Fiori app from a template in Web IDE

2. Click Next, enter a name for your project on the next page, and click Next again. Now you have the option to specify a view type (XML, JSON, JavaScript, or HTML). In this example, select the XML view. Then enter a namespace and a name for your view (see Figure 6-65). Click Next and then click Finish.

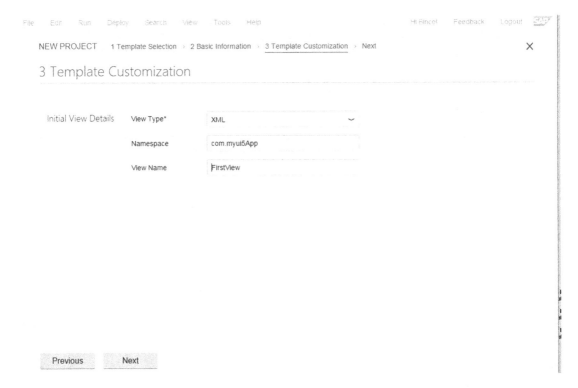

Figure 6-65. *Creating a UI5 app project from a template*

3. The app appears in the project explorer pane of Web IDE. It has a new view and a controller named `FirstView` (see Figure 6-66).

Figure 6-66. *The new app is created in Web IDE*

4. To add controls to the UI, Web IDE has a built-in Layout Editor (this feature is not available in Eclipse). You can drag-and-drop any control you want directly into the preview pane in the middle of the Layout Editor (see Figure 6-67). To the right of the preview pane are the properties of all the controls you have added. To its left are all the available UI5 controls. This is a useful feature for beginners to check the code that is generated for each control, but it only allows you to build basic controls.

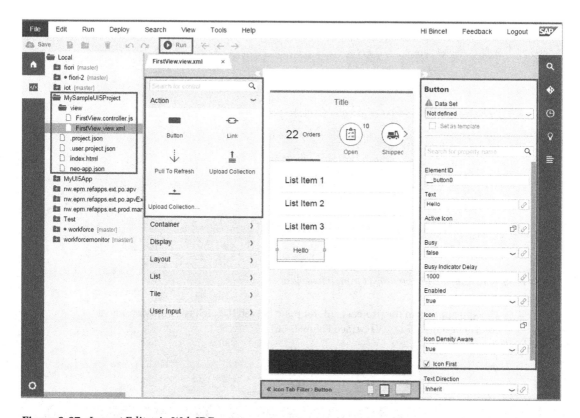

Figure 6-67. *Layout Editor in Web IDE*

5. Once you have added the controls, click the green Run icon on the toolbar to preview the app (see Figure 6-68).

Figure 6-68. *Application preview in Web IDE*

Creating a Sample Application Using Web IDE

You also have the option to generate a fully functional UI5 app from a set of samples. Doing so will help you understand how a full-fledged app is built and the coding standards used in these apps. Here are the steps to create a sample app:

1. Go to File ➤ New ➤ Project From Sample Application. On the wizard page, select the sample app you want to create. In this case, choose the Manage Products app (see Figure 6-69). Click Next, accept the terms and conditions, and click Finish.

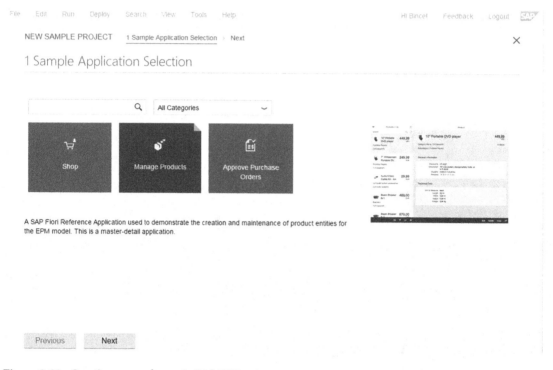

Figure 6-69. *Creating a sample app in Web IDE*

2. The sample app's source code appears in Web IDE (see Figure 6-70). You can run the app just as you previewed the template project app earlier.

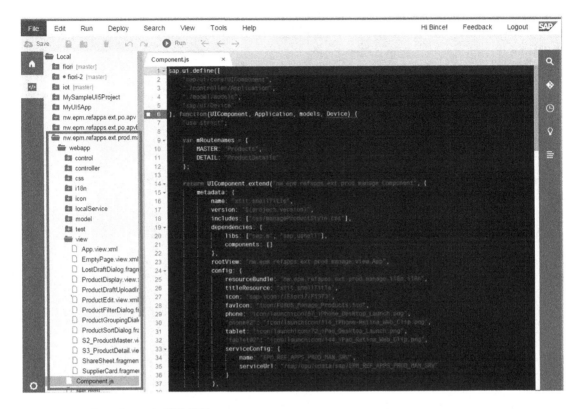

Figure 6-70. *Sample app in Web IDE*

Using Quick Start with the Layout Editor

Instead of creating a project from a template or sample, you can jump directly into app development using the Layout Editor in Web IDE. To create a Quick Start project, go to File ➤ New ➤ Quick Start With Layout Editor. A Quick Start app is immediately created and opens in the Layout Editor (see Figure 6-71).

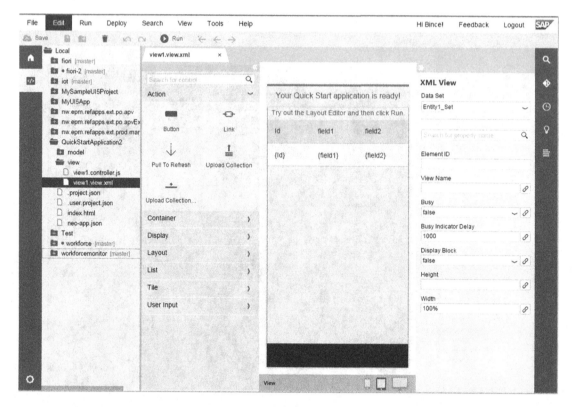

Figure 6-71. *Quick Start app in the Layout Editor in Web IDE*

In the next chapter, you learn about SAP Smart Business and how to create a project on the Internet of Things using a Raspberry Pi connected to a UI5 app.

■ ■ ■

CHAPTER 7

Introduction to HANA Smart Business and the Internet of Things

HANA Smart Business apps give users the option to analyze and evaluate strategic or operational key performance indicators (KPIs) in real time and help users make the right decisions based on the data. Because SAP HANA is designed to process real-time data, it can be used in the Internet of Things. SAP HANA Cloud Platform provides the necessary tools to use this feature. The Internet of Things is the next big step toward connected devices via the Internet. This chapter shows you how to build your own UI5 application and connect it to different sensors using a Raspberry Pi, with SAP HANA as the channel between UI5 and the sensors.

Analytical and Fact Sheet Applications Overview

In addition to Fiori transactional apps, which primarily deal with task-based activities like changing, creating, or approving a set of processes, there are Fiori fact sheets and analytical apps. These apps require a HANA back-end DB to run:

- *Fact sheets*: Used to search and explore essential information, such as viewing details about an object and navigating between similar objects.

- *Analytical apps*: Help you to visualize a complex scenario by processing a huge amount of data in a short time for tracking or monitoring purposes. For example, you can see the purchase history of a certain commodity over the last ten years as a chart by processing the data in a few seconds. Analyzing such an immense volume of data helps you monitor the purchase pattern and make decisions based on the data.

Smart Business Apps Overview

Smart Business apps show real-time information such as charts and analytics. These apps are represented by a set of KPI tiles (for of HANA Smart Business installation details, see http://help.sap.de/ssb). Although it may look similar to a dynamic tile, a KPI tile can show much more than just a number. KPI tiles can show micro-charts and other real-time data, as shown in Figure 7-1.

Electronic supplementary material The online version of this chapter (doi:10.1007/978-1-4842-1335-3_7) contains supplementary material, which is available to authorized users.

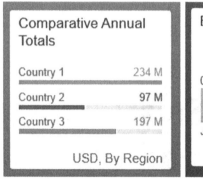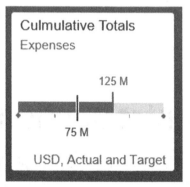

Figure 7-1. KPI tiles

These tiles process gigabytes of data every second and give you a summary. You can drill down to see more information, just like clicking any other Fiori tile. For example, suppose you are looking at a KPI tile that shows an expense report in real time, and suddenly the expense begins to increase and turns red. You feel something is not right, and you want to investigate further. This is where drilldown views come into play. These views let you analyze critical KPIs in real time, as shown in Figure 7-2.

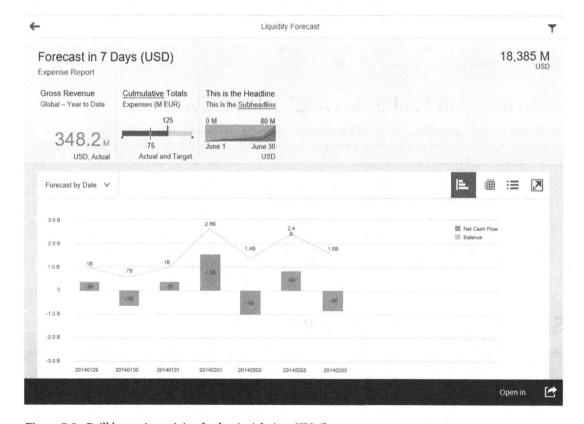

Figure 7-2. Drilldown views giving further insight into KPI tiles

KPI Modeler Overview

Although prebuilt Smart Business apps are available, you may want to make custom apps to meet your business requirements. You cannot build KPI tiles with the usual Fiori launchpad designer; to create Smart Business apps, you need to use the KPI Modeler. The KPI Modeler is a set of eight apps that helps you create KPI tiles (for configuration information, see http://help.sap.com/fiori_bs2013/helpdata/en/d1/c44b527fb7077de10000000a445394/content.htm). You can see the KPI Modeler tools in Figure 7-3. They are as follows:

- *Create KPI*: Creates KPI or OPI definitions

- *Create Evaluation*: Defines filters and targets

- *Configure KPI Drill-Down*: Creates further drilldown views for KPI tiles by defining charts or tables

- *Configure KPI Tiles*: Configures the controls needed to visualize KPI tiles, such as using micro-charts or comparison charts to represent information

- *Manage KPI Authorizations*: Grants access rights for KPIs and KPI evaluations

- *Manage KPI Associations*: Sets associations for managing KPI relationships

- *KPI Workspace*: Shows KPIs and evaluations

- *Migration Tool*: Migrates existing KPIs to the new data model

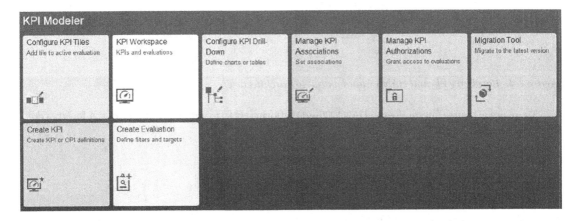

Figure 7-3. *KPI Modeler tiles*

Internet of Things

SAP HANA Cloud Platform has native support for the Internet of Things, so let's look at how you can use it. The Internet of Things is perhaps the most talked about tech in the connected world. It simply means communicating with devices over the Internet: for example, reading measurements such as temperature, humidity, water pressure, and so on from a fleet of sensors over the Internet; or automating your home and connecting devices like your garage door, bedroom lamps, water sprinklers in the garden, and the smoke detector. These smart devices can receive data over the Internet and send data to your smartphone or computer in any part of the world.

In the world of SAP, this concept of connected devices can be used for scenarios like real-time tracking of a customer's shipping freighter, monitoring the temperature of high-value items, tracking the gas pressure in an oil rig, monitoring the RPM of heavy machinery in a plant, and so on. Today, whoever has the latest real-time data has the upper hand in the market.

Anyone can make their own Internet of Things–based devices, thanks to affordable miniature PCs designed to communicate with digital and analog sensors. Two of the leading and most widely used such miniature PCs are the Raspberry Pi and BeagleBone Black. There are other cost-effective alternatives, such as the ESP8266 WiFi module with a programmable 32-bit microcontroller on board, but setting up this dongle to meet your requirements is more complicated than going with a Raspberry Pi (there is a lot of wiring and programming involved). The examples in this chapter use a Raspberry Pi. Your aim is to switch on an LED light from a smartphone and get the room temperature from a digital thermometer connected to the Raspberry Pi.

To send and receive data between a smartphone and the Raspberry Pi device over the Internet, you need a mediator in the cloud that can store and send data between the smartphone and the device. This example uses an SAP UI5 app as the mobile app so it will work on any device. The cloud mediator is the excellent SAP HANA Cloud Platform, which has a service dedicated to the Internet of Things (IoT). The architecture diagram in Figure 7-4 shows my vision of achieving this scenario.

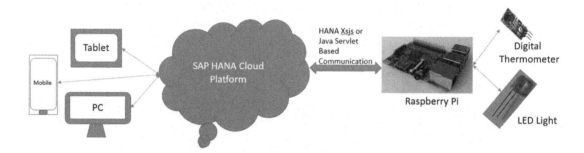

Figure 7-4. *Raspberry Pi- and HANA Cloud-based IoT architecture*

There are of course alternatives to HANA Cloud Platform (HCP) to connect your devices. A few that are worthy of mentions are as follows:

- Parse: www.parse.com

- Firebase: www.firebase.com

- PubNub: www.pubnub.com

- Scaledrone: www.scaledrone.com

- Pusher: www.pusher.com

- ThingSpeak: https://thingspeak.com

To get an idea of the ever-growing list of IoT-based devices on the market, check out http://iotlist.co.

UI5 Apps with SAP HANA and Raspberry Pi

Before starting the tutorial, this section presents a summary of what a Raspberry Pi device is. The latest model, Raspberry Pi 2, is a credit-card-sized PC with 1GB RAM, a 900MHz processor, four USB ports, one HDMI out, and an Ethernet port. It can run multiple operating systems from Linux to Windows 10 (not full-fledged Windows 10—Microsoft custom-developed a version for the Raspberry Pi).

When I started testing with HCP, I used an XSJS service to send and receive data between my UI5 app and the Raspberry Pi device. It worked fine, because the UI5 app was hosted on HCP. But problems began when I tried to consume the XSJS service from my Raspberry Pi. The reason was that I was using a HANA Cloud Platform trial, and SAP redirects incoming XSJS service requests after authenticating; when I tried to get the response in my Raspberry Pi Python app, it received the SAML 2.0 authentication key. This is a known issue with the HCP trial in the SCN community. If you have a fully licensed version of HCP, you will not face this issue. Because most readers of this book will have access to an HCP trial account rather than an on-premises or fully licensed cloud edition, I had to figure out an alternative.

After some digging around in `http://help.hana.ondemand.com`, I found an option to deploy a Java app with a persistence storage option. I downloaded some tutorials from the HANA help website (`https://help.hana.ondemand.com/help/frameset.htm?e4c52854bb571014aeb88753d0dad158.html`) and modified the sample Java App to meet my custom requirements.

I used the following components for this project:

- Raspberry Pi 2 (see Figure 7-5); older models should also work fine.

Figure 7-5. *Raspberry Pi 2*

- 16GB microSD card. The Raspberry Pi doesn't come with internal memory, so you have to buy a card.

- Digital thermometer (DS18B20; see Figure 7-6). The Raspberry Pi doesn't have an analog input, so you have to use digital sensors. Otherwise you have to buy an analog-to-digital convertor chip.

Figure 7-6. DS18B20 digital thermometer

- LED lights, a breadboard, and a basic wiring kit. I used the Sunfounder Project Super Kit for Raspberry Pi (see Figure 7-7).

Figure 7-7. Sunfounder Project Super Kit for Raspberry Pi

- Case for the Raspberry Pi (optional; see Figure 7-8).

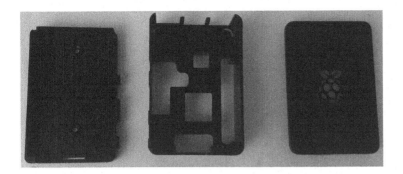

Figure 7-8. *Custom case for the Raspberry Pi*

- HANA Cloud Platform trial account. You can create a new HANA trial account at `https://account.hanatrial.ondemand.com`.

Now that know what hardware and software you need to develop your own IoT project, let's look at the steps involved:

1. Set up the Raspberry Pi.

2. Connect sensors to the Raspberry Pi.

3. Deploy the Java Persistence API in HANA Cloud Platform.

4. Write Python scripts to pass data from the Raspberry Pi to HANA Cloud.

5. Create a Fiori front end for IoT.

Setting Up the Raspberry Pi

Setting up the Raspberry Pi is a fairly simple task. The Raspberry Pi doesn't comes with a preinstalled operating system, so you need to install the OS first.

My choice of OS for the Raspberry Pi is Raspbian. It is the most commonly used OS for the Raspberry. And because it's Linux based, it has more open source community support. Although Microsoft's Windows 10 flavor for the Raspberry Pi is also available, it is a newcomer to the IoT, and open source community support for it is not large at the moment.

You can download and install the Raspbian OS from `https://www.raspbian.org/RaspbianImages`, but the recommended method is to install it via NOOBS. NOOBS is an installer with Raspbian built in; it's much easier to install Raspbian with NOOBS than to install it yourself. You can download NOOBS from `https://www.raspberrypi.org/downloads`. Detailed steps for installing the Raspbian OS via NOOBS is available at `https://www.raspberrypi.org/documentation/installation/noobs.md`.

I connect my Raspberry Pi directly to a monitor via its HDMI port. There are other ways to connect to the Raspberry Pi via apps like PuTTY, but I prefer to boot into the Raspbian GUI. Figure 7-9 shows the Raspbian home screen.

Figure 7-9. Raspberry Pi Raspbian OS

Once you have logged in to Raspbian, you need to install the following libraries in Python. (One advantage of Raspbian is that is comes preloaded with Python 2.7 and Python 3.0, so you don't have to set up Python from scratch.)

pip

To install pip, go to `https://pip.pypa.io/en/stable/installing.html` and download the `get-pip.py` file. Open the terminal window in Raspbian (similar to `cmd` in Windows), and navigate to the downloaded `get-pip.py` folder via `sudo python get-pip.py` (see Figure 7-10).

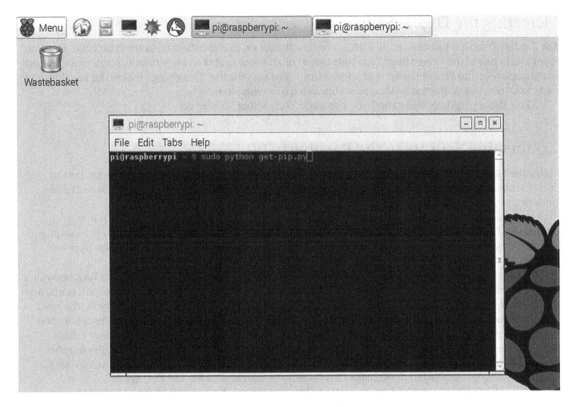

Figure 7-10. Installing pip for Python

Requests Library

After pip is installed, you can install any Python plug-in without downloading the Python file manually from the website. To install Requests, type `sudo pip install requests` in the terminal.

Parse

Type `sudo pip install` parse in the terminal.

Requests

Type `sudo pip install` requests in terminal.

W1ThermSensor

This is an open source library for reading digital thermometers. Type `sudo pip install w1thermsensor` in the terminal.

Detecting the Digital Sensor

For the digital sensor, you need to do a little more configuration to make the Raspberry Pi detect it. First you need to edit one of the system files. Type `sudo nano /boot/config.txt` in the terminal, scroll to the bottom of the page, and add `dtoverlay=w1-gpio`. Press Ctrl + X to save the file. This change makes the Raspberry Pi detect any new digital thermometer sensor connected to it when it restarts.

Once these plug-ins are installed, you can begin connecting the sensors.

Connecting Sensors to the Raspberry Pi

To connect sensors to the Raspberry Pi, you need to be familiar with some basics of electronics. It's not rocket science, though it may seem that way at the beginning; you just need some patience to read and understand the wiring concepts.

You can solder the sensors onto a board with the required wirings, but I prefer the much less complicated approach of using a breadboard. Figure 7-11 shows the layout of a breadboard. You can align your sensors on the breadboard with zero soldering and get the system up and running in less than ten minutes.

Before connecting sensors to the Raspberry Pi, you need an introduction to its pins. The Raspberry Pi has a set of digital input and output pins, generally referred to as GPIO (general pin input output) ports. Any digital sensors connected to these pins can be read into a program running on the Raspberry Pi (the most commonly used programs are Python and Java). You can get the readings from the digital sensors or send commands to a digital device connected to any of these ports (for example, you can send a 0 or 1 digital signal to one of the pins and switch on an LED light or a fan, and so on.). Each pin has a unique number assigned to it. The Raspberry Pi has a total of 40 pins, including the GPIO pins as well as a few 3.3V and 5V pins for powering small digital devices like LED displays, small DC motors, and LED lights.

When you access the GPIO pins via programs like Python, you have multiple choices of third-party plug-ins that give you direct access without much coding. One commonly used plug-in is RPi. Generally, there is a difference between the pin number on the Raspberry Pi and the name of the GPIO port. For example, the 11th pin on the Raspberry Pi (the 11th pin from the top of the Raspberry Pi, where the top is the side closest to the display port for connecting LCD devices; see Figure 7-8) has the GPIO name GPIO17. With the help of plug-ins like RPi, you can use pin number 11 in the code, which matches the actual port number.

■ **Note** For a detailed reference to the GPIO ports, see `www.element14.com/community/docs/DOC-73950/1/raspberry-pi-2-model-b-gpio-40-pin-block-pinout`.

You can see the GPIO wiring layout chart in Figure 7-11.

NAME	PINs On Raspberry Pi		NAME
3.3v DC Power	1	2	5v DC Power
GPIO02	3	4	5v DC Power
GPIO03	5	6	Ground
GPIO04	7	8	GPIO14
Ground	9	10	GPIO15
GPIO17	11	12	GPIO18
GPIO27	13	14	Ground
GPIO22	15	16	GPIO23
3.3v DC Power	17	18	GPIO24
GPIO10	19	20	Ground
GPIO09	21	22	GPIO25
GPIO11	23	24	GPIO08
Ground	25	26	GPIO07
ID_SD	27	28	ID_SC
GPIO05	29	30	Ground
GPIO06	31	32	GPIO12
GPIO13	33	34	Ground
GPIO19	35	36	GPIO16
GPIO26	37	38	GPIO20
Ground	39	40	GPIO21

Figure 7-11. *GPIO layout for the Raspberry Pi*

Now, let's start connecting the sensors and the LED:

1.   First let's connect the LED. I am using a different color of wire for each pin (see Table 7-1). Figure 7-12 shows the wires from the LED to the Raspberry Pi.

Table 7-1. *Wire Color Connected to Each Pin*

Wire Color	PIN Number
Red	11
Brown	17 (3.3V power)

Figure 7-12. *Connecting wires to the Raspberry Pi GPIO pins*

2. Connect the other end of the wires to the LED. Instead of soldering the wires and the resistor required to connect to the LED, use a breadboard to connect the wires to the LED and a 220-ohm resistor (you can check the resistor's ohms by checking its color code at https://physics.ucsd.edu/neurophysics/courses/ physics_120/resistorcharts.pdf). A breadboard is a solderless board you can use to connect the ends of wires and other electronic devices via a series of underlying vertical and horizontal wires. In Figure 7-13, you can see that the underlying wires on either side of the breadboard are marked with + and - at the top and are vertically connected; the middle section of the breadboard is horizontally connected.

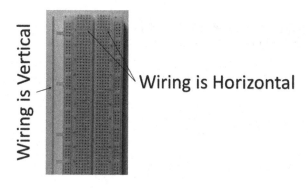

Figure 7-13. *Breadboard generic wiring layout*

3. Place the LED on the middle portion of the breadboard. Connect the red wire (the wire connected to pin 11 on the Raspberry Pi) to the short side of the LED pin (one leg of the LED is shorter than the other), and connect the brown wire to one side of the breadboard marked with a + sign (you can connect to any hole on that row vertically). Now connect one end of the 220-ohm resistor to any one of the holes in the vertical row on the same side where you plugged the brown wire. Connect the other end of the resistor to the longer leg of the LED in the horizontal row. See Figure 7-14.

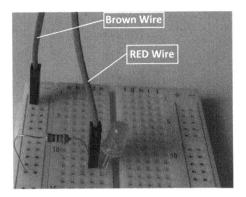

Figure 7-14. *Breadboard wiring for the LED*

Figure 7-15 shows the layout for the LED connection on the breadboard.

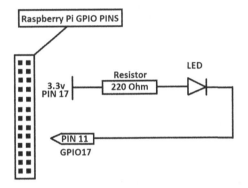

Figure 7-15. *LED connection layout*

4. Similarly, you need to connect your digital temperature sensor (DS18B20). I wired it to the Raspberry Pi with colored wires, as shown in Table 7-2. Connect the wires to the Raspberry Pi pins.

Table 7-2. *Digital Sensor Wire Colors*

Wire Color	pin Number
Purple	1 (3.3V DC power port)
Grey	7 (GPIO04)
Blue	6 (ground)

5. The advantage of this particular version of DS18B20 is that it can be directly connected to the Raspberry Pi without using a breadboard as a mediator. Connect the other end of the wires to the three pins of the digital thermometer. Connect the purple wire to the + pin, the grey wire to the middle pin (the data pin), and the blue wire to the - pin. See Figure 7-16.

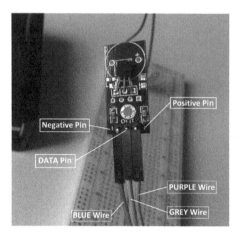

Figure 7-16. *DS18B20 wiring layout*

Once you have made all the connections, reboot your Raspberry Pi so that it will detect the connected digital thermometer.

Deploying the Java Persistence API in HANA Cloud Platform

To deploy the Java Persistence API in the cloud, you need to develop the app using Eclipse and then directly publish it into HCP from Eclipse.

Installing the HANA Cloud Platform SDK

To develop the Java Persistence API, download the SAP HANA Cloud Platform SDK (Java web version) from the HANA Cloud support page at `https://tools.hana.ondemand.com/#cloud` and extract the file. You will need the extracted file later to add Server Runtime in Eclipse.

In addition, you need to add a few plug-ins to Eclipse Luna. To do so, go to Help ➤ Install New Software, and enter the URL `https://tools.hana.ondemand.com/luna` in the wizard (see Figure 7-17). Select the following check boxes:

- SAP HANA Cloud Integration Tools

- SAP HANA Cloud Platform Tools

- SAP HANA Tools

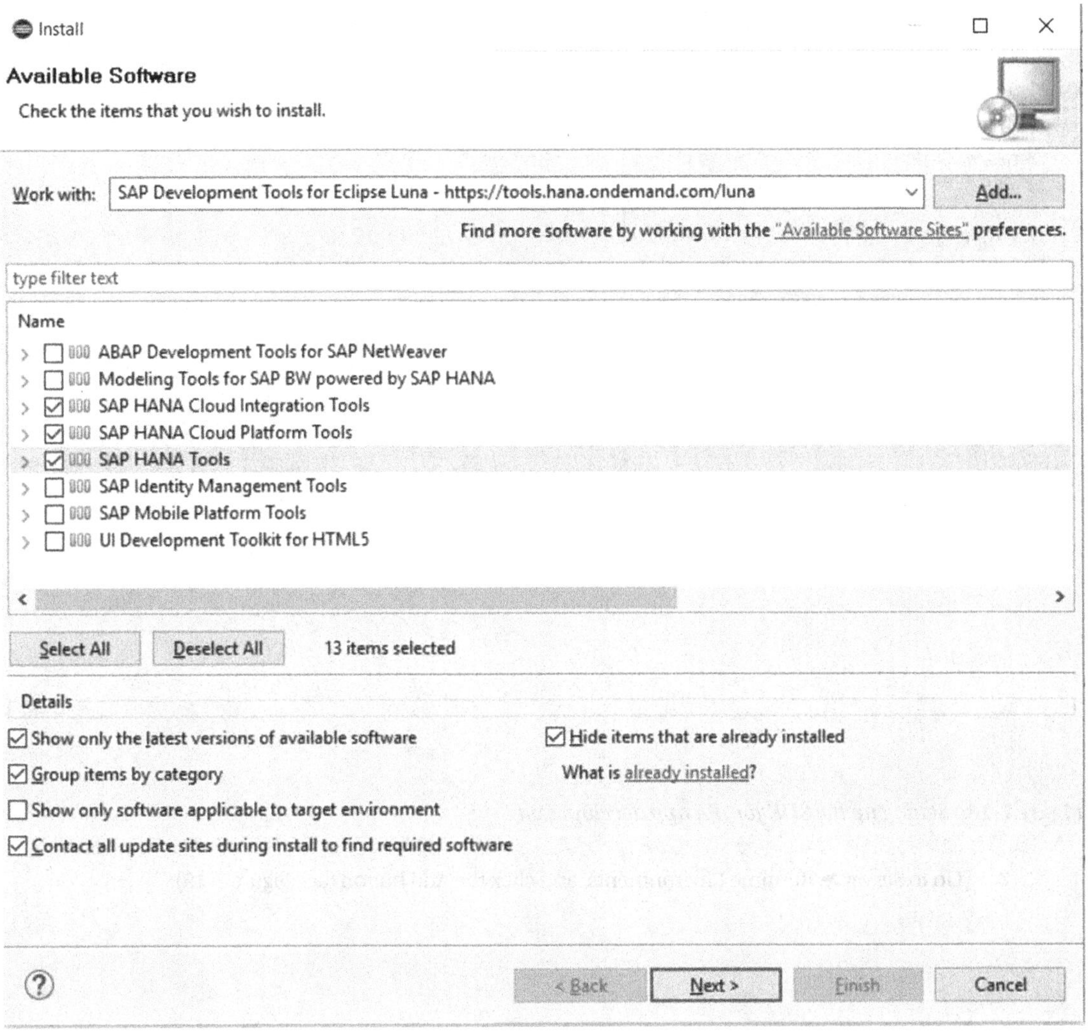

Figure 7-17. Install the required HANA tools

When the installation is finished, download the MyIot zip file from the Apress website and import the project into Eclipse. This example does not go into the basics of developing a Java Persistence API program; instead, I have built the app, and you need to modify parts of the project to make it work with your HANA trial account. (To learn about using the Java Persistence API from scratch, see http://hcp.sap.com/developers/TutorialCatalog/jav100_01_java_setup_eclipse.html.)

Once you have installed the required plug-ins, it's time to set up the SDK as a Runtime environment:

1. Go to Window ➤ Preferences in Eclipse (see Figure 7-18).

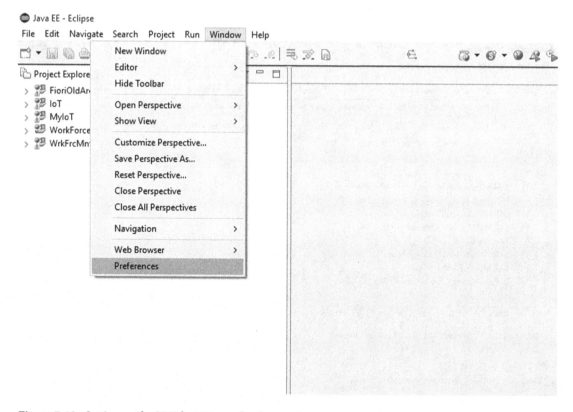

Figure 7-18. *Setting up the SDK for JPA app development*

    2.   Go to Server ➤ Runtime Environments, and click the Add button (see Figure 7-19).

Figure 7-19. *Adding Runtime environments*

3. In the New Server Runtime Environment window, expand the SAP tree, select Java Web, and click Next (see Figure 7-20).

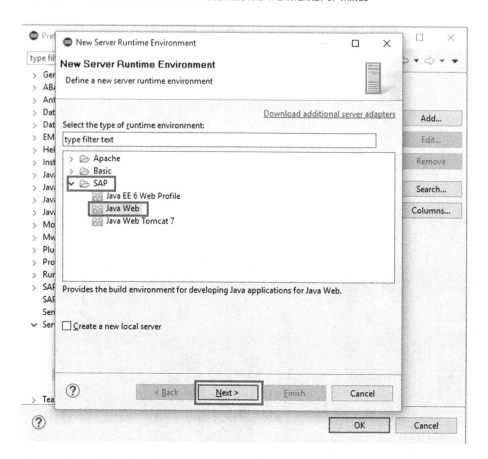

Figure 7-20. *Add the Java web server*

4. On the next screen, click Browse, and select the neo-java-web-sdk-1.86.27 folder where you downloaded the SAP HANA Cloud Platform SDK (https://tools.hana.ondemand.com/#cloud). Click Finish (see Figure 7-21).

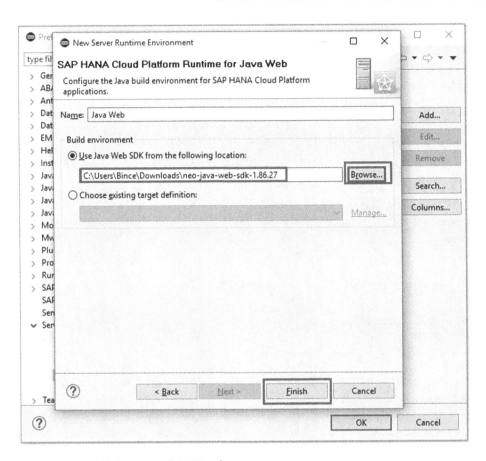

Figure 7-21. *Add the Java web SDK path*

Importing the Java App Source Code into Eclipse

You are all set to develop a Java Persistence app. If you are familiar with Java programming, you can refer to the sample app for the Java Persistence API on the SAP HANA help page `https://help.hana.ondemand.com/help/frameset.htm?e4c52854bb571014aeb88753d0dad158.html` and make the modifications I have made to the app manually. If you are from an ABAP or HTML5 background, you can download the modified version of the project, named `MyIoT_Java_App`, from the Apress website. Go to File ➤ Import in Eclipse, and select General ➤ Existing Projects into Workspace (see Figure 7-22).

Figure 7-22. *Import the sample project into Eclipse*

> 5. On the next screen, browse to the path of the project file you downloaded from the Apress website, select the Copy Projects Into Workspace check box, and click Finish (see Figure 7-23).

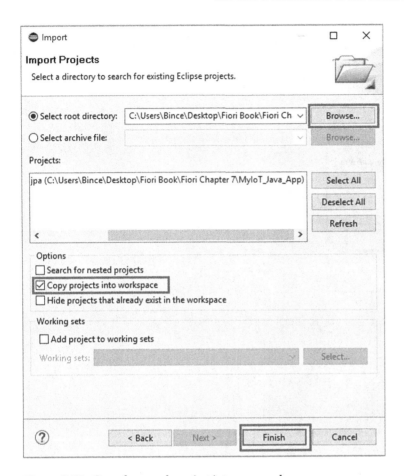

Figure 7-23. *Copy the sample project into your workspace*

6. After the project is imported, navigate to the project folder in the project explorer pane at left in Eclipse. In the project, navigate to Java Resources ➤ src ➤ com. sap.cloud.sample.persistence. Here you can see two files (see Figure 7-24): PersistenceWithJPAServlet.java and Raspberry.java.

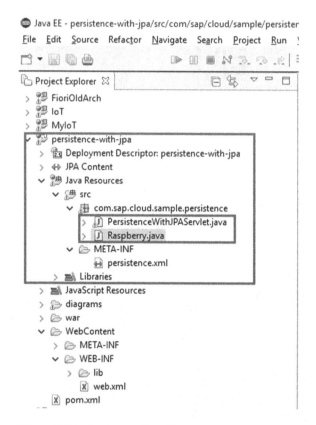

Figure 7-24. Persistence Java files

These two files act as a web server when deployed into the HANA Cloud. `PersistenceWithJPAServlet.java` acts as the server, and `Raspberry.java` contains the structure of the database table in which you will store the values from your sensors; and it also contains the JPA SQL queries required to fetch data from or post data to the database. Listing 7-1 shows the code snippet from `Raspberry.java` containing the database name and the JPA SQL queries for retrieving and saving data. If you want to further explore the JPA SQL queries, see `www.objectdb.com/java/jpa/query/jpql/structure`.

Listing 7-1. `Raspberry.java` Code Snippet

```
@Entity
@Table(name = "RaspberryTable") //The name of your Database Table
@NamedQueries({
@NamedQuery(name = "AllReadings", query = "select p from Raspberry p ORDER BY p.id DESC"),
//JPA SQL Queries
@NamedQuery(name = "SpecificReadings", query = "select p from Raspberry p where
p.raspberrydevice = :valueRaspberrydevice"),
@NamedQuery(name = "CurrentReading", query = "select p from Raspberry p where
p.raspberrydevice = :valueRaspberrydevice and p.id = (SELECT MAX(v.id) from Raspberry v
where v.raspberrydevice = :valueRaspberrydevice)")
})
```

Deploying a Java App to HANA Cloud

To deploy the app into HANA Cloud, you need to register for a HANA trial account. You can go to
https://account.hanatrial.ondemand.com and simply register for a new account. Once you have created
an account, you can deploy the app to HANA Cloud from Eclipse:

1. Right-click your project, and go to Run As ➤ Run on Server (see Figure 7-25).

Figure 7-25. *Deploy the app on the HANA Cloud*

2. On the next screen, select the SAP HANA Cloud Platform under the SAP tree, and enter the Landscape Host value **hanatrial.ondemand.com**. For Sever Name, enter a one letter word in lowercase; for some reason, the HANA Cloud trial platform is not accepting the default long name that appears in the field (This might be a bug in the server). Click Next (see Figure 7-26).

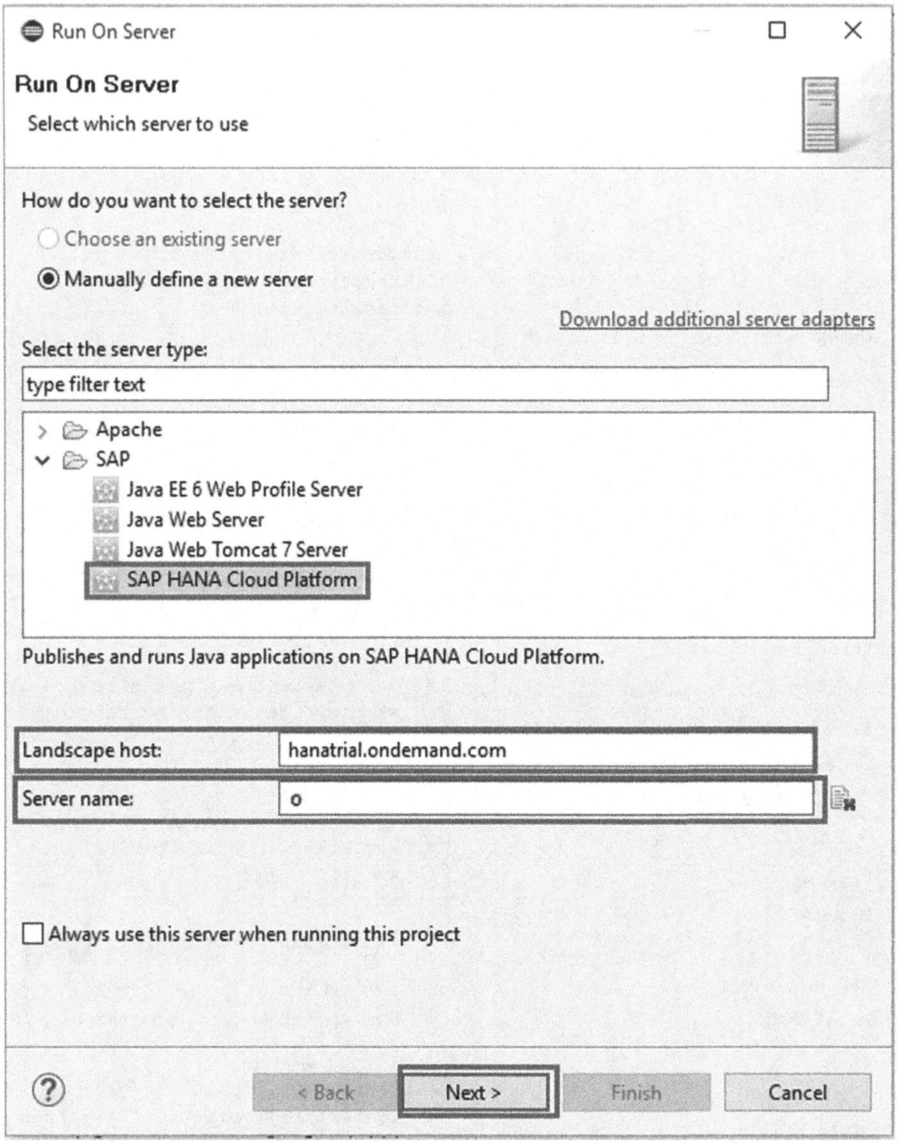

Figure 7-26. Select the HANA Cloud Platform for deployment

3. On the next screen, give the app a name; keep it short. In the Account Name field, enter your HANA trial account name (for example, the HANA trial account name p12345trial and the username p12345). After you enter the account name, a new blue hyperlink appears at the bottom. Click it; this is very important, because otherwise the wizard will try to reach hana.ondemand.com instead of hanatrial.ondemand.com. Fill in your username and password, and click finish (see Figure 7-27).

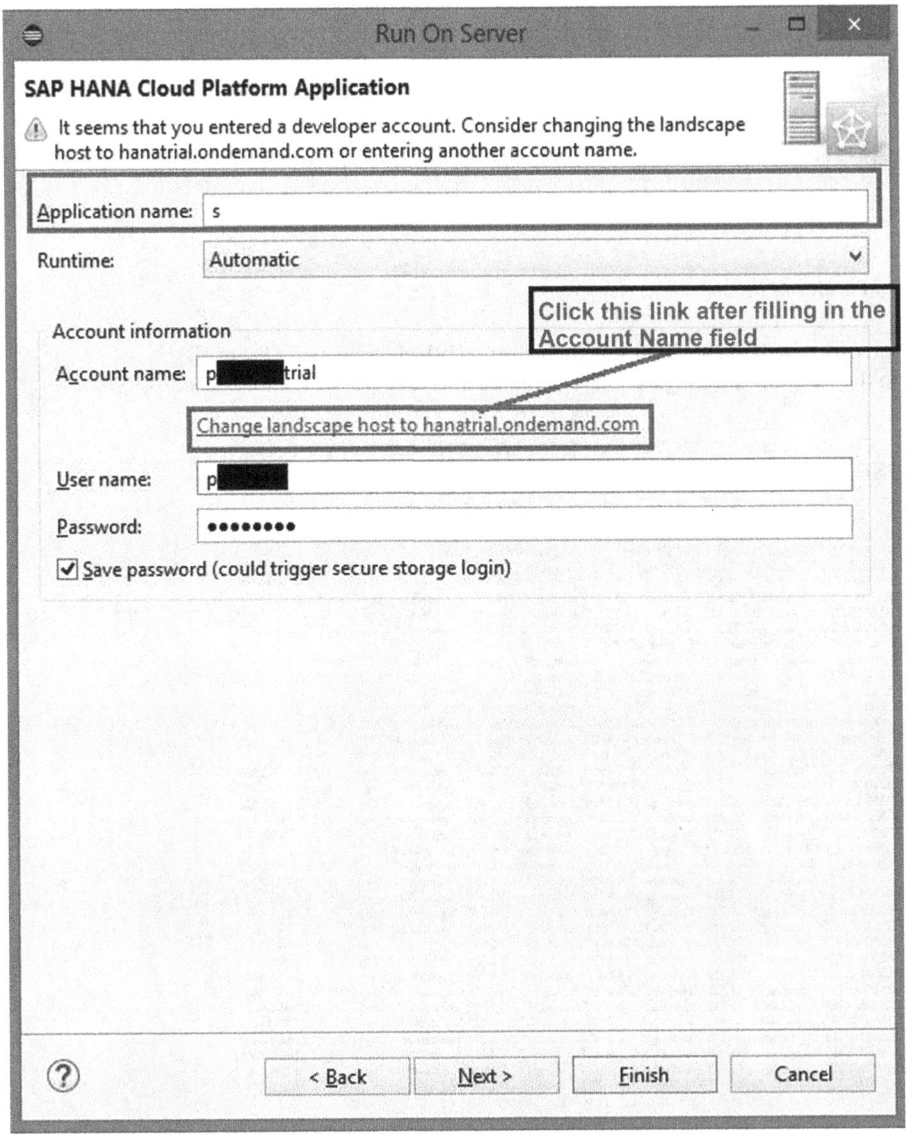

Figure 7-27. *Enter your HANA trial credentials to deploy the app in the cloud*

4. You can see the status of the server upload in the Servers tab at the bottom in Eclipse. When the upload is complete, right-click the server, and go to Application URL ➤ Open (see Figure 7-28).

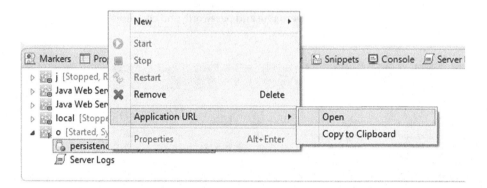

Figure 7-28. *Check the status of the server*

5. When you open the URL, you can see the Java app URL giving you the list of all values in the database (see Figure 7-29). I created a few records in the database.

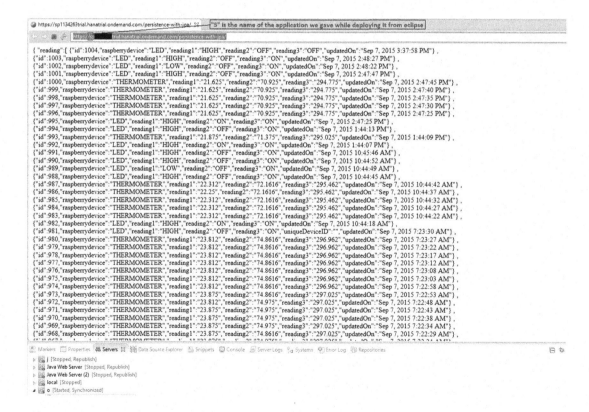

Figure 7-29. *The JPA app is up and running from the HANA server*

6. To see the app from your HANA Cloud Cockpit, log in to `https://accounts.sap.com/saml2/idp/sso/accounts.sap.com` with your HANA trial ID and go to Java Apps. There you see the list of Java apps running in HANA Cloud (see Figure 7-30). Click your app at right, and you get the same app URL that you got in the previous step. In this example, the URL is `https://s<yourhanatrialaccountname>.hanatrial.ondemand.com/persistence-with-jpa/`. If the URL starts with `s`, this is the app name you specified while deploying to the HANA Cloud from Eclipse.

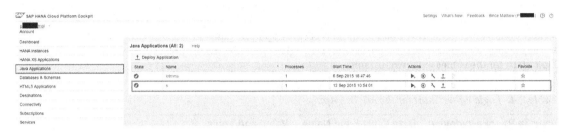

Figure 7-30. *Java apps running in HANA Cloud*

7. With the app up and running, there are few parameters you should be aware of in order to modify the app logic for your custom requirements. First, the app accepts a set of commands other than the standard OData CRUD methods. For example, I have modified the JPA app to use an HTML interface to manually create records instead of passing all the necessary fields in the URL (which is tedious). When you run the app for the first time, be sure to make at least one entry. To get the HTML interface for the JPA app, pass the URL like this:

    `https://s<yourhanatrialaccountname>.ondemand.com/persistence-with-jpa/?action=ShowUI`

    Be sure you replace *<yourhanatrialaccountname>* with your HANA trial account name. You see an interface like the one shown in Figure 7-31. On the web page, make entry shown in Table 7-3, and click Add Readings.

Raspberrydevice:LED	Reading1:HIGH	Reading2:OFF	Reading3:ON	UniqueDeviceID:	Add Readings

305 Entries in the Database

Id	Raspberrydevice	Reading1	Reading2	Reading3	UniqueDeviceID	UpdatedOn
1051	LED	HIGH	OFF	ON	null	2015-09-12 09:23.39.653
1004	LED	HIGH	OFF	OFF	null	2015-09-07 15:37:58.385
1003	LED	HIGH	OFF	ON	null	2015-09-07 14:48:27.824
1002	LED	LOW	OFF	ON	null	2015-09-07 14:48:22.197
1001	LED	HIGH	OFF	ON	null	2015-09-07 14:47:47.777
1000	THERMOMETER	21.625	70.925	294.775	null	2015-09-07 14:47:45.246
999	THERMOMETER	21.625	70.925	294.775	null	2015-09-07 14:47:40.39
998	THERMOMETER	21.625	70.925	294.775	null	2015-09-07 14:47:35.536
997	THERMOMETER	21.625	70.925	294.775	null	2015-09-07 14:47:30.711
996	THERMOMETER	21.625	70.925	294.775	null	2015-09-07 14:47:25.877
995	LED	HIGH	ON	ON	null	2015-09-07 14:47:25.498
994	LED	HIGH	OFF	ON	null	2015-09-07 13:44:13.837
993	THERMOMETER	21.875	71.375	295.025	null	2015-09-07 13:44:09.862
992	LED	HIGH	ON	ON	null	2015-09-07 13:44:07.621
991	LED	HIGH	OFF	ON	null	2015-09-07 10:45:46.011
990	LED	HIGH	OFF	ON	null	2015-09-07 10:44:52.715
989	LED	LOW	OFF	ON	null	2015-09-07 10:44:49.683
988	LED	HIGH	OFF	ON	null	2015-09-07 10:44:45.903
987	THERMOMETER	22.312	72.1616	295.462	null	2015-09-07 10:44:42.062

Figure 7-31. *JPA App URL with HTML interface*

Table 7-3. Make One Entry Each for the LED and the Thermometer

Raspberrydevice	Reading1	Reading2	Reading3
LED	HIGH	OFF	ON
THERMOMETER	0	0	0

Now let's look at the logic behind these values. The aim is to make an interface with a button to switch on the LED; in addition, you want to activate the thermometer only when you need to get a reading and then switch it off to prevent data overload on the server (the app posts data to HANA Cloud every second to make the app switch on the LED without any latency). You also switch off the Raspberry Pi from the UI5 app. The logic chart for the values is shown in Table 7-4.

Table 7-4. Logic Value Chart for the IoT UI5 App

Value in Raspberrydevice Field	Data Value Field Name	Value and Logic
LED	Reading1	HIGH: LED is switched off.
LED	Reading1	LOW: LED is switched on.
LED	Reading2	OFF/ON: This field is constantly monitored by the Thermometer Python app to know when it should start. When the value is ON, the thermometer starts posting values to the HANA Cloud DB. It keeps posting the temperature every second until a new record is created in the table with the value OFF.
LED	Reading3	ON/OFF: This value tells the Raspberry Pi to switch on or shut down.
THERMOMETER	Reading1	Temperature in Celsius.
THERMOMETER	Reading2	Temperature in Fahrenheit.
THERMOMETER	Reading3	Temperature in Kelvin.

With the Java app built, it's time to build the app that will run on the Raspberry Pi and communicate with your Java App running on the HANA server. Table 7-5 shows the features supported by the custom Java Persistence app. All the app features can be accessed via `https://s<yourhanatrialaccountname>.ondemand.com/persistence-with-jpa/?action=<feature>`. For example, to get the current latest entry in the database table based on the `Raspberrydevice` field, the URL is `https://s<yourhanatrialaccountname>.ondemand.com/persistence-with-jpa/?action==GetCurrentReading&Raspberrydevice=<device name>`. To get all the readings, use the URL `https://s<yourhanatrialaccountname>.ondemand.com/persistence-with-jpa/`; it returns all the records in the database.

Table 7-5. *Java Persistence App Feature List*

Feature	Description
ShowUI	HTML interface
GetCurrentReading&Raspberrydevice=*<device name>*	Gets the latest reading based on a key field
CreateReading&Raspberrydevice=*<device name>*&Reading1 =*<Value>*Reading2=*<value>*&Reading3=*<value>*	Creates a new record

Python Scripts for Passing Data from the Raspberry Pi to HANA Cloud

To communicate between the Raspberry Pi and HANA Cloud, I chose Python as the programming language instead of Java due to the sheer amount of open source community support and the number of open source plug-ins available for Python. You don't need to do much coding other than some simple if and else conditions due to the strong third-party open source plug-ins. All the plug-ins were described in the section "Connecting Sensors to the Raspberry Pi."

I wrote three Python scripts. Initially I put all the code in a single Python app, but that led to a lag in the app while listening to commands from the UI5 app (for example, the LED light took close to 1.5 seconds to switch on after I gave the command from the UI5 app). So, I wrote an app for each sensor to run separately:

- LED_Single.py

- DSb8120.py

- SystemPower.py

I used Pushbullet for Android (https://play.google.com/store/apps/details?id=com.pushbullet. android&hl=en) to use a Notify.sh file to push notifications directly to my Android device every time the Raspberry device shut down after receiving the shutdown command from the UI5 app. I used this link to configure Pushbullet with my Android device and the Raspberry Pi (see http://www.pratermade. com/2014/08/use-pushbullet-to-send-notifications-from-your-pi-to-your-phone). This is not a mandatory step; it's up to you to decide whether to use the Notify.sh file.

All the files, including the Python scripts and other sample projects mentioned in the book, can be downloaded from Apress website. Once you have downloaded the files, open the terminal of your Raspberry Pi, navigate to the path of the downloaded files, and type the following three commands in separate terminals:

```
sudo python LED_Single.py
sudo python DSb8120.py
sudo python SystemPower.py
```

SystemPower.py is configured to call the additional Notify.sh file, which is used to push a notification to your mobile device once it initiates its shutdown procedure. These apps continue to run in the background even if you close the window (see Figure 7-32).

Figure 7-32. *Start all the Python scripts from the Raspberry Pi*

Once you execute the scripts in the terminal, you can see them listening and broadcasting values to HANA Cloud, as shown in Figure 7-33. Check your Java app HTML interface to simulate commands for switching on the LED light or activating the thermometer.

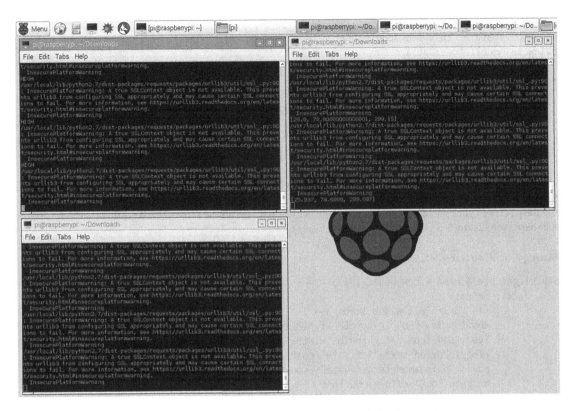

Figure 7-33. Sensors broadcasting and listening to signals from HANA Cloud

Your Raspberry Pi is now communicating with your Java app deployed in HANA Cloud. Next, you build the Fiori UI5 app to send commands to HANA Cloud.

Creating a Fiori Front End for IoT

In this section, you build the UI5 app for the IoT example. Download the `MyIoT` file from the Apress website, and import it into Eclipse. Let's look at the main parts of the logic used in the UI5 app to send data to and receive data from HANA Cloud.

IoT UI5 App Logic

The `Component.js` file of the UI5 app source code you downloaded binds the Java Persistence app service URL from HANA Cloud to the model of the UI5 app. Listing 7-2 shows the URL for the Java app bound to the root view.

Listing 7-2. `Component.js`

```
sap.ui.getCore().HANA = new Object();
sap.ui.getCore().HANA.URL = "https://<Your Hana Trial Account Name>.hanatrial.ondemand.com/
persistence-with-jpa";
var url = sap.ui.getCore().HANA.URL;
```

```
var oModel = new sap.ui.model.json.JSONModel();
var oModelData =  this.loadModel(url);
oView.setModel(oModelData);

loadModel: function(url) {
        var url = url;
      var oModel = new sap.ui.model.json.JSONModel();
      oModel.loadData(url, null, false);
      return oModel;
    }
```

Home.view.xml has the buttons required to switch on the LED and get temperature readings from the sensor. In the footer area of the page, you place buttons for powering on the Raspberry Pi, shutting down the Raspberry Pi, and navigating to the next page, which displays all the sensor readings in the HANA Cloud database (see Listing 7-3).

Listing 7-3. Home.view.xml

```
sap.ui.getCore().HANA = new Object();
        <l:content>
            <!-- Half/Full width items -->
            <Button id="LED" text="LED Light" type="Emphasized" press="onSwitch"
            icon="sap-icon://lightbulb" width="100%" height="100%"></Button>
            <ToggleButton text="Activate" enabled="true" pressed="false"
            press="onThermometerActivate" icon="sap-icon://measure" width="100%"
            height="100%"></ToggleButton>
            <ObjectListItem id="LEDSwitch"
                title="LED Light"
                intro="LED"
                icon="sap-icon://lightbulb"
                type="Active"
                press="onSwitch" >
            </ObjectListItem>
            <ObjectListItem id="Temperature"
                title=""
                intro="Thermometer"
                icon="sap-icon://temperature"
                number=""
                type="Active"
                press="onTherm" >
            </ObjectListItem>
        </l:content>
    </l:Grid>
    </content>
    <footer>
    <Bar>
    <contentRight>
        <Button text="Power On" icon="sap-icon://sys-monitor" type="Accept"
        press="onPowerOn"></Button>
```

```
<Button text="ALL Readings" type="Emphasized" press="onAllReadings"></Button>
<Button text="Shutdown" icon="sap-icon://log" type="Reject" press="onShutDown">
</Button>
</contentRight>
    </Bar>
</footer>
```

The controller of the Home view (Home.view.controller.js) has six methods (see Listing 7-4):

- onSwitch: Switches the LED on and off

- onPowerOn: Boots up the Raspberry Pi

- onShutdown: Sends a command to the Raspberry Pi to shut down

- onThermometerActivate: Sends a signal to the digital thermometer to start
  broadcasting temperature readings

- onTherm: Displays the current temperature reading on the screen

- onAllReadings: Navigates to the next view, which displays all the sensor readings in
  the HANA Cloud database

Listing 7-4. Home.view.controller.js

```
onSwitch: function(oEvent){
      var oBtn = this.getView().byId("LED");
      var statusModel = this.checkStatus(this.url + "/?action=GetCurrentReading&
      Raspberrydevice=LED");
      if(statusModel.oData["result"])
          {
      var LEDStat = statusModel.oData["result"].reading1;
      var oModel = new sap.ui.model.json.JSONModel();
      if (LEDStat ==="LOW"){
      var result1 = oModel.loadData(this.url +  "/?action=CreateReading&Raspberrydevice=
      LED&Reading1=HIGH&Reading2=OFF&Reading3=ON");
      var msg = 'Light Switched Off';
      sap.m.MessageToast.show(msg);
      }
      else if(LEDStat ==="HIGH"){
      var result1 = oModel.loadData(this.url + "/?action=CreateReading&Raspberrydevice=LED
      &Reading1=LOW&Reading2=OFF&Reading3=ON");
      var msg = 'Light Switched On';
      sap.m.MessageToast.show(msg);
      }
      else{
          var result1 = oModel.loadData( this.url + "/?action=CreateReading&Raspberry
          device=LED&Reading1=HIGH&Reading2=OFF&Reading3=ON");
          var msg = 'Light Switched Off';
          sap.m.MessageToast.show(msg);
      }
        }
}
```

```
onPowerOn: function(){
        var oModel = new sap.ui.model.json.JSONModel();
        var result1 = oModel.loadData(this.url + "/?action=CreateReading&Raspberrydevice=LED
        &Reading1=HIGH&Reading2=OFF&Reading3=ON");
        var msg = 'Raspberry Is Online';
        sap.m.MessageToast.show(msg);
    },

onShutDown: function(){
        var oModel = new sap.ui.model.json.JSONModel();
        var result1 = oModel.loadData(this.url + "/?action=CreateReading&Raspberrydevice=LED
        &Reading1=HIGH&Reading2=OFF&Reading3=OFF");
        var msg = 'Raspberry Shutting Down';
        sap.m.MessageToast.show(msg);
    },

checkStatus: function(url) {
        var url = url;
        var oModel = new sap.ui.model.json.JSONModel();
        oModel.loadData(url, null, false);
        return oModel;
    },

onThermometerActivate: function(oEvent){
        this.temp;
        var statusModel = this.checkStatus(this.url + "/?action=GetCurrentReading&Raspberry
        device=LED");
        var LEDStat = statusModel.oData["result"].reading1
        this.temp = statusModel.oData["result"].reading2
          if (this.temp === "ON"){
                var deactivateThermometer = this.checkStatus(this.url + "/?action=
                CreateReading&Raspberrydevice=LED&Reading1="+LEDStat +"&Reading2=OFF&
                Reading3=ON");
                oEvent.getSource().setPressed(false);
                var msg = 'Thermometer Deactivated';
                sap.m.MessageToast.show(msg);
        }
        else
            {
            var activateThermometer = this.checkStatus(this.url + "/?action=CreateReading&
            Raspberrydevice=LED&Reading1="+LEDStat +"&Reading2=ON&Reading3=ON");
            oEvent.getSource().setPressed(true);
            var msg = 'Thermometer Activated';
              sap.m.MessageToast.show(msg);
            }
    },

onTherm: function(oEvent){
        var statusModel = this.checkStatus(this.url +  "/?action=GetCurrentReading&Raspberry
        device=THERMOMETER");
        var Temperature = statusModel.oData["result"].reading1
```

```
        Temperature = Temperature + " Â°C "
        var oTemp= this.getView().byId("Temperature");
        oTemp.setNumber(Temperature);
    },
```

```
onAllReadings: function(oEvent){
        this.router.navTo("AllReadings");
    }
```

AllReadings.view.xml displays all the sensor readings from HANA Cloud as a List (see Listing 7-5). The total number of records shown at a time is limited to 20; it is a growing list so that it pulls more records as you scroll down. This improves performance on mobile devices because it loads more records only on demand.

Listing 7-5. AllReadings.view.xml

```
<List id="list" mode="{device>/listMode}" items="{/reading}" select="handleListSelect"
growing = "true" busyIndicatorDelay="400" growingThreshold="20">

<ObjectListItem icon="{path: 'raspberrydevice',formatter: 'com.iotApp.util.Formatter.
deviceIcon'}"
            number="{id}" numberUnit="{path: 'reading1',
                    formatter: 'com.iotApp.util.Formatter.deviceText'}"
            press="handleListItemPress" title="{raspberrydevice}" type="Active">

<attributes>
        <ObjectAttribute text="{path: 'reading2',formatter: 'com.iotApp.util.Formatter.
        deviceTextF'}"/>
        <ObjectAttribute text="{path: 'reading3',formatter: 'com.iotApp.util.Formatter.
        deviceTextK'}"/>
        <ObjectAttribute text="{uniqueDeviceID}"/>
        <ObjectAttribute text="{updatedOn}"/>
</attributes>
</ObjectListItem>
</List>
```

Now that you have gone through the logic used in the IoT app, you need to make a small change in the app before you execute it.

Running the Program

You need to replace the URL for the HANA Cloud Java app with your app URL. Open the Component.js file of the project, and edit the line with the app's default URL (https://<*Your HANA Trial Account Name*> .hanatrial.ondemand.com/persistence-with-jpa). See Figure 7-34.

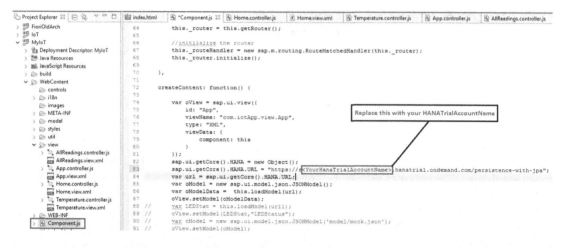

Figure 7-34. *Replace the URL with your HANA app UR.*

When the changes are made, you can run the app. Right-click the project, and go to Run As ➤ Web App Preview. You can see the output in Figure 7-35.

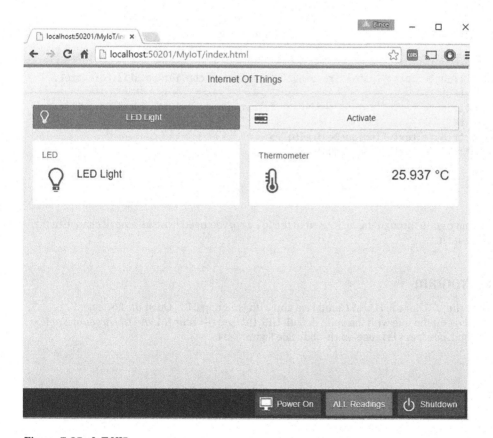

Figure 7-35. *IoT UI5 app*

Let's try to switch on the LED light and activate the thermometer. I converted the app into a native app using Cordova; you can try the same thing by referring to Chapter 9.

When you start the app, you see the last recorded temperature and the LED status. Click the LED icon to create a new entry in the HANA Cloud database, which is in turn monitored by the Raspberry Pi (see Figure 7-36).

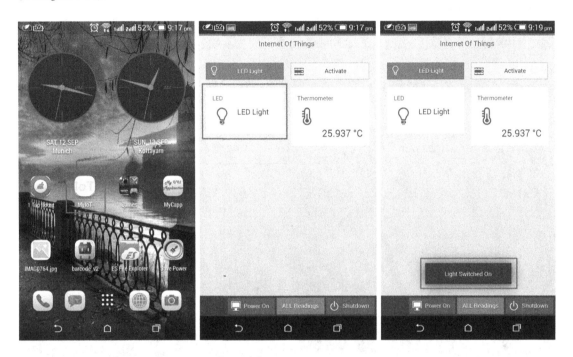

Figure 7-36. *Switching on the LED via the mobile app*

At the same time, you can also monitor the database records via the HTML interface of your Java app running on HANA Cloud. You can confirm whether it's the latest entry by checking the `UpdatedOn` timestamp field in the table. You also see the LED switch on (see Figure 7-37).

Id	Raspberrydevice	Reading1	Reading2	Reading3	UniqueDeviceID	UpdatedOn
1096	LED	LOW	OFF	ON	null	2015-09-12 19:19:47.078
1095	LED	HIGH	OFF	ON	null	2015-09-12 19:19:42.912
1094	LED	LOW	OFF	ON	null	2015-09-12 19:19:38.147
1093	LED	HIGH	OFF	ON	null	2015-09-12 19:18:56.25
1092	LED	HIGH	OFF	ON	null	2015-09-12 19:04:12.087
1091	LED	HIGH	ON	ON	null	2015-09-12 19:04:00.373
1090	LED	HIGH	OFF	ON	null	2015-09-12 19:03:54.0
1089	LED	LOW	OFF	ON	null	2015-09-12 19:03:44.453
1088	LED	HIGH	OFF	ON	null	2015-09-12 17:37:16.705
1087	LED	HIGH	ON	ON	null	2015-09-12 17:37:08.718

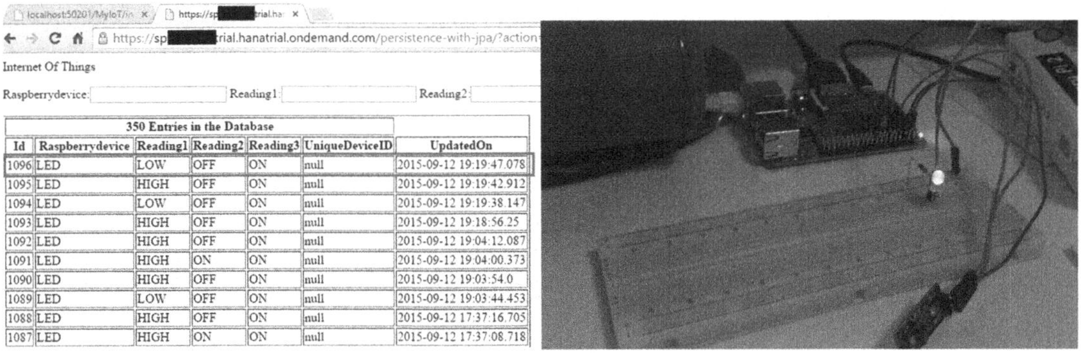

Figure 7-37. *A new record is created in HANA Cloud, and the LED switches on*

Now let's try activating the thermometer. Click the Activate Toggle button, and you see a toast message saying "Thermometer Activated". Click the Thermometer button to refresh the temperature. If the temperature is being updated to the server from the Raspberry Pi, you see the new temperature (see Figure 7-38). Click Activate Toggle again to deactivate the thermometer, to avoid too many records being created on the server. The Python app updates the value every second; you can modify the duration and set it to every hour or so if you wish.

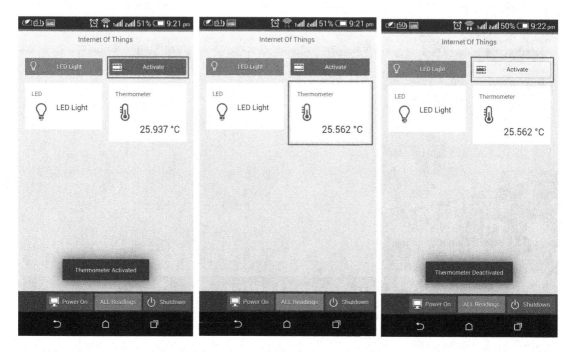

Figure 7-38. *Activating the digital thermometer*

You can double-check the data using the HTML interface of the Java app (see Figure 7-39).

Internet Of Things

Raspberrydevice: Reading1:   Reading2:

362 Entries in the Database						
Id	Raspberrydevice	Reading1	Reading2	Reading3	UniqueDeviceID	UpdatedOn
1108	LED	LOW	OFF	ON	null	2015-09-12 19:22:14.076
1107	THERMOMETER	25.562	78.0116	298.712	null	2015-09-12 19:22:13.641
1106	THERMOMETER	25.562	78.0116	298.712	null	2015-09-12 19:22:08.849
1105	THERMOMETER	25.562	78.0116	298.712	null	2015-09-12 19:22:04.015
1104	THERMOMETER	25.562	78.0116	298.712	null	2015-09-12 19:21:59.21
1103	THERMOMETER	25.562	78.0116	298.712	null	2015-09-12 19:21:54.424
1102	THERMOMETER	25.562	78.0116	298.712	null	2015-09-12 19:21:49.606
1101	THERMOMETER	25.562	78.0116	298.712	null	2015-09-12 19:21:44.81
1100	THERMOMETER	25.562	78.0116	298.712	null	2015-09-12 19:21:40.027
1099	THERMOMETER	25.562	78.125	298.712	null	2015-09-12 19:21:35.24
1098	THERMOMETER	25.562	78.0116	298.712	null	2015-09-12 19:21:30.445
1097	LED	LOW	ON	ON	null	2015-09-12 19:21:26.782
1096	LED	LOW	OFF	ON	null	2015-09-12 19:19:47.078

Figure 7-39. New temperature records created by the Raspberry Pi

You can also see all the records in the table in the app. Click the All Readings button, and you get a list view containing the latest 50 records from the database (see Figure 7-40).

Figure 7-40. *List of the latest 50 records in the HANA Cloud database*

Finally, let's try to shut down the Raspberry Pi device. Click the Shutdown button: you get a toast message saying "Raspberry Shutting Down"; and, if Pushbullet is configured for your mobile device, you get a push notification directly from the Raspberry Pi when the shutdown sequence is initiated (see Figure 7-41).

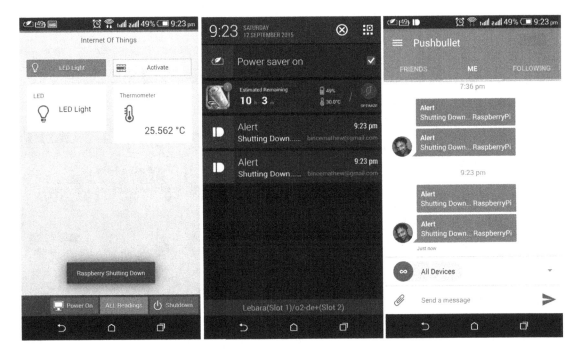

Figure 7-41. *Push notifications sent directly to mobile from the Raspberry Pi*

Now you have a full-fledged IoT-enabled device connected to the Internet. You can access these sensors from anywhere in the world. A much simpler solution to create an online database using HPC's IoT service is available, but it's very basic at the moment (a beta version as of the time of writing). I wanted to execute custom SQL queries and limit the maximum data from HANA Cloud to 50 records at any time due to performance constraints on mobile devices; and I needed an entity that gives me only the latest entry based on the device ID I send to the server. These custom features cannot be implemented on the beta version of the IoT subscription service in HANA Cloud. So I had to stick with the Java Persistence API for this example. You can access the IoT services from your HANA Cloud Cockpit (`https://account.hanatrial.ondemand.com/cockpit`) under Services (see Figure 7-42). For more information about the IoT service, see `https://help.hana.ondemand.com/iot/frameset.htm`.

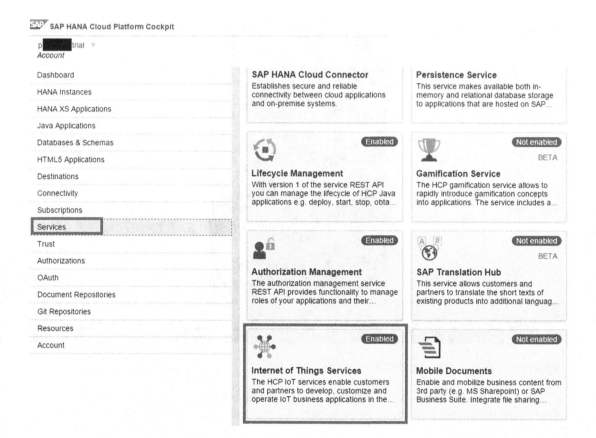

Figure 7-42. *Internet of Things services*

The next chapter discusses troubleshooting and debugging techniques commonly used in Fiori development.

CHAPTER 8

Debugging and Troubleshooting Fiori Applications

After developing a custom Fiori app or enhancing a standard Fiori app, you need to thoroughly test it. This chapter explains the debugging methods and troubleshooting techniques you can use with Fiori apps.

Supported Web Browsers

Because SAP Fiori is an HTML5 framework, older browser versions are not compatible with Fiori apps. Table 8-1 shows the compatibility of mobile OSs, different browsers, and Fiori client apps.

Table 8-1. *Fiori Browser Compatibility Chart for Mobile OSs*

OS	Versionn	Fiori Client	Apple Safari	Android Native Browser	BlackBerry Native Browser	Microsoft IE	Google Chrome
Apple IOS	7.x , 8.x,9.x	Yes	Yes	NA	NA	NA	NA
Android	4.1–5.x	Yes	NA	Yes	NA	NA	Yes
Windows Phone	8.1 GDR1 and above	Yes	NA	NA	NA	Yes, from 11.x	NA
BlackBerry	10.x	NA		NA	Yes, from 10.x	NA	NA

For desktop OSs, Table 8-2 shows the compatibility chart.

Table 8-2. *Fiori Browser Compatibility Chart for Desktop OSs*

OS	Type	Version	IE	Safari	Chrome	Firefox
Microsoft Windows	Desktop	7	9.x–11.x (IE 9 has compatibility issues with some Fiori apps, such as KPI tiles and Modeler tools)	NA	Yes (latest version)	Yes (latest version)
Apple Mac OS X	Desktop	10.9 and above	NA	Yes	NA	NA
Microsoft Windows	Touch + Desktop	8.0 and above	10.x–11.x	NA	Yes (latest version)	Yes (latest version)

© Bince Mathew 2015
B. Mathew, *Beginning SAP Fiori*, DOI 10.1007/978-1-4842-1335-3_8

Debugging Methods

Debugging is a way of finding out what went wrong with your code. It's the first thing to do when your app is not functioning the way you want it to. UI5 apps are based on HTML5, so you can debug the code using your browser's Developer Tools. You can put breakpoints in your JavaScript code via the browser.

Press the F12 key on your UI5 app output in the browser, and the debugger console opens as shown in Figure 8-1. The F12 shortcut is the same for every Fiori-supported browser. For Firefox, you have to download an additional plug-in called Firebug to see the app source code at runtime.

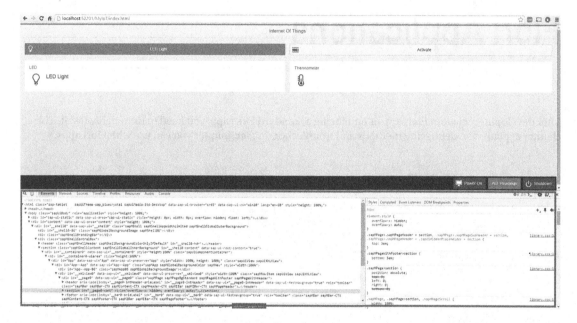

Figure 8-1. *Chrome browser Developer Tools*

The Developer Tools let you see the source code of your UI5 app and any errors or warnings that happen at runtime (see Figure 8-2).

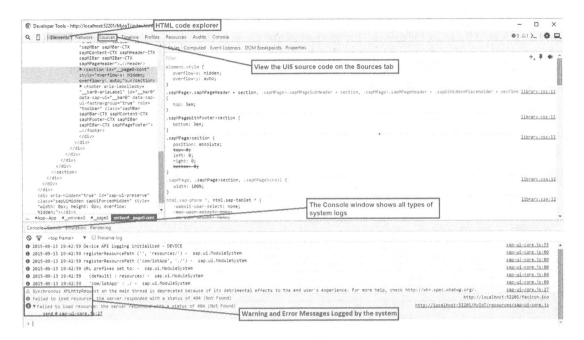

Figure 8-2. Source code and logs

You can view the UI5 app JavaScript source code on the Sources tab at upper left in the Developer Tools, as shown in Figure 8-3. You can put breakpoints directly in the source code: to do so, click to the left of the line where you want to put the breakpoint. A blue icon appears, indicating that the breakpoint is set.

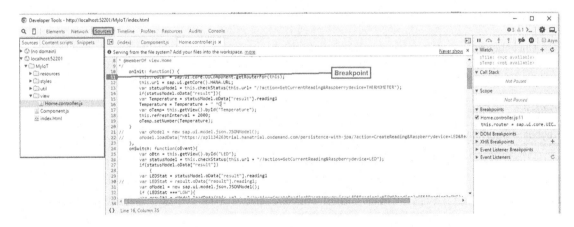

Figure 8-3. Setting a breakpoint in the browser

After you add the breakpoint, reload the UI5 app URL with the Developer Tools window open. The code will pause at the line where you set the breakpoint. You can view the value loaded into each variable at runtime either by adding the variables to the Watch window at upper right side in the debugger or by adding the variable name in the Console window (see Figure 8-4). Investigating the variable values can help you pinpoint exactly where your code has gone wrong.

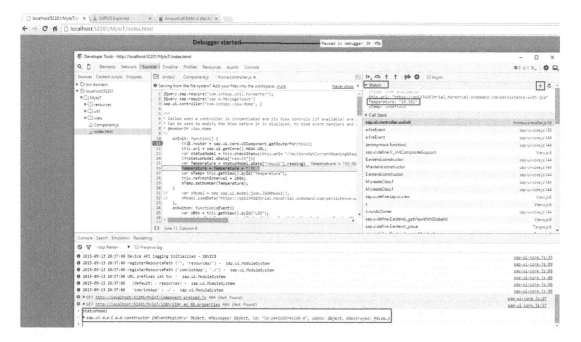

Figure 8-4. *Add variables to watch*

Once the code is in Debug mode, you can make the compiler execute the next line and push the code execution step by step or make the compiler step in and out of functions and loops. Table 8-3 lists the keyboard shortcuts for the debugger.

Table 8-3. *Debugger Keyboard Shortcuts*

Keyboard Shortcut	Description
F11	Step-by-step execution. Makes the compiler step into functions and loops.
F10	Step-by-step execution. The compiler steps over functions, rather than into them.
Shift + F11	Steps out of the current function. Can be used to step out of a function that you made the compiler step into.
F8	Resumes execution.

Debug Mode in UI5 Apps

If you try to debug any of the standard Fiori apps, in the Sources tab, the JavaScript code is a minimized version of the actual code (meaning it's not written in a developer-friendly way). The reason is that Fiori loads with a minimized, optimized version of the standard code by default, for the sake of faster loading and performance optimization. But this makes the code difficult for developers to debug and understand. Fortunately, Fiori has a Debug mode you can set by sending an additional parameter at the end of the standard app URL with the flag `sap-ui-debug=x`. Another copy of the source code is loaded with the extension `-dbg.js` (see Figure 8-5).

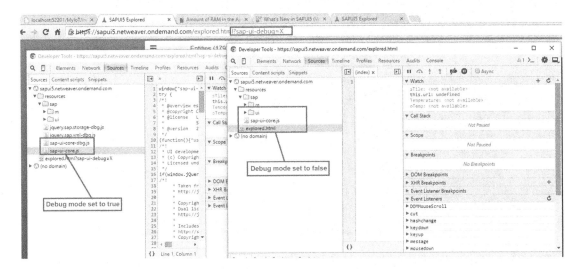

Figure 8-5. *Debug mode*

You can also manually check and set the debug flag in your UI5 app code, as shown as Listing 8-1.

Listing 8-1. Checking and Setting the Debug Flag

```
Var checkDebugStatus = jQuery.sap.debug();
if (checkDebugStatus === false)
{ jQuery.sap.debug(true); }
```

Another way to easily switch the debug flag is to use the keyboard shortcut Ctrl + Shift + Alt + P. When you do, a pop-up window opens with multiple options in addition to enabling the debug flag. You see information about the SAPUI5 version; you can examine the various UIAreas, controls, and properties of the app; you can enable the log viewer; and so on (see Figure 8-6).

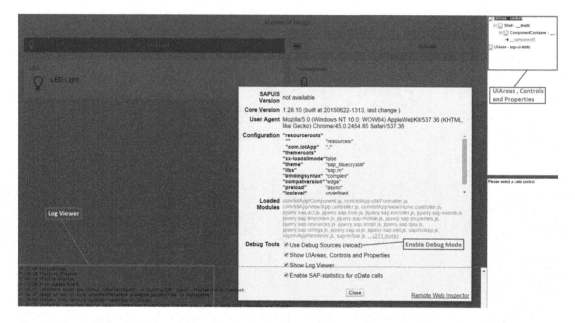

Figure 8-6. *Enabling the debug flag using a keyboard shortcut*

Logging and Network Tracing

You can use your UI5 app to set logs that let you know a certain piece of functionality has successfully completed, which can help with debugging (see Figure 8-7).

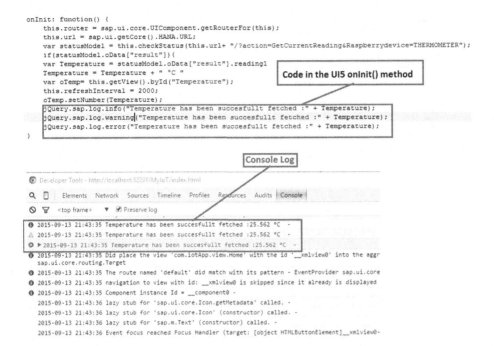

Figure 8-7. Different types of logs for an SAPUI5 app

You can push logs to the console using the code snippet in Listing 8-2.

Listing 8-2. Creating Logs

```
jQuery.sap.log.info("Your custom log message);
jQuery.sap.log.warning("Your custom log message);
jQuery.sap.log.error("Your custom log message);
```

To trace a network (OData calls), you can check the Network tabs of the browser Developer Tools. It shows the status of a network call, whether it was successful, the request header, the response message and so on (see Figure 8-8).

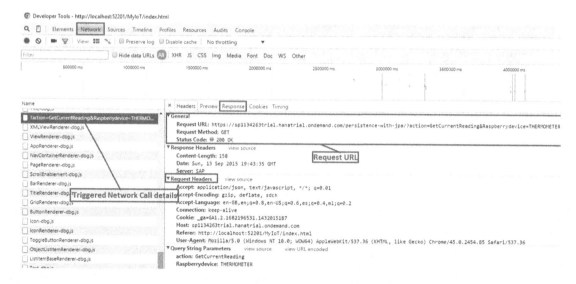

Figure 8-8. *Network trace in the browser debugger*

Diagnostics

SAPUI5 has a Diagnostics tool for both desktop and mobile browsers. To enable desktop browser diagnostics, use the keyboard shortcut Ctrl + Alt + Shift + S (see Figure 8-9). The Diagnostics tool helps you toggle Debug mode, trace the JavaScript code, and view the control tree (which contains details of all the controls used in the view you are in). It also has a feature that gets an XML version of the code if the view is written in JavaScript instead of XML; click the root control on the Control Tree tab, and then click the Export button to get the XML code.

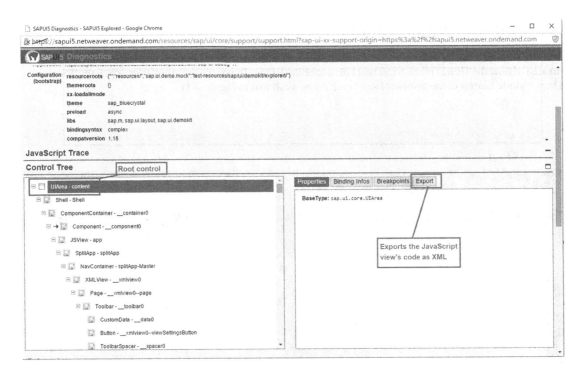

Figure 8-9. *Diagnostics tool for the desktop browser*

You can enable the mobile Diagnostics tool by using the multi-touch feature of the mobile device (see Figure 8-10). Follow these steps:

1. Press two fingers on a non-interactive screen area of the UI5 app for at least three seconds.

2. While holding the two fingers on the screen, tap a third finger on the screen.

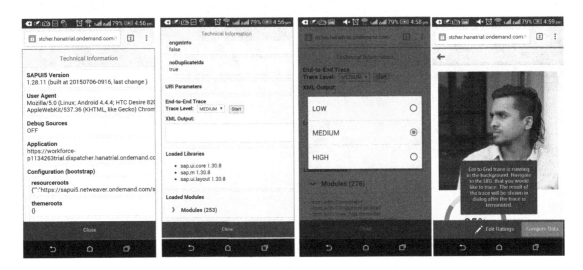

Figure 8-10. *Diagnostics tool for a mobile browser*

Simulating Mobile Devices

You can simulate any mobile device and screen size in the browser Developer Tools. Doing so gives you an idea of how the UI will render and react on a mobile device. To enable the simulation, click the Toggle Device Mode button in the browser Developer Tools, as shown in Figure 8-11.

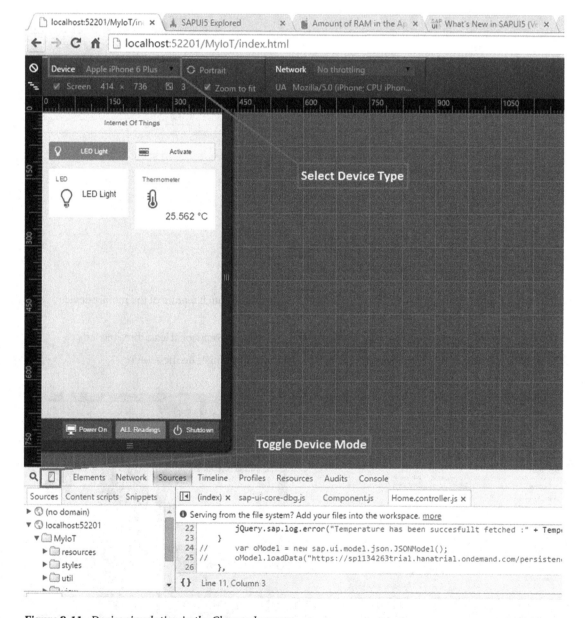

Figure 8-11. Device simulation in the Chrome browser

Troubleshooting Errors in Fiori Apps

Suppose you run the IoT app from Chapter 7 and try to turn on the LED by clicking the LED button, but there is no confirmation message that the LED is switched on. To figure out the issue, open your browser's debugger and check for errors in the Console window (see Figure 8-12). The Console log shows the error "Uncaught ReferenceError: LEDSta is not defined" for the `Home.controller.js` file.

Figure 8-12. *Error log in the Console window*

Now let's check the Sources tab of the debugger tool and examine the code in `Home.controller.js`. It shows that the error is on line 35: it looks like I typed a flag name as `LEDSta` instead of `LEDStat` in a condition statement (see Figure 8-13).

Figure 8-13. *Source file in the debugger showing a typo in the code*

Similarly, you can use the browser debugger to troubleshoot different types of errors in your UI5 apps.

Troubleshooting Errors in the Fiori Configuration

As in any implementation, you may face some errors while implementing SAP Fiori. This section discusses common errors and their possible solutions. Let's divide the process into the following steps:

1. Fiori installation and add-ons on the front-end server:

    a. Double-check whether all the prerequisite components and add-ons are installed. You can check the installation guides for Fiori at `http://help.sap.com/fiori`.

    b. If a specific Fiori app is not opening or the tile is missing on the Fiori launchpad, check whether the app-specific configuration has been done. You can get app configurations details at `https://fioriappslibrary.hana.ondemand.com/sap/fix/externalViewer/#/home`.

    c. Check the app catalog to find the Fiori applications that are available for your specific ERP system version at `http://help.sap.com/fiori_bs2013/helpdata/en/ed/e1e153ddf60466e10000000a423f68/frameset.htm` and `http://help.sap.com/fiori_bs2013/helpdata/en/59/69c553c9519638e10000000a44176d/frameset.htm`.

    d. Always check whether a note has been released for your specific issue. (Most issues in Fiori are due to missing notes.) You can keep track of the latest notes for your SAP Fiori apps at `http://service.sap.com/notes`. If you need to know how to search for a note, see `https://websmp101.sap-ag.de/~sapidb/011000358700005576692003`.

    e. Check whether you are using the latest Support package

2. SAP Gateway and back-end connectivity:

   a. One of the most common mistakes when setting up the Fiori landscape occurs while configuring a trusted RFC. To configure a trusted RFC in Gateway, see `https://help.sap.com/saphelp_nw74/helpdata/en/50/ f72651c294256ee10000000a445394/content.htm?frameset=/en/88/ f72651c294256ee10000000a445394/frameset.htm&current_toc=/en/ad/6 12bb3102e4f54a3019697fef65e5e/plain.htm&node_id=28` and Chapter 2.

   b. A second common mistake is related to the system alias definition. Make sure your system alias definitions in both Gateway and the back end point to the correct system. See the section "Creating a System Alias" in Chapter 2.

   c. If you encounter CSRF token issues, make sure the HTTP and HTTPS for the SAP Gateway are maintained properly. See note 1896961: `https://websmp130.sap-ag.de/sap(bD1lbiZjPTAwMQ==)/bc/bsp/sno/ ui_entry/entry.htm?param=69765F6D6F64653D3030312669765F7361706E6 F7465735F6E756D6265723D3138393639363126`.

   SAP back-end server configuration. In some cases, even after you set up a Fiori app and can see it in the Launchpad, users still get errors while trying to execute the apps. For example, when you try to create a leave request using a Fiori app and you get an error in return, chances are a configuration is missing on the functional side. Make sure all the necessary configurations from the back end are done properly for that scenario. The issue may be due to a missing authorization for the user ID you used to log in to the Fiori app for that specific task. For the latest information about Fiori configurations, see `https://fioriapps-rds.dispatcher.hana.ondemand.com`.

Fiori is a niche technology, but you can find an active forum in SCN that discusses ongoing issues, updates, and documents. The SCN community for Fiori (`http://scn.sap.com/community/fiori`) is always a good place to begin. You can also follow my blog at `http://scn.sap.com/people/bince.mathew2/content`.

The below Table 8-4 lists some of the most frequently used t-codes that comes in handy while troubleshooting and maintaining Fiori Applications.

Table 8-4. *Fiori T-Codes*

T-Code	Description
/IWFND/CACHE_CLEANUP	Clears the metadata cache on the Gateway
/IWBEP/CACHE_CLEANUP	Clears the metadata cache on the Gateway and back end
/UI2/CACHE_DEL	Deletes cache entries
/UI2/PERS_DEL	Clears the personalization settings on the server
/UI2/SEMOBJ	Defines a custom semantic objects
/UI2/SEMOBJ_SAP	Defines a custom semantic object—SAP
/UI2/GW_MAINT_SRV	Performs Gateway service maintenance
/UI2/GW_SYS_ALIAS	Manages Gateway system aliases
/UI2/GW_ACTIVATE	Activates the Gateway
/UI2/GW_ERR_LOG	Gateway error log
/UI2/GW_APPS_LOG	Gateway application log
/UI2/FLPD_CUST	Fiori launchpad designer

Table 8-5 shows some useful ABAP report programs related to Fiori.

Table 8-5. *ABAP Report Programs Related to Fiori*

Report Name	Description
/UI2/CHIP_SYNCHRONIZE_CACHE	Synchronizes the chip cache
/UI5/UPDATE_CACHEBUSTER	Updates the cache buster information
/UI5/UI5_REPOSITORY_LOAD	Uploads and downloads UI5 apps into the Gateway server

The next chapter explores how to use Cordova and plug-ins to port UI5 apps into native mobile apps.

■ ■ ■

CHAPTER 9

Developing Fiori Applications Using Cordova and Kapsel

Fiori is a set of browser-based, platform-independent applications, but Fiori apps can be converted into native mobile applications using Cordova plug-ins and SAP Kapsel plug-ins. This gives the Fiori apps access to native device hardware such as GPS, accelerometer, camera, device orientation, and so on. Using SAP's Kapsel plug-in, Fiori applications can be used to connect to the SAP Mobile Platform (SMP), which provides access to additional SMP features.

Connecting to the SMP Architecture with Fiori

SMP is a product line from SAP that offers integration of native mobile apps with SAP. It also has a hybrid web container app available for mobile OSs. The hybrid web container is a client mobile app that is a customized Cordova app, with custom Kapsel plug-ins developed by SAP to access SMP features. SAP offers a solution that lets you deploy Fiori apps with SMP Server. Accessing Fiori apps through SMP Server is more secure and adds many features that are not available natively with the Fiori platform:

- Requiring a PIN to access an app.

- A cross-platform hybrid app for multiple mobile OSs.

- SMP Management Cockpit to monitor all devices connected to SMP Server.

- Ability to add SAP Afaria to the SMP architecture for added security as a mobile device management solution.

- Ability to connect to non-SAP back ends.

- Ability to configure Fiori apps to fetch data from the back end via mobile business objects (MBOs) and OData.

- Support for offline OData.

- Push notification via Fiori Client with the Kapsel Push plug-in.

- Better cache management. Fiori Client detects any changes to Fiori apps and automatically updates its cache.

- Ability to access native mobile hardware and features.

© Bince Mathew 2015
B. Mathew, *Beginning SAP Fiori*, DOI 10.1007/978-1-4842-1335-3_9

Figure 9-1 shows a high-level overview of how mobile devices connect to SMP Server. Connections to Fiori apps in the SAP Gateway server happen via SMP Server. This way, you have a more secure connection to the SAP back end, because the initial authentication happens at the SMP Server level.

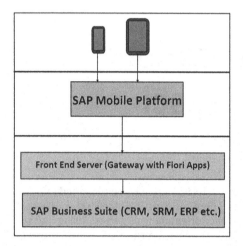

Figure 9-1. *SMP architecture with Fiori*

You can monitor devices and apps that access the SMP Server via its SMP Management Cockpit. In Figure 9-2, you see two apps, one user, and one app registration on the SMP Server. The Management Cockpit screen also has a small chart that gives the administrator an overview of the different mobile platforms registered with SMP Server.

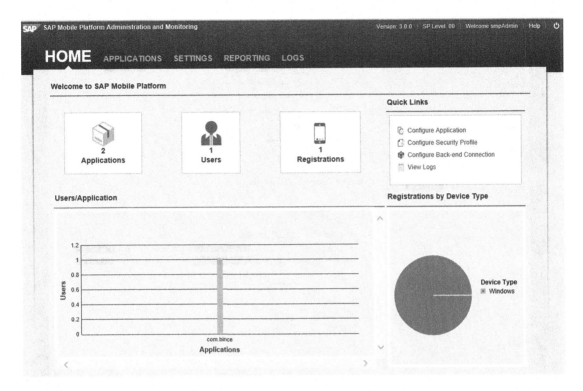

Figure 9-2. *SMP Management Cockpit home page*

You can configure settings individually for each app. And you have the option to configure the back-end URL and authentication required for each app to connect the SAP Gateway or other back-end systems. When it comes to Fiori on SMP, you configure the hybrid app with your SMP Server URL; on SMP Server, you configure the Fiori back-end URL on the app's settings page. Figure 9-3 shows the configuration for an app registered with SMP Server.

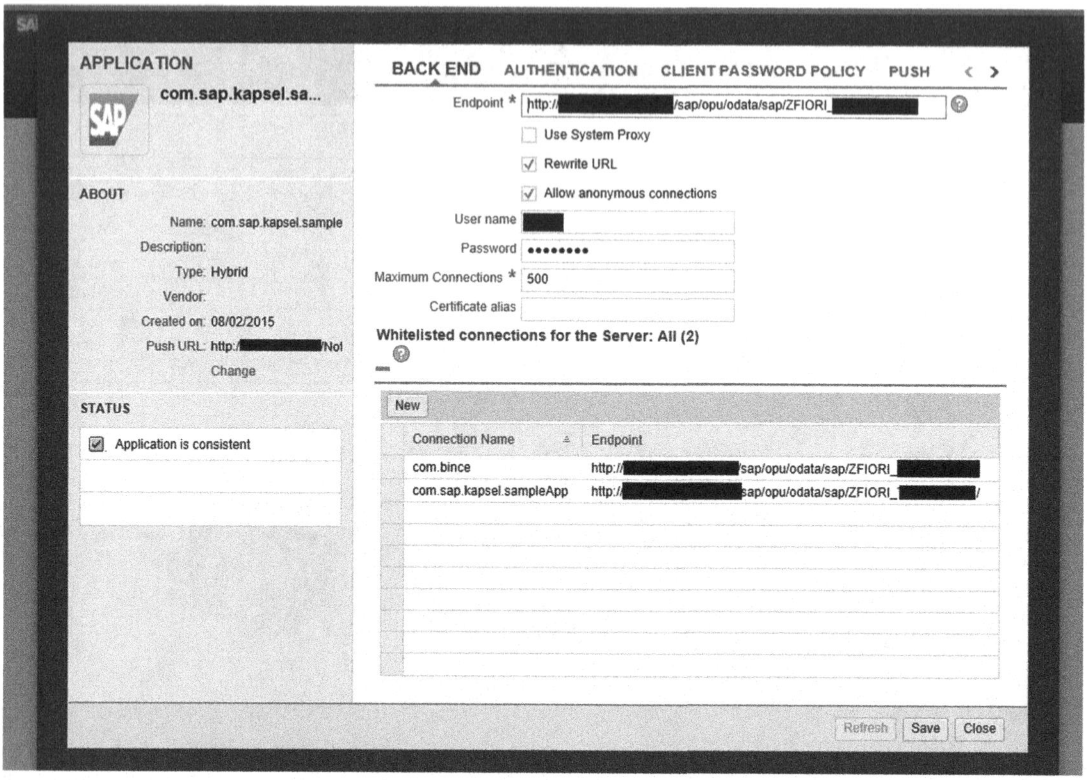

Figure 9-3. *SMP hybrid app settings page*

There is even an option to log all the activities of apps that connect through SMP Server. Figure 9-4 shows the different kinds of logs you can view via the SMP Management Cockpit. This feature is very handy when it's critical to monitor data sent through Fiori apps due to security concerns.

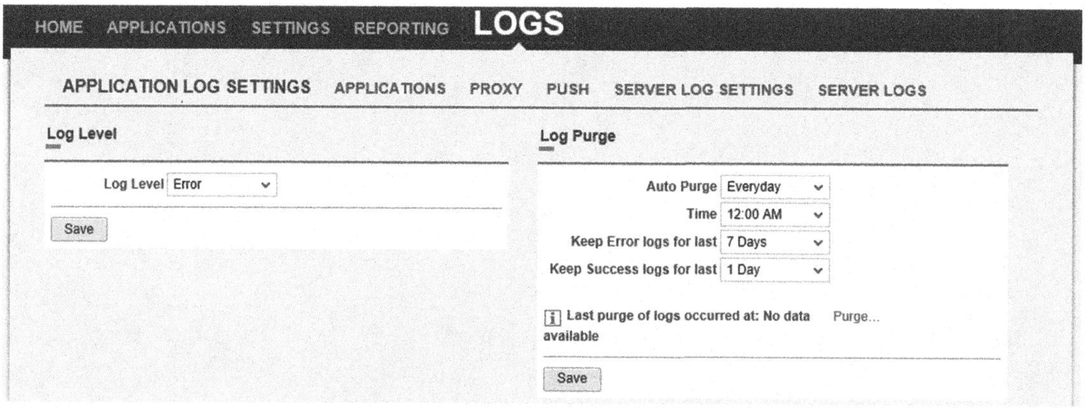

Figure 9-4. *Log management in the SMP Cockpit*

SAP has published a customized hybrid web container based on Cordova specifically for Fiori. It's called Fiori Client.

Fiori Client Application for Mobile

The Fiori Client app is available for download in the iOS, Android, and Windows mobile marketplaces. Fiori Client has all the standard Kapsel plug-ins for SMP preconfigured. It can be installed and accessed like any native app on your mobile device, which makes it easy to use compared with accessing the Fiori Launchpad via your mobile browser. Figure 9-5 shows the Fiori Client app interface. You give the Fiori Launchpad URL on the first screen; the app saves the URL, so you only have to enter it once. It even offers passcode-based security to access the app.

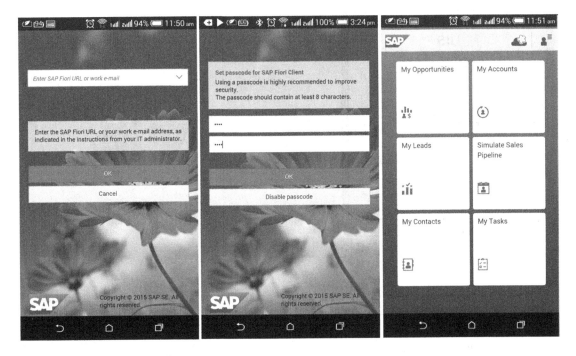

Figure 9-5. *Fiori Client mobile app*

Introduction to Cordova and Kapsel

One of the limitations of Fiori UI5 apps is that they're HTML5-based. Although the UI is optimized to work with mobile devices, it lacks the ability to talk directly to a mobile device's hardware or native features. This is where Cordova comes into play. You can embed your Fiori apps into a Cordova container app that can interact with your device's native features and hardware. Cordova acts as a middlemen between your UI5 apps and your mobile OS's native APIs (camera, accelerometer, location details, network status, and so on). The UI5 apps talk to the device APIs via JavaScript-based plug-ins that can be added to the apps. It's similar to adding a third-party JavaScript file to an app. Once these plug-ins are added to a UI5 app, you can access a series of methods and functions that let your app access device features.

Figure 9-6 shows the architecture of a Cordova hybrid app with a UI5 app embedded in it. The UI5 app talks to the Cordova native plug-ins via the added JavaScript plug-ins. The Cordova native plug-ins communicate with the device's native platform API and finally access hardware features such as the device's camera.

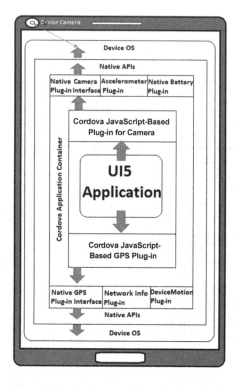

Figure 9-6. *Cordova architecture overview*

The Kapsel plug-ins are a set of Cordova-based plug-ins provided by SAP specifically to integrate UI5 apps with SMP (basically, these are Cordova apps with Kapsel plug-ins added to them). The Fiori Client app is a Cordova app with the Kapsel plug-ins already installed. The Kapsel plug-ins provided by SAP are as follows:

- Logon
- AppUpdate
- Push
- EncryptedStorage
- Logger
- Settings
- AuthProxy
- Online Application
- Toolbar
- Barcode Scanner

- Application Preferences

- Cache Manager

- SAP Fiori Client

- Offline OData

- End-To-End Trace

- Attachment Viewer

- Calendar

- Printer

- Usage

- OData

- i18n

- In App Browser

Creating a New Project with Cordova and Kapsel Plugins

This section looks at creating a Cordova app with Kapsel plug-ins. Before you begin Cordova development,   [AL
there are a few prerequisites.

To install Cordova, you need the following:

- Node.js, available from `https://nodejs.org`

- Java Runtime Environment 7, available from `www.oracle.com/technetwork/java/` `javase/downloads/jre7-downloads-1880261.html`

- Android SDK or your preferred mobile platform SDK for which you want to generate the native app

- Apache Ant 1.9 or higher, available from `http://ant.apache.org/bindownload.cgi`

Install the Cordova CLI using Node.js. Then, on Windows, open the command prompt (CMD) on your system and type

```
npm install –g cordova
```

Linux users, open the terminal and type

```
sudo npm install –g cordova
```

Once you have installed all the prerequisites, ensure that the necessary system environment variables are set. Usually, Node.js and Cordova are automatically registered in the system; make sure the Apache Ant and Android SDK tool paths are registered in the system environment variables as well. Figure 9-7 shows how to enter those values: right-click My Computer, click Properties, and follow the numbered steps in the figure.

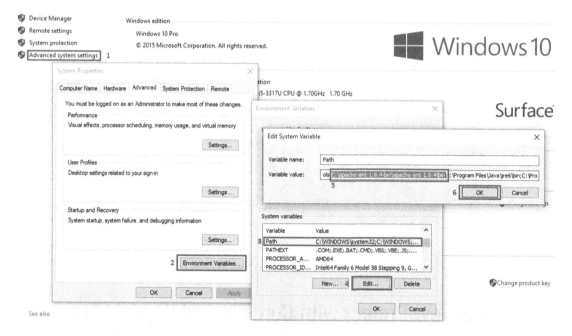

Figure 9-7. *Update the Apache Ant and Android paths in your system properties*

Now you can create your first Cordova-based app. Follow these steps:

1. Open CMD on your PC and type the following, as shown in Figure 9-8

   ```
   cordova create MyCordovaApp com.sap.mycordova MyCordovaApp
   ```

Figure 9-8. *Create a new Cordova project*

2. Navigate to the new Cordova app folder. Type the following:

   ```
   cd MyCordovaApp
   ```

3. You need to add a few Cordova plug-ins to your UI5 app, such as the barcode scanner, camera, geolocation, device, and so on. To do so, type this for the barcode scanner:

```
cordova plug-in add com.phonegap.plug-ins.barcodescanner
```

Similarly, for the other plug-ins, type

```
cordova plug-in add org.apache.cordova.camera
cordova plug-in add org.apache.cordova.geolocation
cordova plug-in add org.apache.cordova.device
cordova plug-in add org.apache.cordova.file
cordova plug-in add org.apache.cordova.network-information
cordova plug-in add org.apache.cordova.battery-status
cordova plug-in add org.apache.cordova.device-motion
cordova plug-in add org.apache.cordova.device-orientation
cordova plug-in add org.apache.cordova.console
cordova plug-in add org.apache.cordova.inappbrowser
```

4. To see the list of plug-ins you added to the Cordova app, type

```
cordova plug-ins
```

5. To add Kapsel plug-ins, you need to download the SMP SDK from https://store.sap.com/sap/cp/ui/resources/store/html/ SolutionDetails.html?pid=0000013098&catID=&pcntry=US&sap-language=EN&_cp_id=id-1409756206625-0.

Once you download and install the SMP SDK, you can see the Kapsel plug-ins in the SAP folder of the drive which you installed the SDK. The path is something like C:\SAP\MobileSDK3\KapselSDK\plugins (see Figure 9-9).

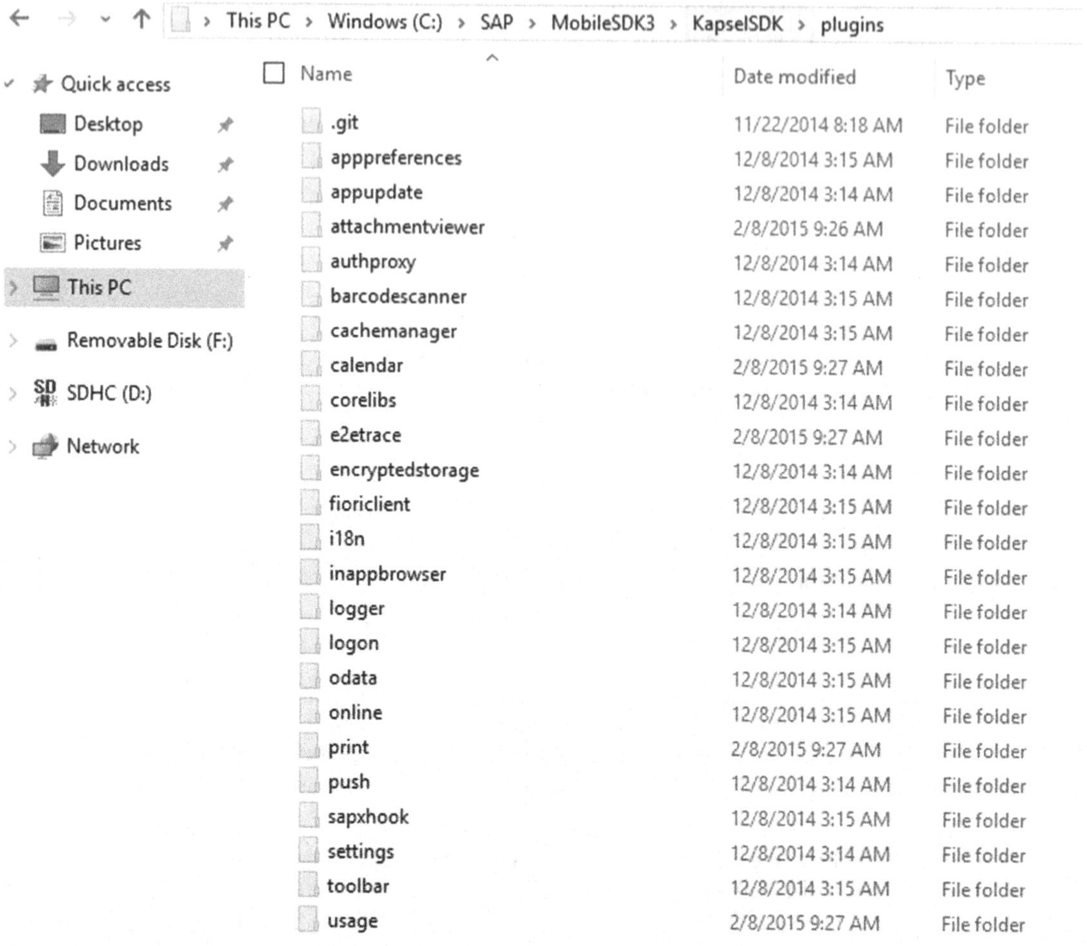

Figure 9-9. *SAP Kapsel plug-ins that come with the SMP SDK*

6. To add the Kapsel plug-ins to your Cordova app, type

```
cordova plug-ins <path to your specific kapsel plug-in>
```

For example, to add the Logon Kapsel plug-in to the Cordova app, type
`C:\SAP\MobileSDK3\KapselSDK\plug-ins\logon` for the path in this command.

7. You need to add platform support for your app. In this case, you are building for
the Android platform. To add it, type the following (see Figure 9-10):

```
cordova platform add android
```

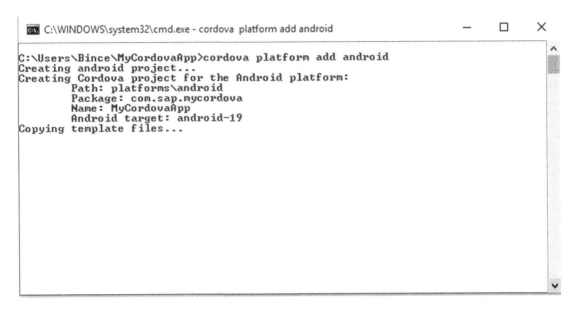

Figure 9-10. *Adding the Android platform to your Cordova app*

8. Go to the project folder. You should see the folder structure shown in Figure 9-11. The platforms folder contains individual folders for every platform you add to the Cordova app.

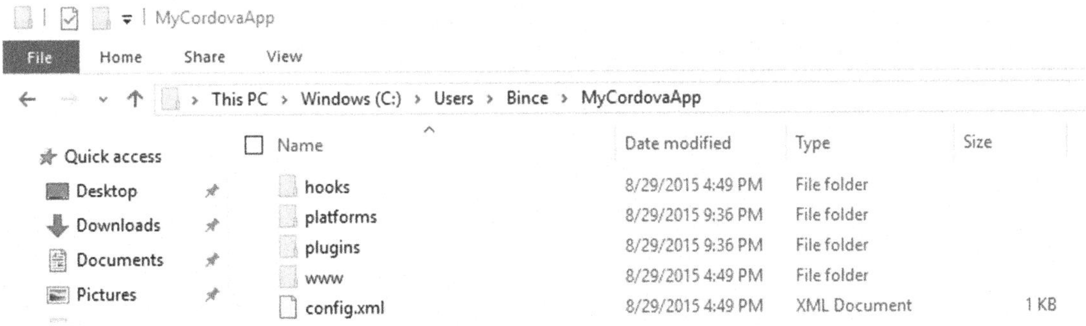

Figure 9-11. *Cordova app folder structure*

9. To prepare the Cordova project, type

   cordova prepare

   When you run this command, Cordova copies all the files in the www folder (as shown in Figure 9-12) into the www folder under the path <Your Cordova app root folder>\ \platforms\android\assets\www. In this example, the path is C:\Users\Bince\MyCordovaApp\platforms\android\platform_www.

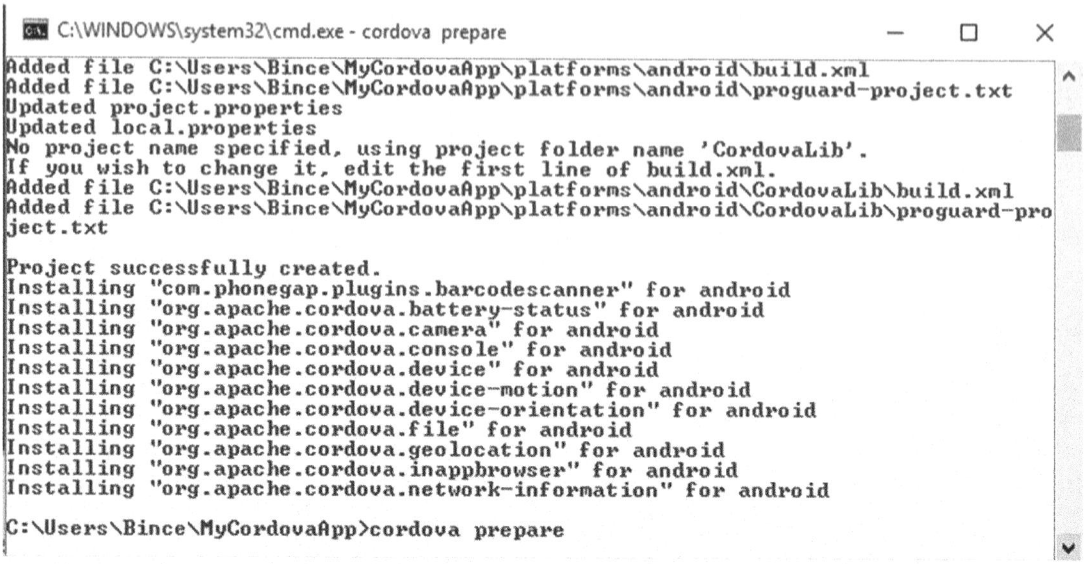

Figure 9-12. *Preparing Cordova for the first time*

10. To compile the Cordova app, type

```
cordova compile
```

This command compiles the code and gives you an installable native app file under the platforms folder (see Figure 9-13). This example uses the Android platform, so the installable mobile app package is under C:\Users\Bince\MyCordovaApp\platforms\android\ant-build.

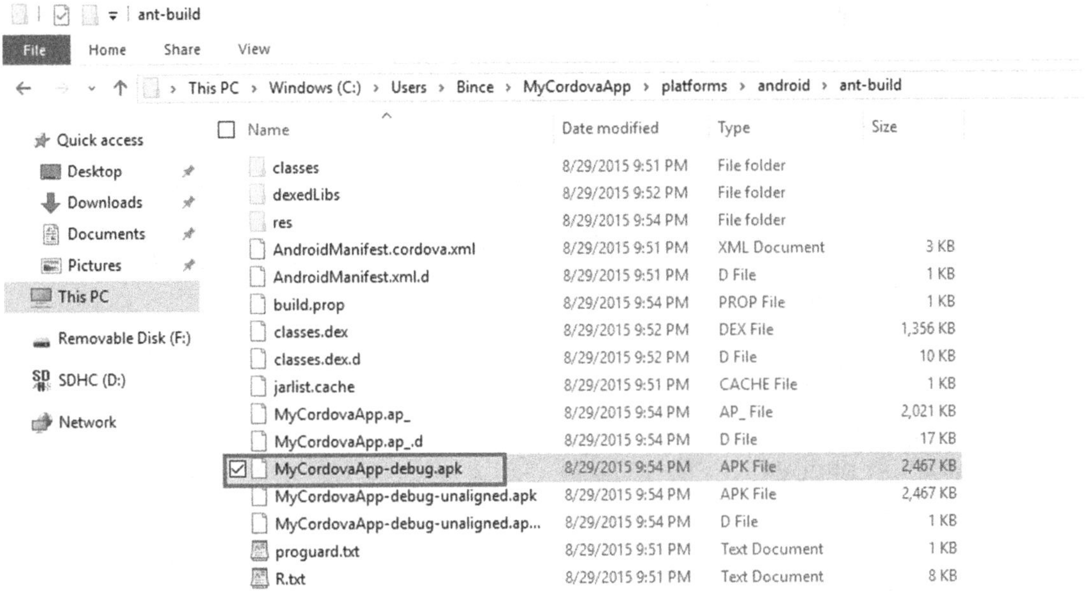

Figure 9-13. *Installable* .apk *file after compiling the Cordova project*

11. Install the .apk file on your Android device and run it. You see the default Cordova app splash screen, as shown in Figure 9-14.

Figure 9-14. *Default splash screen for the Cordova app*

Your aim next is to replace this standard sample app and put your UI5 app in the Cordova container.

Building Fiori Apps Using Cordova

You've created a Cordova project, and it's time to import this app into Eclipse. Follow these steps:

1. Open Eclipse, go to File ➤ import ➤ Existing Android Code Into Workspace (see Figure 9-15), and click Next.

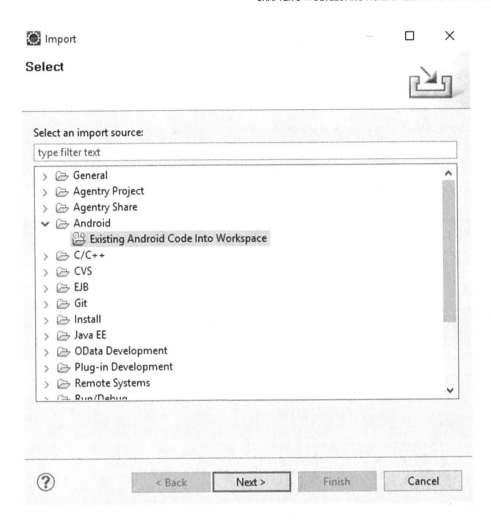

Figure 9-15. *Import your Cordova project into Eclipse*

2. Browse to the Android platform project folder of your Cordova app. In this example, the path is C:\Users\Bince\MyCordovaApp\platforms\android. Uncheck CordovaLib on the Projects tab, and check Copy Projects Into Workspace, as shown in Figure 9-16.

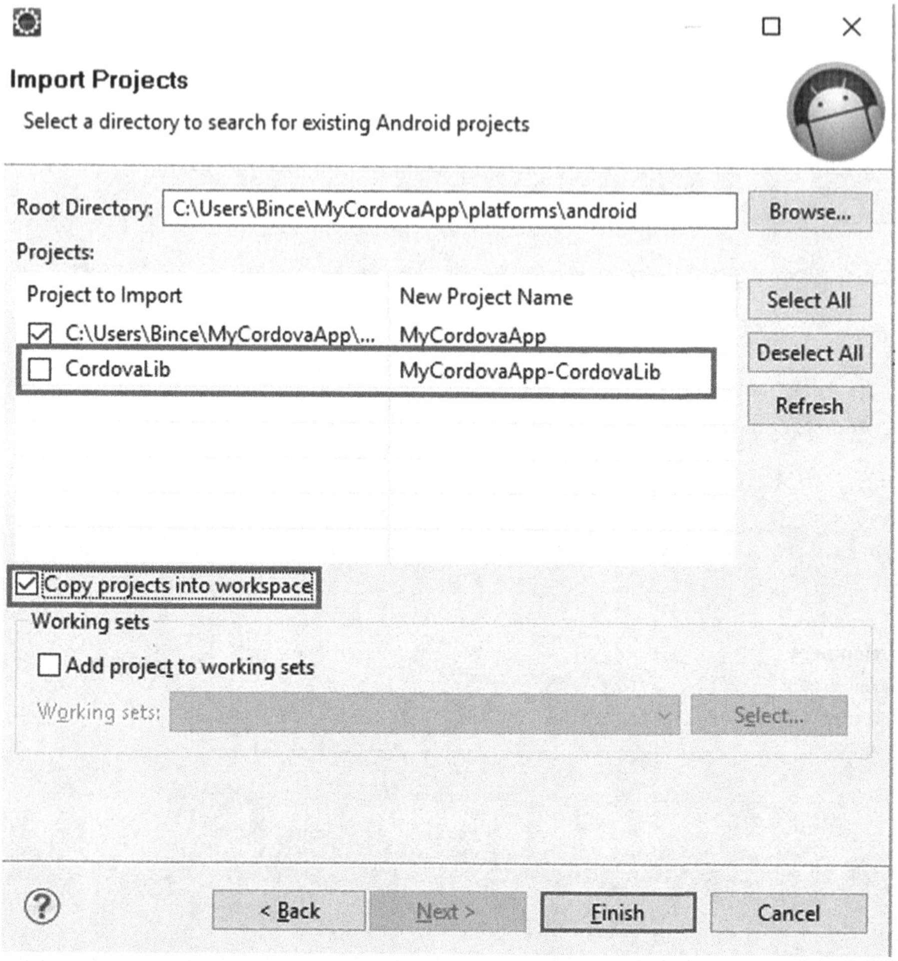

Figure 9-16. *Do not import CordovaLib*

3. Go to the properties of the project you imported, and go to Java Build Path ➤ Source tab ➤ Add Folder ➤ CordovaLib folder, as shown in Figure 9-17.

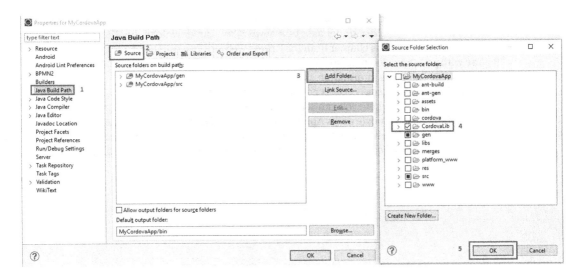

Figure 9-17. Add CordovaLib *to the project's source folder*

4. Go to Resource ➤ Resource Filters in the same window, and delete all the Exclude filter values, as shown in Figure 9-18.

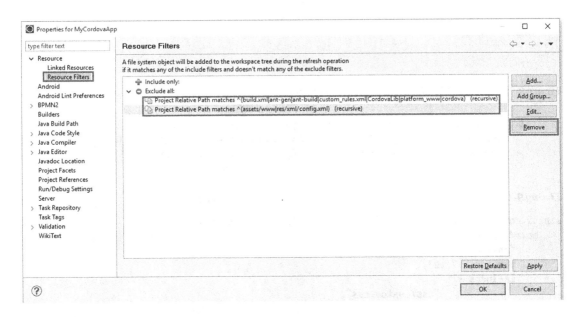

Figure 9-18. *Remove all the resource filters*

5. Copy/paste the webcontent folder's contents for your SAP UI5 app into the Cordova project's www folder, under assets ➤ www. (You can download the UI5 source code shown in this chapter from the Apress web site.) To use the geolocation feature with your app, you need to get the Google Maps API from the Google accounts page. You can find more information about the Google Maps API and key at https://developers.google.com/maps/documentation/javascript/tutorial. In the below Figure 9-19 where you can see the Google maps Api is being initialized in the index.html, every Google maps Api requires a unique key to use the Google maps services. To know more about obtaining a unique key for your project, go-to this link https://developers.google.com/maps/documentation/javascript/tutorial.

Figure 9-19. *Imported Cordova folder structure in Eclipse*

6. You need to connect your imported UI5 app to the Cordova plug-ins. To do that, you reference the cordova.js file in your index.html or Component.js file. This example links the cordova.js file in Component.js. You have to add the reference to the metadata section under includes, as shown in Listing 9-1.

Listing 9-1. Code to Link cordova.js in the UI5 App's Component.js File

```
sap.ui.core.UIComponent.extend("sap.ui.cordova.app.Component", {
    metadata: {
        "abstract": true,
        version : "1.0",
        includes : [
                    "css/custom.css",
                    "/cordova.js",
                    "js/index.js",

                    ]
                }
}
```

Now you are ready to access the features and hardware of the native Android OS via your UI5 app.

Example App Using the Device's Camera, GPS, and Google Maps

In this section's example app, you access the mobile device's camera, barcode scanner, geolocation feature, and Google Maps.

Accessing the Camera

To access the camera, you call the `navigator.camera.getPicture()` method. Listing 9-2 shows the code. Here, the `handle_camera` method is invoked when the camera button is clicked.

Listing 9-2. Accessing the Camera API in the UI5 App

```
handle_camera : function (evt){
        navigator.camera.getPicture(          function (imageURL) {
            console.log("Entering cameraSuccess");
              image.setValue(imageURL);
              img.setSrc(imageURL);
                success(), fail());

            console.log("Leaving cameraSuccess");
        }, function (error) {
            alert("Camera failed: " + error);
        });
    },
```

Accessing the Barcode Scanner

To access the barcode scanner, you invoke the `cordova.plug-ins.barcodeScanner.scan()` method. The code is shown in Listing 9-3.

Listing 9-3. Accessing the Barcode Scanner API

```
cordova.plug-ins.barcodeScanner.scan(
                function (result) {
                    barcode_result = result.text;
                    barcode_val.setValue(result.text);
                },
                function (error) {
                    alert("Scanning failed: " + error);
                }
            );
```

Accessing the GPS and Google Maps

The Cordova Geolocation plug-in only gives you access to the GPS. This example uses the Google Maps API along with Geolocation, to display a map on the UI5 app's screen. You access the geolocation feature using the navigator.geolocation.getCurrentPosition() method. To use Google Maps, you need to reference the Google Maps JavaScript plug-in in your app. For example, reference the Google Maps API in index.html as follows:

```
<script src="https://maps.googleapis.com/maps/api/js?key=<your Google Maps API key>"></script>
```

The code for accessing Geolocation and Google Maps in your UI5 app is shown in Listing 9-4.

Listing 9-4. Accessing the Geolocation API

```
navigator.geolocation.getCurrentPosition(function(position){
        var mapOptions = {
            mapTypeId: google.maps.MapTypeId.ROADMAP
        };
    // Info Window Content
        var infoWindowContent = [
            ['<div class="info_content">' +
            '<h3>OST Asset</h3>' +
            '<p>Property Of Open Source Tech' +           '</div>'],
            ['<div class="info_content">' +
                '<h3>OST Asset</h3>' +
                '<p>Property Of Open Source Tech' +           '</div>'],
            ['<div class="info_content">' +
            '<h3>OST Asset</h3>' +
            '<p>Property Of Open Source Tech</p>' +
            '</div>']
        ];
// Display multiple markers on a map
        var infoWindow = new google.maps.InfoWindow(), marker_new, i;
        var MapRef = sap.ui.getCore().Map.Ref;
        var map_new = new google.maps.Map(document.getElementById(MapRef.byId("maps_new").sId),
                mapOptions);
        map_new.setTilt(45);
        for( i = 0; i < records.length; i++ ) {
//          debugger;
            var position = new google.maps.LatLng(records[i].Longitude,records[i].Latitude );
                bounds.extend(position);
                marker_new = new google.maps.Marker({
                    position: position,
                    map: map_new,
                    title:'Location'+i});
                // Allow each marker to have an info window
                google.maps.event.addListener(marker_new, 'click', (function(marker, i) {
                    return function() {
                        infoWindow.setContent(infoWindowContent[i][0]);
                        infoWindow.open(map_new, marker);
                    }
                })(marker_new, i));
```

```
    // Automatically center the map fitting all markers on the screen
    map_new.fitBounds(bounds);
  }
});
```

When your changes to the UI5 app are complete, copy the contents of your project from Eclipse under the www folder in the Project Explorer, and paste them into the www folder of your Cordova project at the path `<defaultpath>\MyCordovaApp\platforms\android\assets\www`. Open CMD, navigate to MyCordovaApp, and compile the project once more using this command:

```
cordova compile
```

Your new app package file appears on the path `<defaultpath>\MyCordovaApp\platforms\android\ant-build`. Install it on your mobile device: you now have a Fiori UI5 app, complete with all the features of a native mobile app.

Figure 9-20 shows the custom Cordova-based UI5 app accessing the Google Maps API and displaying coordinates via the Cordova Geolocation plug-in.

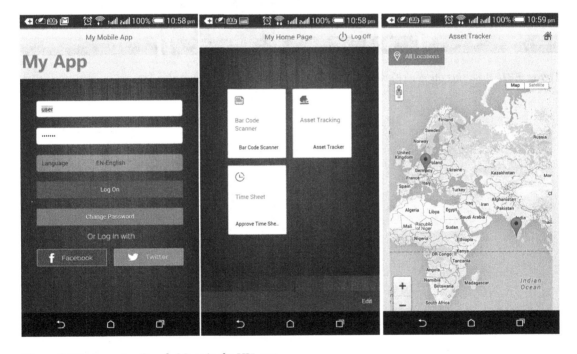

Figure 9-20. *Accessing Google Maps in the UI5 app*

In Figure 9-21, the UI5 app is accessing the camera and displaying a picture on the UI5 app page. The figure also demonstrates the use of the barcode scanner.

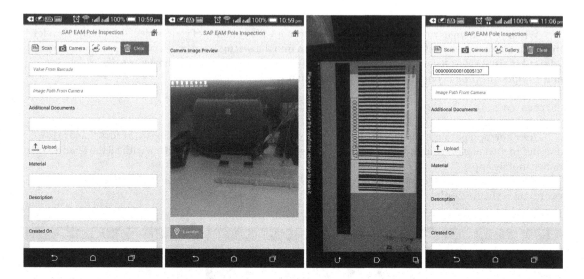

Figure 9-21. *Accessing the device's camera and barcode scanner via Cordova plug-ins*

Index

■ W, X, Y, Z

Get the eBook for only $5!

Why limit yourself?

Now you can take the weightless companion with you wherever you go and access your content on your PC, phone, tablet, or reader.

Since you've purchased this print book, we're happy to offer you the eBook in all 3 formats for just $5.

Convenient and fully searchable, the PDF version enables you to easily find and copy code—or perform examples by quickly toggling between instructions and applications. The MOBI format is ideal for your Kindle, while the ePUB can be utilized on a variety of mobile devices.

To learn more, go to www.apress.com/companion or contact support@apress.com.

Printed in the United States
By Bookmasters